WILD EDIBLE PLANTS OF THE SOUTHWEST

LOCATE, IDENTIFY, STORE, AND PREPARE YOUR FORAGED FINDS

FORAGE AND FEAST SERIES: COMPREHENSIVE GUIDES TO FORAGING ACROSS AMERICA

BOOK 5

SHANNON WARNER

ALSO BY SHANNON WARNER

<u>**Individual Books:**</u>

Wild Edible Plants of the Mid-Atlantic

Wild Edible Plants of New England

Wild Edible Plants of California

Wild Edible Plants of the Pacific Northwest

Wild Edible Plants of Texas

Wild Edible Plants of the Great Lakes *(Coming Soon)*

Wild Edible Plants of the Great Plains *(Coming Soon)*

Wild Edible Plants of the Southeast *(Coming Soon)*

Wild Edible Plants of the Gulf Coast *(Coming Soon)*

Wild Edible Plants of the Upper Midwest *(Coming Soon)*

Wild Edible Plants of the Rocky Mountains *(Coming Soon)*

<u>**2-in1 Guides:**</u>

Wild Edibles of the West Coast (California & the Pacific Northwest)

Wild Edibles of the Northeast (Mid-Atlantic & New England)

Foraging the Wild South (Texas & the Southwest)

Foraging the Midwest *(Coming Soon)*

Foraging the Southeast *(Coming Soon)*

Foraging the North *(Coming Soon)*

THE ALLURE OF THE ARID WILDERNESS

Discover the uncharted marvels of the American Southwest, where barren deserts and grandiose peaks conceal precious gems. Beyond the blazing heat and the captivating dance of light and darkness lies a wealth of mouthwatering flora eagerly awaiting the daring adventurer. Set out on an enthralling expedition through this untamed wilderness with "Wild Edible Plants of the Southwest" as your faithful guide, uncovering the mysteries within.

Rediscovering the art of foraging has recently become popular as we seek to establish a stronger bond with nature, minimize our carbon footprint, and adopt locally sourced foods. This age-old practice presents an exhilarating opportunity to accomplish all of these objectives. The Southwest region boasts diverse ecosystems and native cultures, which have a rich history of utilizing wild plants for sustenance, healing, and ceremonial purposes. By embracing this tradition, we nourish our bodies, deepen our connection with the land, and pay homage to the indigenous communities who have nurtured it for centuries.

However, embarking on this thrilling adventure comes with its fair share of challenges. The Southwest boasts a wide variety of mouthwatering plants, but it also hides a multitude of poisonous impostors. The line between a delectable wild salad and a dangerous mistake is incredibly delicate. That's why this book serves a dual purpose: to unveil the tantalizing edible treasures of the Southwest and to equip you with the knowledge to forage safely and responsibly.

Come along with us as we embark on an extraordinary adventure through the breathtaking landscapes of the Southwest. Prepare to be amazed as we unveil the hidden treasures of the Sonoran Desert and the awe-inspiring Rockies. From the towering cacti that stand proudly in the desert to the vibrant meadows that adorn the mountains, we will immerse ourselves in the enchanting flora that flourishes in this remarkable region.

During our journey, we will unravel the cultural significance of plants that have played a vital role in the lives of indigenous communities for centuries. Discover the fascinating story behind the agave, a plant that has been a staple in these communities, providing sustenance and resources. We will also uncover the secrets of the prickly pear. This succulent offers delectable fruits and tender young pads that have been cherished for generations.

Join us on a journey of discovery through the Southwest, where we'll explore the rich flavors and textures of wild edible plants. By the end of this guide, you'll have a deep understanding of their value and culinary applications. You'll also learn how to safely and responsibly identify and harvest these plants with a healthy dose of caution and respect for the environment. Armed with this knowledge, you'll be ready to embark on your foraging adventures and prepare delicious and nutritious meals. Whether you're a seasoned forager or a curious beginner, there's something here for everyone. So, let's set out together with open hearts and curious spirits and uncover the wonders of the Southwest!

PART ONE
FORAGING 101

CHAPTER 1

STARTING YOUR FORAGING JOURNEY

Before we plunge into the captivating world of Southwest wild edibles, let's set some fundamental ground rules. Foraging is more than a delightful pastime; it's a craft interwoven with respect, knowledge, and responsibility.

Know Before You Go:

Before you start foraging, it's essential to do your research. Just like diving into a pool without checking its depth can be dangerous, jumping into foraging without proper knowledge can be risky. Don't take any chances with your health - make sure you know which plants are safe to eat and which ones to avoid. Remember, many edible plants have toxic look-alikes, so it's better to be safe than sorry. Take the time to educate yourself, and you'll be able to enjoy nature's bounty without any unpleasant surprises.

Start Small, Think Big:

Embark on your foraging adventure by acquainting yourself with some readily identifiable and plentiful flora. Dandelions and prickly pear cactus are two beloved Southwestern staples that are unmistakable. As you become more self-assured, you can broaden your horizons and explore new options.

Forage in Safe Places:

When choosing a spot for your plants, remember the importance of location. Steer clear of areas near bustling roads, industrial zones, or places where pesticides have been used. Why? Well, plants can absorb whatever is in the soil around them, including harmful pollutants. So, to ensure the health and well-being of your green companions, it's best to find them a safe and clean environment to thrive in.

Tool Time:

Ensure you're well-prepared for your adventure by gathering a few essential items. Firstly, arm yourself with a top-notch field guide tailored to the Southwest region.

This invaluable resource will be your trusty companion, helping you identify and learn about the diverse flora you encounter along the way.

Next, don't forget to shield your hands from any potential thorns or prickles that may cross your path. Sturdy gloves will be your best defense, ensuring your hands remain unscathed and ready for further exploration.

To ensure precise and clean cuts, it's wise to have a reliable knife or a pair of scissors. These handy tools will come in handy when you stumble upon the perfect specimen to add to your collection or when you need to extract a sample for further examination carefully.

Lastly, be prepared to bring your bountiful harvest back home by carrying containers or baskets. These vessels will keep your precious findings safe and secure and allow you to showcase your botanical treasures with pride.

Remember, equipping yourself with these essentials will enhance your experience and ensure you're fully prepared to delve into the wonders of the Southwest. So, gather your gear and embark on a botanical journey like no other!

1. **Nature's Calendar:**

Discover the natural rhythms of your favorite plants to ensure a bountiful harvest. Each season brings its unique bounty, from the vibrant blooms of spring to the crisp autumn air. By understanding the optimal harvest time for each plant, you can savor your homegrown produce's full flavor and nutritional benefits.

1. **When in Doubt, Leave it Out:**

When it comes to foraging, one rule stands above all others - the golden rule. Suppose you ever find yourself unsure about the identity of a plant. No matter how tempting it may appear, you must resist the urge to consume it. Remember, it is always wiser to err on caution regarding your safety and well-being.

Embark on an enthralling gastronomic adventure as you lace up your hiking boots and delve into the Southwest's vast deserts and lush meadows. With a basket in hand and the sun gently caressing your face, you'll discover that foraging is more than a means to an end. It's a captivating journey, a dance with nature that allows you to connect with the Earth in the most primal way.

As you wander through this breathtaking landscape, don't just think of yourself as a collector of plants. Instead, embrace the opportunity to absorb centuries-old wisdom and immerse yourself in the secrets of the ancient world. The Southwest holds myriad flavors and hidden treasures waiting to be discovered.

So, let the allure of foraging guide you as you explore this enchanting region. Happy foraging, and may your journey be filled with unforgettable experiences and delectable delights!

CHAPTER 2
HARVESTING RESPONSIBLY
PRACTICES FOR ETHICAL AND SUSTAINABLE GATHERING

As we explore the untamed terrains of the Southwest, it's impossible not to be mesmerized by the plethora of mouth-watering treats Mother Nature has bestowed upon us. From the tangy berries of the desert wolfberry to the crispy, nutty seeds of the chia sage, the culinary options are endless. However, before indulging in this natural feast, let's pause and ponder: What steps can we take to guarantee that our actions don't strip away the pantry for future generations?

Understanding the Plant's Life Cycle

Understanding the plant's life cycle is crucial for responsible harvesting. Take a moment to consider this: when a plant is in full bloom, it signifies that it is in the process of producing seeds. However, if we were to harvest it at this stage, we would be risking its chances of reproducing. Therefore, we must familiarize ourselves with the growth stages of the plants we intend to harvest and carefully plan our harvest accordingly. By doing so, we can ensure that we are responsible stewards of nature and allow the plants to thrive and propagate as intended.

Leave More than You Take

Remember the 'One in Three' rule regarding harvesting plants. Instead of mindlessly collecting every plant you see, adopt a more sustainable approach. For every three plants you encounter, only take one. This simple practice ensures the long-term health and regeneration of the plant population. By being mindful of our actions, we become responsible stewards of the land, safeguarding it from overharvesting and preserving its natural beauty for years.

Tread Lightly

The delicate desert landscape demands your utmost care. As you embark on your foraging journey, be mindful of your every step, treading lightly to preserve the precious ecosystem. Take caution not to trample upon the surrounding flora, and be considerate of the local wildlife, ensuring you do not disrupt their harmonious existence. Remember that you are a humble guest in their magnificent home, and treat it with the respect it deserves.

Respect Elder Plants

When it comes to the ecosystem, older, mature plants play a vital role. They not only serve as the primary seed producers but also guarantee the survival of their species. Although it may be tempting to harvest a gigantic cactus or a well-aged yucca, it's essential to reconsider. Instead, choose younger plants (excluding the little ones!) that can bounce back swiftly from a gentle harvest.

The Water Element

When venturing into the desert, it's crucial to remember that the resilient plants that call this arid landscape home depend greatly on rare rainfall. It's fascinating how these plants have adapted to survive such harsh conditions. However, it's important to be mindful of the impact we can have on their water absorption when we disturb the ground around them. So, if you find yourself harvesting in the desert, take care not to uproot or harm the plant's vital source of sustenance. Let's appreciate and protect the remarkable resilience of these desert dwellers.

Know Local Guidelines

In certain regions, there might be particular guidelines or restrictions in place regarding foraging, particularly in protected lands or national parks. It is crucial to stay well-informed and adhere to these rules. Disregarding them and engaging in illegal harvesting can result in grave consequences, not only for yourself but also for the environment.

Harvest with Gratitude

Approach every foraging expedition with a heart full of gratitude, and take a moment to thank the plant you're harvesting from. This small act may seem whimsical, but it can transform your foraging experience and make you more attuned to nature's rhythm. Remember, responsible harvesting is all about balance.

Let's enjoy the bounties of the Southwest while ensuring our actions today pave the way for a green and abundant tomorrow. Happy and ethical foraging!

PART TWO
WHERE WE ARE VISITING

CHAPTER 3
ARIZONA

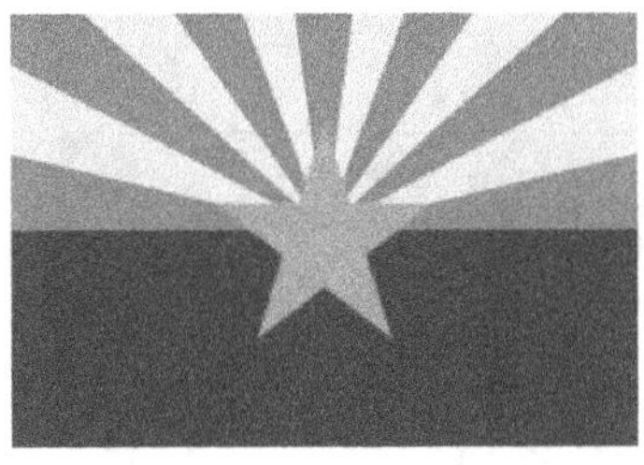

Arizona is a treasure trove of natural wonders, steeped in a rich history and brimming with a vibrant culture. Its diverse landscape, blessed with warm weather and unique wildlife, creates an idyllic setting for thrilling outdoor escapades. Whether you seek the awe-inspiring beauty of the renowned Grand Canyon or hidden gems waiting to be discovered, Arizona becomes an exceptional destination for exploration.

Yearly Weather Patterns by Season

- *Spring (March-May)*: During springtime in Arizona, the weather is pleasantly mild with intermittent showers. The temperature typically varies between the mid-60s and mid-80s, and the state's diverse range of wildflowers come into full bloom during this season.
- *Summer (June-August)*: During the scorching Arizona summers, temperatures frequently surpass 100 degrees Fahrenheit, making it advisable to seek refuge indoors, especially in the lower elevations.
- *Fall (September-November)*: During the fall season, temperatures become cooler, and the foliage transforms. The temperature range varies from the mid-60s to the mid-80s, while the state's abundant trees display vibrant red, orange, and yellow hues.
- *Winter (December-February)*: In the southern parts of Arizona, winters can be relatively mild, while in the northern regions, they tend to be colder. The temperature range during this season varies from the mid-30s to the mid-60s,

depending on the specific location. It is worth noting that certain areas, particularly those at higher elevations, may even witness snowfall.

Land Topography

- **Grand Canyon:** The Grand Canyon, a renowned natural wonder, stretches over 270 miles and spans up to 18 miles in width. Situated in northern Arizona, this majestic canyon attracts hikers, campers, and nature enthusiasts from around the globe.
- **Sonoran Desert:** Located in southern Arizona, it is renowned for its scorching temperatures and remarkable biodiversity. It harbors many distinctive plant and animal species, including the iconic saguaro cactus and the elusive Gila monster.
- **Mogollon Rim:** A steep escarpment that divides the highlands of northern Arizona from the low-lying desert of the southern region, running through central Arizona as a prominent geological feature.
- **Painted Desert:** A popular destination for hikers, photographers, and nature enthusiasts, this northern Arizona region is renowned for its vibrant rock formations and breathtaking vistas.

"Arizona is a land of contrasts, from the deep canyons cut by the Colorado River to the rugged mountains and forests of the north."

- JANET NAPOLITANO, 21ST GOVERNOR OF ARIZONA

Foraging Hotspots

- **Oak Creek Canyon:** is a sought-after spot for foragers due to its copious wild berries, including blackberries and raspberries, and its diverse cacti and succulent plants.
- **Chiricahua Mountains:** located in southeastern Arizona, it is a popular destination foragers thanks to its abundance of edible mushrooms, such as the chanterelle and the morel.
- **Mount Lemmon:** located just outside of Tucson, is known for its abundance of wild berries, such as strawberries and huckleberries, as well as its variety of edible mushrooms and other wild edibles.
- **Saguaro National Park:** Located in southern Arizona, it is known for its towering saguaro cacti, a traditional Tohono O'odham food. The park also has many other edible plants, such as the prickly pear cactus and mesquite beans.
- **Coconino National Forest:** Located in central Arizona, it is a popular destination for foragers thanks to its abundance of wild berries, such as raspberries and blueberries, as well as its variety of mushrooms and other wild edibles.

- **Arizona Mushroom Society:** covers various areas of the state, including Phoenix, Tucson, Flagstaff, and more. They offer exciting workshops, classes, and hikes for all ages. During these events, you can discover different types of mushrooms, learn how to identify them, and understand their role in the ecosystem. The society has knowledgeable guides who will teach you about the importance of mushrooms and how to stay safe while exploring. Whether you're a beginner or an experienced mushroom enthusiast, the Arizona Mushroom Society has something for everyone. You can participate in hands-on activities, join guided hikes to find mushrooms in their natural habitats, and even attend lectures by experts in the field. Visit their website to get more information and stay updated on their upcoming events.
- **Reevis Mountain School of Self-Reliance**: Peter Bigfoot founded the Reevis Mountain School of Self-Reliance, which imparts knowledge on natural healing, self-sufficiency techniques, growing one's food, and other related topics. The school provides courses on identifying and utilizing wild edibles and medicinal and practical plants. For more information, please visit their website.
- **The Forager's Path:** Mike Masek, the founder of The Forager's Path, has established a community herb store in Flagstaff, Arizona. This unique establishment aims to empower individuals in the field of Bio-Regional Herbalism. The Forager's Path provides diverse classes covering medicinal and edible plants, survival skills, and herbal medicine. For further details, please visit their website.

Arizona is brimming with natural wonders, from the awe-inspiring Grand Canyon to the extraordinary wildlife of the Sonoran Desert. Arizona offers something for everyone, whether you seek the finest foraging hotspots or local foraging groups. With a state as captivating as Arizona, there's an adventure waiting to be discovered. So, pack your bags and embark on an unforgettable journey in the Grand Canyon State!

CHAPTER 4
NEVADA
THE BATTLE BORN STATE

In the United States' western region, Nevada is brimming with natural wonders, a rich history, and a vibrant culture. Its diverse landscapes, warm weather, and unique wildlife make it an ideal destination for outdoor enthusiasts and those seeking exploration opportunities. From the renowned city of Las Vegas to the hidden gems of foraging hotspots, Nevada is a state that holds countless treasures eagerly awaiting discovery.

Yearly Weather Patterns by Season

- *Spring (March-May)*: Spring in Nevada is characterized by mild temperatures and occasional rainfall. Temperatures range from the mid-50s to the mid-70s, and the state's many wildflowers begin to bloom during this time.
- *Summer (June - August)*: Summers in Nevada can be scorching, with temperatures often exceeding 100 degrees Fahrenheit. It is best to stay indoors during the hottest parts of the day, particularly in the lower elevations.
- *Fall (September - November)*: Fall in Nevada is characterized by cooler temperatures and changing foliage. Temperatures range from the mid-50s to the mid-70s, and the state's many trees begin to turn vibrant shades of red, orange, and yellow.
- *Winter (December - February)*: Winters in Nevada can be mild in the southern parts of the state but cold in the northern regions. Temperatures can range from the mid-20s to the mid-50s, depending on the location. Some parts of the state, particularly higher elevations, may experience snowfall during this time.

Land Topography

- **Great Basin:** The Great Basin in Nevada is known for its elevated terrain, arid weather, and distinctive biodiversity. Numerous uncommon and threatened flora and fauna species thrive within this vast expanse, including the sagebrush and pronghorn antelope.
- **Lake Tahoe:** Located on the border of Nevada and California, Lake Tahoe is a vast freshwater lake renowned for its crystal-clear water, picturesque views, and plentiful recreational activities such as fishing, boating, and hiking.
- **Red Rock Canyon:** Located just outside Las Vegas, Red Rock Canyon boasts towering rock formations, breathtaking vistas, and scenic hiking trails.
- **Valley of Fire State Park:** Valley of Fire State Park, situated in southeastern Nevada, is a renowned hotspot for hikers, campers, and nature enthusiasts. This captivating park is celebrated for its vibrant rock formations and breathtaking vistas.

"Las Vegas is a city built on hopes, dreams, and a little bit of crazy."

- MICHAEL MCDONALD, SINGER/SONGWRITER

Foraging Hotspots

- **Mount Charleston:** situated near Las Vegas, is a renowned spot for foragers due to its plentiful supply of wild berries like raspberries and huckleberries, alongside a diverse range of edible mushrooms and other wild edibles.
- **Red Rock Canyon:** a favored spot among foragers due to its plentiful supply of wild berries, including elderberries and gooseberries, and a diverse range of edible plants like the prickly pear cactus.
- **Humboldt-Toiyabe National Forest:** in eastern Nevada is a vast and expansive forest that attracts many foragers. It is renowned for its plentiful supply of wild mushrooms, including the morel and the chanterelle, as well as a diverse range of wild berries and other edible plants.
- **Ruby Mountains:** are a favored spot for foragers due to the plentiful wild mushrooms, including morel and porcini, and diverse edible plants like wild onion.
- **Spring Mountains:** Just outside of Las Vegas, the Spring Mountains boast a rich array of wild berries like strawberries and raspberries, along with a diverse selection of edible plants, including the desert parsley and the Indian potato.

Local Foraging Groups

- **Nevada Herbalist Guild:** the Guild serves herb enthusiasts throughout the state, from bustling cities to the serene countryside. Whether you live in Las

Vegas, Reno, or anywhere else, the Nevada Herbalist Guild is here to guide you on your herbal journey. The Guild offers many exciting workshops, classes, and hikes for aspiring herbalists of all ages. Join them for immersive workshops where you'll learn how to identify and harvest medicinal plants, prepare herbal remedies, and discover the ancient wisdom of herbal healing. Take part in informative classes taught by experienced herbalists who will share their knowledge on topics such as herbal teas, natural skincare, and herbal first aid. And don't miss out on their refreshing hikes, where you can explore the bountiful flora and learn about the plants that thrive in Nevada's unique ecosystems. For more information about the Nevada Herbalist Guild, upcoming events, and how to join, visit their website.

- **Foragers of Northern Nevada:** offers a range of captivating workshops, informative classes, and exhilarating hikes that unveil the hidden treasures of our local flora and fauna. Join their knowledgeable guides and fellow enthusiasts as you immerse yourself in wild edibles, medicinal plants, and natural resources in our backyard. Through their workshops, you will gain invaluable insights into identifying, harvesting, and preparing various edible plants, mushrooms, and herbs. Uncover these natural wonders' diverse flavors and healing properties and discover how to seamlessly incorporate them into your daily life. For those yearning for hands-on experience, their guided hikes allow them to explore the breathtaking landscapes of Northern Nevada while discovering wild edibles and deepening their understanding of the region's ecology. Please visit their website to explore more about the Foragers of Northern Nevada and their upcoming events.

- **Southern Nevada Wild Edibles:** Discover the wonders of Southern Nevada's wild edibles with exciting workshops, classes, and hikes offered by Southern Nevada Wild Edibles. Gain fascinating insights into the native plants of the region and learn how they can be used for food, medicine, and other practical purposes. Explore the different species, their nutritional values, and how to identify them in the wild during their workshops. Take informative classes on sustainable harvesting, plant preservation, and creating delicious recipes using wild edibles. Join their knowledgeable guides on guided hikes to explore scenic trails, identify edible plants, and gain valuable insights into the region's unique ecosystem. Visit their website to learn more about upcoming events.

- **Reno Tahoe Wild Edibles:** Based in the stunning region of Reno and Tahoe, our group encompasses a vast area, including the awe-inspiring landscapes and diverse biodiversity of the surrounding forests, meadows, and mountains. We provide an array of captivating workshops, classes, and hikes to assist aspiring nature enthusiasts and adventurous food lovers in exploring the realm of wild edibles. Our workshops offer immersive learning experiences where you will learn about these natural treasures' nutritional and medicinal properties. Uncover the art of foraging, sustainable harvesting practices, and delectable recipes that showcase the flavors of the wilderness. Reno Tahoe Wild Edibles caters to all individuals, offering an opportunity to fully immerse yourself in the marvels of the great outdoors and forge a unique connection with the natural world. Please visit our website for further details on our upcoming workshops, classes, and hikes.

Nevada offers a plethora of natural marvels, ranging from the dazzling lights of Las Vegas to the breathtaking landscapes of the Great Basin. With abundant foraging hotspots and local groups, the state caters to the diverse interests of all individuals.

CHAPTER 5
NEW MEXICO
THE LAND OF ENCHANTMENT

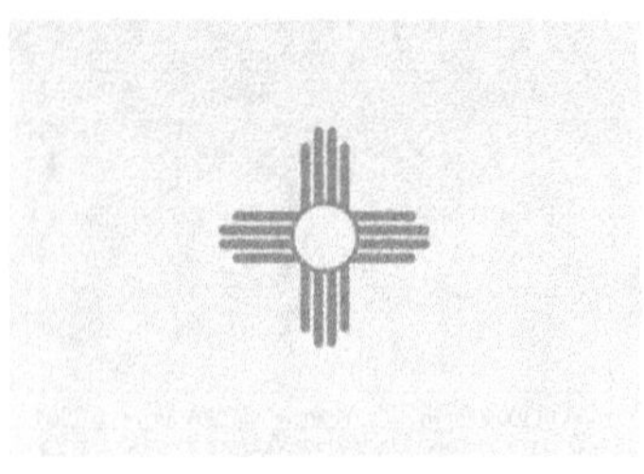

New Mexico, located in the southwestern region of the United States, is full of natural beauty, rich history, and vibrant culture. With its diverse landscapes, warm weather, and unique wildlife, New Mexico offers endless outdoor adventures and exploration opportunities. From the famous Santa Fe to the lesser-known foraging hotspots, New Mexico is a state that is just waiting to be discovered.

Yearly Weather Patterns by Season

- *Spring (March-May):* Spring in New Mexico is characterized by mild temperatures and occasional rainfall. Temperatures range from the mid-50s to the mid-70s, and the state's many wildflowers begin to bloom during this time.
- *Summer (June - August):* Summers in New Mexico can be sweltering, with temperatures often exceeding 100 degrees Fahrenheit. It is best to stay indoors during the hottest parts of the day, particularly in the lower elevations.
- *Fall (September - November):* Fall in New Mexico is characterized by cooler temperatures and changing foliage. Temperatures range from the mid-50s to the mid-70s, and the state's many trees begin to turn vibrant shades of red, orange, and yellow.
- *Winter (December - February):* Winters in New Mexico can be cold, particularly in the northern parts of the state, with temperatures sometimes dropping below freezing. Some parts of the state, particularly higher elevations, may experience snowfall during this time.

Land Topography

- **Sangre de Cristo Mountains:** The Sangre de Cristo Mountains are a mountain range in northern New Mexico. They are known for their beautiful vistas, alpine forests, and abundant wildlife.
- **Chihuahuan Desert:** The Chihuahuan Desert is a large desert region that covers much of southern New Mexico. It is known for its unique plant and animal species, such as the yucca and roadrunner.
- **Rio Grande Valley:** The Rio Grande Valley is a large valley that runs through central New Mexico. It is known for its fertile soil, beautiful scenery, and abundant wildlife.

"The country itself, through its legends and mythology, has always been a source of inspiration and awe."

- GEORGIA O'KEEFFE, AMERICAN ARITIST

Foraging Hotspots

- **Santa Fe National Forest:** Located in northern New Mexico, it is a popular destination for foragers thanks to its abundance of wild berries, such as raspberries and huckleberries, as well as its variety of edible mushrooms and other wild edibles.
- **Valles Caldera National Preserve:** is a large, sprawling preserve that is located in northern New Mexico. It is a popular destination for foragers thanks to its abundance of wild mushrooms, such as the morel and the chanterelle, as well as its variety of wild berries and other edible plants.
- **Gila National Forest:** is a large, sprawling forest in southwestern New Mexico. It is a popular destination for foragers thanks to its abundance of wild mushrooms, such as the porcini and the lobster mushroom, as well as its variety of wild berries and other edible plants.
- **Carson National Forest:** Located in northern New Mexico, it is a popular destination for foragers thanks to its abundance of wild mushrooms, such as the morel and the chanterelle, as well as its variety of wild berries and other edible plants.
- **Organ Mountains-Desert Peaks National Monument:** located in southern New Mexico, is a popular destination for foragers thanks to its abundance of wild plants, such as the agave and the prickly pear cactus.

Local Foraging Groups

- **New Mexico Wildcrafters:** A group focused on promoting the sustainable use of New Mexico's natural resources through wildcrafting and foraging. They offer a variety of classes and workshops on wildcrafting, herbalism, and other natural health practices and are an excellent resource for those interested in foraging in New Mexico. Visit their website for more information.

- **Albuquerque Herbalism:** A group focused on promoting the use of medicinal plants and herbs found in the wilds of New Mexico. They offer a variety of classes and workshops on herbalism, foraging, and other natural health practices. They are an excellent resource for those interested in the healing properties of New Mexico's wild plants. Visit their website for more information.
- **Foraging New Mexico:** A group focused on exploring the wilds of New Mexico and foraging for wild edibles. They offer a variety of events and workshops throughout the year, including foraging hikes and plant identification classes, and are an excellent resource for those interested in learning more about foraging in the state. Visit their website for more information.
- **Los Alamos Mountaineers:** A group focused on exploring the wilderness of New Mexico and surrounding areas. They offer a variety of events and workshops throughout the year, including foraging hikes and plant identification classes, and are an excellent resource for those interested in foraging in the state. Visit their website for more information.
- **Farmington Wildcrafters:** A group focused on promoting the sustainable use of New Mexico's natural resources through wildcrafting and foraging. They offer a variety of classes and workshops on wildcrafting, herbalism, and other natural health practices and are an excellent resource for those interested in foraging in the Farmington area. Visit their website for more information.
- **High Desert Foraging:** A group focused on exploring the wilds of northern New Mexico and foraging for wild edibles. They offer a variety of events and workshops throughout the year, including foraging hikes and plant identification classes, and are an excellent resource for those interested in learning more about foraging in the state. Visit their website for more information.
- **New Mexico Mycological Society:** A group focused on promoting the study and enjoyment of wild mushrooms in New Mexico. They offer a variety of events and workshops throughout the year, including mushroom identification classes and foraging hikes, and are an excellent resource for those interested in learning more about mushroom foraging in the state. Visit their website for more information.

New Mexico is full of natural wonders and opportunities for outdoor exploration, including foraging wild edibles. From the Santa Fe National Forest to the Gila National Forest, there are plenty of foraging hotspots throughout the state for those interested in wildcrafting. And with various local foraging groups, plenty of resources are available to learn more about foraging in the Land of Enchantment. So pack your bags and head out to New Mexico for an adventure you will never forget!

CHAPTER 6
UTAH
THE BEEHIVE STATE

Utah is a state that carries a rich and colorful history. It is known for its vibrant landscapes and unique past. In the mid-1800s, a group of pioneers called the Mormons traveled to Utah to find freedom to practice their religion. Brigham Young led this group, and Salt Lake City became their home. Later on, Utah played a big part in the Western expansion of the United States, with the famous Golden Spike marking the completion of the first Transcontinental Railroad in 1869. Utah became the 45th state of the U.S. in 1896.

Yearly Weather Patterns by Season

- *Spring (March-May):* Spring in Utah is characterized by mild temperatures and occasional rainfall. Temperatures range from the mid-40s to the mid-60s, and the state's many wildflowers begin to bloom during this time.
- *Summer (June - August):* Summers in Utah can be scorching, with temperatures often exceeding 100 degrees Fahrenheit. It is best to stay indoors during the hottest parts of the day, particularly in the lower elevations.
- *Fall (September - November):* Fall in Utah is characterized by cooler temperatures and changing foliage. Temperatures range from the mid-40s to the mid-60s, and the state's many trees begin to turn vibrant shades of red, orange, and yellow.
- *Winter (December - February):* Winters in Utah can be frigid, particularly in the northern parts of the state, with temperatures sometimes dropping below freezing. Some parts of the state, particularly higher elevations, may experience heavy snowfall during this time.

- **Wasatch Range:** The Wasatch Range is a mountain range in northern Utah. It is known for its beautiful vistas, alpine forests, and abundant wildlife.
- **Red Rock Country:** Red Rock Country is a region in southern Utah known for its unique rock formations and rugged landscapes. It is home to several national parks, including Zion and Arches.
- **Great Salt Lake:** The Great Salt Lake is a large saltwater lake in northern Utah. It is the largest saltwater lake in the Western Hemisphere and is known for its unique ecosystem and wildlife.

"Utah, the only state where you can be a Democrat, a doctor, and a skier."

- MICHAEL DUKAKIS, FORMER GOVERNOR OF
MASSACHUSETTS

Foraging Hotspots

- **Wasatch Mountain State Park:** Wasatch Mountain State Park, located in northern Utah, is a popular destination for foragers thanks to its abundance of wild berries, such as raspberries and huckleberries, as well as its variety of edible mushrooms and other wild edibles.
- **Zion National Park:** Zion National Park, located in southern Utah, is a popular destination for foragers thanks to its abundance of wild plants, such as the prickly pear cactus and the elderberry.
- **Grand Staircase-Escalante National Monument:** Grand Staircase-Escalante National Monument, located in southern Utah, is a popular destination for foragers thanks to its abundance of wild mushrooms, such as the morel and the chanterelle, as well as its variety of wild berries and other edible plants.
Capitol Reef National Park: Capitol Reef National Park, located in central Utah, is a popular destination for foragers thanks to its abundance of wild berries, such as the chokecherry and the serviceberry, as well as its variety of edible mushrooms and other wild edibles.
- **Uinta-Wasatch-Cache National Forest:** The Uinta-Wasatch-Cache National Forest is a large, sprawling forest in northern Utah. It is a popular destination for foragers thanks to its abundance of wild mushrooms, such as the porcini and the lobster mushroom, as well as its variety of wild berries and other edible plants.

Local Foraging Groups

- **Salt Lake City Foraging Collective:** The Salt Lake City Foraging Collective is a group of foragers dedicated to exploring the wild edibles of Utah. They offer a variety of events and workshops throughout the year, including foraging hikes and plant identification classes, and are an excellent resource for those interested in foraging in the Salt Lake City area. Visit their website for more information.

- **Ogden Wildcrafters:** Ogden Wildcrafters is a group that promotes the sustainable use of Utah's natural resources through wildcrafting and foraging. They offer a variety of classes and workshops on wildcrafting, herbalism, and other natural health practices and are an excellent resource for those interested in foraging in the Ogden area. Visit their website for more information.
- **Southern Utah Foragers:** Southern Utah Foragers is a group focused on exploring the wilds of southern Utah and foraging for wild edibles. They offer a variety of events and workshops throughout the year, including foraging hikes and plant identification classes, and are an excellent resource for those interested in learning more about foraging in the state. Visit their website for more information.
- **Moab Wildcrafting:** Moab Wildcrafting is a group focused on promoting the sustainable use of Utah's natural resources through wildcrafting and foraging. They offer a variety of classes and workshops on wildcrafting, herbalism, and other natural health practices and are an excellent resource for those interested in foraging in the Moab area. Visit their website for more information.
- **Cache Valley Foragers:** Cache Valley Foragers is a group focused on exploring northern Utah's wilds and foraging for wild edibles. They offer a variety of events and workshops throughout the year, including foraging hikes and plant identification classes, and are an excellent resource for those interested in learning more about foraging in the state. Visit their website for more information.
- **Southern Utah Mycological Society:** The Southern Utah Mycological Society is a group that promotes the study and enjoyment of wild mushrooms in southern Utah. They offer a variety of events and workshops throughout the year, including mushroom identification classes and foraging hikes, and are an excellent resource for those interested in learning more about mushroom foraging in the state. Visit their website for more information.
- **Utah Valley Permaculture:** Utah Valley Permaculture is a group that promotes sustainable living practices in the Utah Valley area, including wildcrafting and foraging. They offer a variety of events and workshops throughout the year, including foraging hikes and plant identification classes, and are an excellent resource for those interested in learning more about sustainable living in the state. Visit their website.

There's much to see and do in Utah, including exploring the outdoors and foraging wild foods. Those interested in wildcrafting can find plenty of foraging hotspots around the state. Many resources are available for people who want to learn more about foraging in the Beehive State. Take a trip to Utah and explore the wild edibles of this beautiful state for an adventure you'll never forget.

NOTE FROM THE PUBLISHER

We completely understand the advantages of using color photos to identify plants. However, to make this book edition more affordable, we decided to use black-and-white photographs, which helped us reduce printing costs, which we passed on to you. But don't worry—we have a solution for you! Scan the QR code below and download a complimentary printable PDF file that includes vibrant, clear, color photos of all the plants featured in the book. Happy Foraging!

PART THREE
FRUITS & BERRIES

Arizona Rosewood

Vauquelinia californica [VAW-KWUH-LIN-EE-UH KAL-UH-FOR-NI-KUH]

Native Americans used the Arizona Rosewood for traditional purposes, such as making fence posts and small tools. It belongs to the Rosaceae (rose) family, and other familiar names include California Rosewood and simply Rosewood.

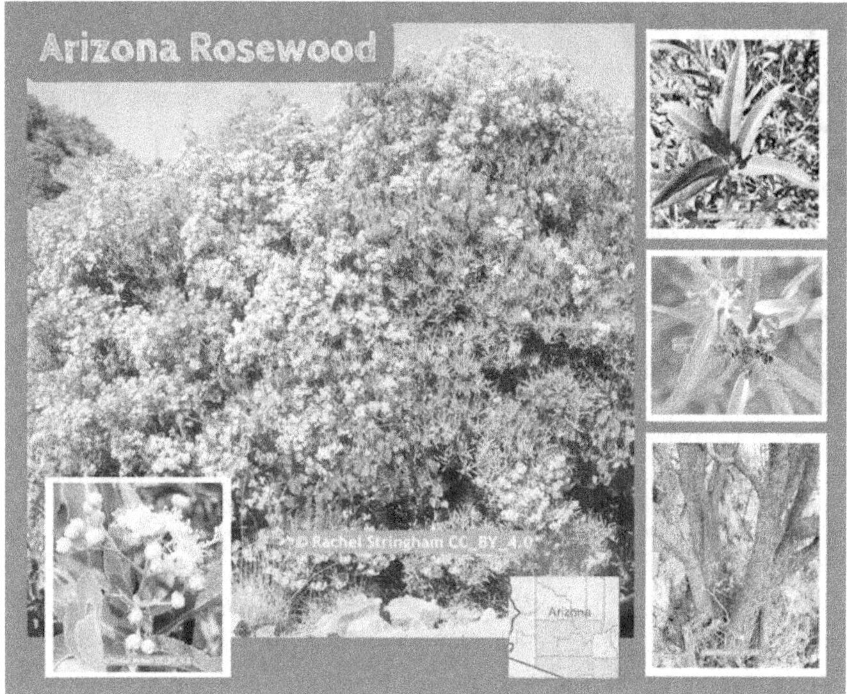

Native to the southwestern region of the United States, including Arizona, New Mexico, Nevada, and parts of Utah. Look for it in canyons, washes, and rocky slopes.

Identification:

GROWTH/SIZE: a shrub that grows compact and bushy. It typically reaches a moderate height of 6 to 10 feet and spreads to a similar width.

BARK/STEM/ROOT: The bark is smooth and often appears grayish-brown. It may have fine lines or shallow ridges running along its surface. The stems are slender and woody, usually with a reddish-brown hue. They grow upright and can reach heights of 10 to 20 feet. They are often covered in small, alternating leaves that give the plant a feathery appearance. The roots are extensive and can be both fibrous and deep-reaching. They spread out in search of water and nutrients in the soil. The roots are essential in anchoring the plant and absorbing necessary resources for its growth and survival.

LEAF: The leaves are vibrant, shiny, and dark green. They are elongated and lanceolate, tapering to a point at the end. They grow in an alternate arrangement along the branches, creating a feathery appearance. They can range in size from 1 to 3 inches long, depending on the age of the plant.

FLOWER: arranged in small clusters called panicles. Each flower has five petals and comes in shades of white or cream, sometimes with a tinge of pink. The flowers bloom in spring, covering the plant in a burst of color and attracting pollinators like bees and butterflies. While the exact size of the flowers may vary, they are typically around half an inch to one inch in diameter.

FRUIT/SEED/NUT: These round or oval fruits are green when unripe, then turn dark brown or black when mature. They grow in clusters on the plant's branches. You'll find hard, dark brown, or black seeds or nuts in each fruit. Fruits and seeds form after the plant blooms with tiny white or pale pink flowers. They're usually small, about 0.25 to 0.5 inches in diameter, but they can vary. Those seeds are even smaller, between 0.1 and 0.2 inches across. The best time to harvest them is in the late summer or early fall when they're mature. The fruits will have turned dark brown or black and may have wrinkles or dried appearances.

Look-a-like(s): Toxic: **Oleander** (*Nerium oleander*) and the **Yellow Oleander** (*Thevetia peruviana*) are two plants that are toxic and can be confused with the Arizona Rosewood. The leaves of both plants are elongated and pointed, but the flowers are different colors. Oleanders have pink, white, or red flowers, while Yellow Oleanders have yellow or orange flowers.

Non-toxic: **Texas Mountain Laurel** (*Sophora secundiflora*) and the **Silk Tassel** (*Garrya spp.*) share similar characteristics with the Arizona Rosewood. The Texas Mountain Laurel has similar leaves and produces fragrant, purple flowers. The Silk Tassel also has dark green leaves, but its flowers are long and pendulous, resembling tassels.

Cautions: There are no significant cautions associated with the Arizona Rosewood.

Culinary Preparations: It's not commonly used as a food ingredient, but its leaves can be used to make tea. To make Rosewood tea, steep the leaves in hot water for a few minutes. The tea has a slightly bitter taste but is refreshing and soothing.

Medicinal Uses: Traditionally used by Native Americans to treat various ailments, including toothaches, stomach aches, and colds. In modern times, the plant has been found to have potential antimicrobial and antioxidant properties. However, further research is needed to determine its full medicinal potential.

Fun/Historical Fact: Arizona Rosewood is highly valued by guitar makers for its beautiful and unique grain pattern and tonal qualities. The wood is hard, dense, and resonant, making it an excellent choice for guitar backs and sides. Many famous guitarists, including Carlos Santana and Doyle Dykes, have guitars made with Arizona Rosewood.

Dog Toxicity: Not considered toxic to dogs. However, ingestion may cause gastrointestinal upset, such as vomiting or diarrhea.

Banana Yucca

Yucca baccata [YUHK-UH BUH-KAH-TUH]

Native Americans have used Banana Yucca for centuries as a source of food and medicine. The roots were used to make soap, while the seeds were ground into flour and used for making bread. It belongs to the Asparagaceae (asparagus) family. Banana Yucca is also known by other common names such as Datil Yucca, Spanish Bayonet, and Soapweed Yucca.

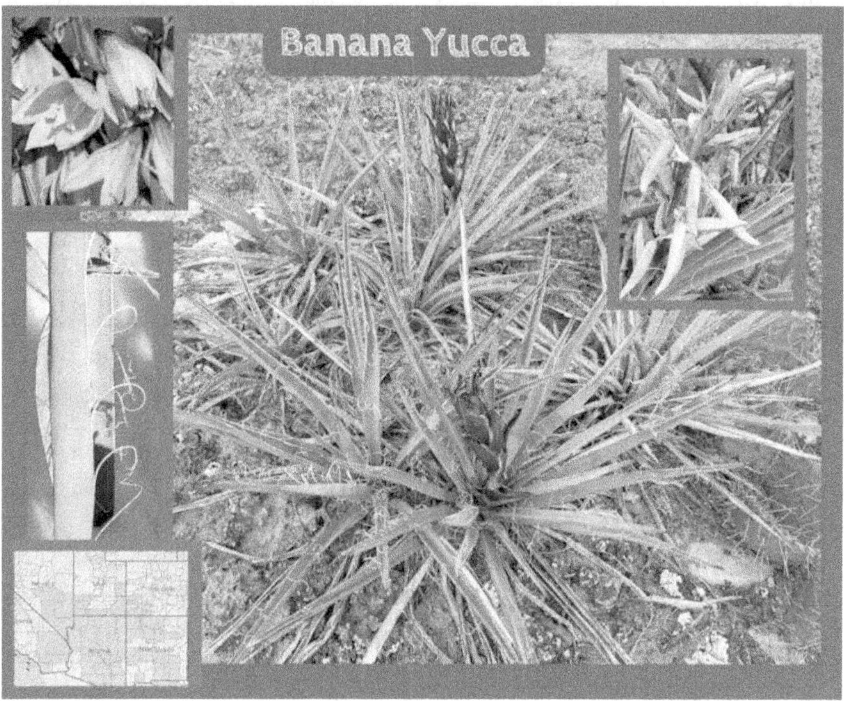

Location: Banana Yucca is native to the southwestern region of the United States, specifically in areas such as Arizona, New Mexico, and Utah. It grows in arid areas, including deserts, rocky slopes, and grasslands.

Identification:

GROWTH/SIZE: It typically clumps, with multiple stems originating from a central base. The plant can reach a height of about 2 to 3 feet with a spread of around 3 to 5 feet, creating a visually striking presence in its arid environment.

BARK/STEM/ROOT: The bark is rough and thick, often displaying a grayish-brown color. It forms a unique pattern with vertical fissures and ridges that add texture to its appearance. The stems are stout, sturdy, and usually woody. They grow upright from the base, resembling thick, spiky trunks with a greenish-brown hue. They can reach heights of several feet. As for the roots, an extensive, fleshy taproot system extends deep into the ground. These robust roots help the plant withstand arid conditions by efficiently absorbing water from the soil.

LEAF: is long, slender, and sword-shaped. They have a vibrant green color and grow in a rosette pattern at the base of the plant. Each leaf is typically 1 to 2 feet long, and the edges are often sharp and pointed. They can curve gracefully or have a slightly rigid appearance.

FLOWER: has a creamy white or pale yellow color, resembling the hue of a banana. They grow in clusters on tall stalks that emerge from the center of the plant. Each flower has six petals and a tubular shape resembling a bell or cup. The flowers are quite large, typically around 2 to 3 inches long. Banana yucca blooms in the spring or early summer,

FRUIT/SEED/NUT: The fruit is a large, oval-shaped, fleshy structure with a greenish-brown color. It grows in clusters on tall stalks that emerge from the center of the plant. As the fruit matures, it turns a golden brown and tastes sweet, indicating it is ready to harvest. Numerous black, flat seeds are shaped like teardrops inside the fruit. It also produces edible nuts that are found within the fruit. The nuts are large, dark brown, and have a hard shell. Harvesting typically occurs in late summer or early fall when they are fully mature and have turned a golden brown. It's essential to wait until this stage to ensure optimal flavor and nutritional value.

Look-A-Likes: Toxic: **Red Yucca** (*Hesperaloe parviflora*) can be mistaken for Banana Yucca. It has a similar shape and pink flowers.

Non-toxic: **Joshua Tree** (*Yucca brevifolia*) and the **Spanish Dagger** (*Yucca gloriosa*) are two plants with similar characteristics. However, the Joshua Tree has a distinctive branching pattern, while the Spanish Dagger has wider leaves with a bluish tint.

Cautions: Foraging for Banana Yucca requires caution, as the plant has sharp, pointed leaves that can cause injury. Additionally, the roots contain saponins, which can be harmful if ingested in large quantities.

Culinary Preparations: Its unique flavor and texture make it a popular ingredient in many Southwestern dishes. Here are just a few ways you can make use of this plant. Boil the fruit with sugar and water to make a delicious jam that can be spread on toast or used as a topping for ice cream. You can boil the roots with vegetables and spices for a hearty and nutritious soup, and after removing the outer shell, you can roast the seeds in a pan or oven to make a healthy snack.

Medicinal Uses: Traditionally, Native Americans used the root to make soap for washing and shampoo to treat dandruff. Some modern research suggests that Yucca extract might have anti-inflammatory properties and could be helpful for arthritis.

Fun/Historical Fact: The fibers from the leaves were used by Native Americans to make rope, baskets, and even clothing. The fibers are strong and durable, making them ideal for these purposes.

Dog Toxicity: Good news, dog owners! Banana Yucca is not toxic to dogs. However, keeping your furry friends away from those sharp leaves is always best to avoid injuries.

Buffaloberry

Shepherdia argentea [SHEP-HER-dee-uh ar-JEN-tee-uh]

Buffaloberry has been used for centuries by Native Americans. It belongs to the Elaeagnaceae (oleaster) family. Buffaloberry is also known as Silver Buffaloberry, Rabbitberry, and Soopolallie [SOO-PUH-LAL-EE].

Buffaloberry is native to North America, and you can find it growing in areas such as the Great Plains, the Rocky Mountains, and the southwestern United States. It grows best in dry regions and is often found in open grasslands, forests, and riverbanks.

Identification:

GROWTH/SIZE: a shrub typically grows in a rounded or bushy shape. It can reach 6 to 10 feet tall and has a similar spread, creating a dense and compact appearance.

BARK/STEM/ROOT: The bark is thin and smooth, often gray or brownish-gray. The stems are slender and woody, covered in tiny silvery hairs that give them a fuzzy appearance. They can grow several feet tall, branching out bushy or spreading. The extensive and fibrose roots extend deep into the soil to anchor the plant and gather nutrients and water. They help the shrub withstand harsh conditions and provide stability.

LEAF: elongated and lance-shaped. They have a distinct silvery-gray color, which gives the plant its name. The leaves are arranged alternately along the branches, growing in an alternating pattern. They can vary in size but are typically around 2 to 4 centimeters long.

FLOWER: The flowers are typically a pale yellow or greenish and have a tubular shape with tiny petals. The flowers can be found blooming in the spring or early summer. Although individually small, they create a beautiful and delicate display when the flowers are clustered together.

FRUIT/SEED/NUT: produces small, bright red berries about 1/4 inch in diameter. The berries are covered in a silvery-gray coating and have a sweet-tart flavor. The fruits are ready to harvest in late summer or early fall when fully ripened and become soft to the touch.

Look-a-like(s): Toxic: **Holly** (*Ilex spp.*) is a shrub or small tree with glossy and dark green spiny leaves that produce small, white flowers that bloom in clusters. The berries are similar in appearance, but they are toxic and can cause nausea, vomiting, and diarrhea if ingested. **Red-berried Elder** (*Sambucus racemosa*) is a deciduous shrub that produces clusters of small, white flowers, which later develop into bright red berries. The berries look similar but are mildly toxic and can cause nausea, vomiting, and diarrhea if ingested in large quantities.

Non-toxic: The **Oregon Grape** (*Mahonia aquifolium*) and the **Autumn Olive** (*Elaeagnus umbellata*) are non-toxic plants that resemble Buffaloberry. The Oregon Grape has prickly leaves and produces blue-black berries. The Autumn Olive has silvery-green leaves and produces red berries with silvery speckles.

Cautions: When foraging for Buffaloberry, be cautious of any nearby toxic look-a-likes.

Culinary Preparations: *Jams and jellies:* The berries can be cooked with sugar and pectin to create a vibrant and flavorful spread. *Beverages:* Extract the juice by blending and straining the berries. The juice can be enjoyed on its own or used as a base for cocktails, mocktails, or fruit-infused water. *Baked goods:* The berries can be added to muffins, scones, pies, or bread, imparting a tart and vibrant flavor. Depending on your preference, they can be used fresh or dried. *Salad dressing:* The bright flavor of silver buffaloberry can enhance salad dressings. Blend the berries with vinegar, oil, honey, and your favorite seasonings to create a tangy, fruity dressing that adds flavor to salads.

Medicinal Uses: The leaves have traditionally been used to treat inflammation and pain. Modern research has found that the plant contains anti-inflammatory compounds that may help reduce inflammation and pain. The fruit has traditionally been used to treat digestive issues like diarrhea and dysentery. The fruit is high in fiber, which may help regulate bowel movements and improve digestive health. The fruit is high in antioxidants, which may help reduce the risk of chronic diseases such as cancer, heart disease, and Alzheimer's. The plant contains compounds that may help stimulate the immune system, improving overall health and well-being.

Fun or historical fact: The Buffaloberry gets its name from its historical use as a food source for buffalo. The berries were a valuable food source for indigenous communities and the animals that roamed the plains.

Dog toxicity: Buffaloberry is not considered toxic to dogs.

oralberry

Symphoricarpos orbiculatus [SIM-FOR-IH-KAR-POHS OR-BIK-YOO-LAY-TUS]

Coralberry is a deciduous shrub that belongs to the Caprifoliaceae (honeysuckle) family. Some other common names for the plant include Buckbrush, Indian Currant, and Waxberry. Historically, Native Americans used coralberry for medicinal purposes, such as treating toothaches and sore throats.

Coralberry is native to North America. It prefers moist, well-drained soils and can tolerate both sun and shade. It grows in various habitats, including forests, woodlands, thickets, and rocky slopes. It can also grow along the edges of fields and roadsides.

Identification:

GROWTH/SIZE: Grows between 2 and 5 feet tall but can reach up to 8 feet sometimes.

BARK/STEM/ROOT: The bark is grayish-brown and may become rough with age. The stems are slender and green, and the roots are shallow.

LEAF: The leaves are simple, oval-shaped, measuring 1-2 inches long.

FLOWER: The flowers are small, pink, or white and are arranged in clusters. It blooms from spring to mid-summer, depending on the region.

FRUIT/SEED/NUT: The fruit is a small, round berry that starts green and turns bright pink or red when ripe. The fruit is in season from September to December.

Look-a-like(s): Toxic: Coralberry is not known to have any toxic look-a-likes.

Non-toxic: **Snowberry** (*Symphoricarpos albus*) and **Creeping Snowberry**

(*Symphoricarpos mollis*) are similar to coralberry. However, they have white berries.

Cautions: Eating a lot of berries may lead to some tummy troubles, but don't worry, they're not fatal.

Culinary Preparations: Explore the versatility of these berries! Mix them with other fruits and sugar to create a delicious jam or jelly. Cook them with sugar and water to make a sweet syrup perfect for pancakes or desserts. Add them to muffins, cakes, or bread for a delightful twist. And don't forget about sauces - cook them down with sugar, vinegar, and spices to create a savory sauce that pairs perfectly with gamey meats. The possibilities are endless!

Medicinal Uses: Indigenous communities traditionally use Coralberry for various medicinal purposes. Here are some potential ways to use Coralberry as medicine: Make tea from the leaves and berries and drink it several times a day to relieve symptoms of cough, asthma, bronchitis, fever, and sore throat. The bark and leaves have been used to treat digestive issues such as diarrhea, constipation, and stomach pain. You can make tea from the bark or leaves and drink it before meals to improve digestion and treat digestive issues such as diarrhea, constipation, and stomach pain. Coralberry has been traditionally used to treat skin conditions such as eczema, rashes, and wounds. Make a poultice from the leaves and apply it to the affected area, or use a lotion from the berries to soothe the skin. Menstrual-related issues can be relieved by making tea from the leaves and drinking it several times daily to help with cramps and other symptoms.

Fun/Historical Fact: Coralberry's scientific name, Symphoricarpos, comes from the Greek words "symphos," meaning "joined together," and "karpos," meaning "fruit." This refers to the plant's clustered fruits. Another fun fact is that the Coralberry's pink or red berries are not actual berries but drupes.

Dog toxicity: Coralberry is not considered toxic to dogs. However, large amounts could cause symptoms of toxicity in dogs, including vomiting, diarrhea, lethargy, and loss of appetite.

D esert Peach

Prunus andersonii [PROO-NUS AN-DER-SO-NEE-EYE]

The Desert Peach is a member of the Rosaceae (rose) family. Another common name includes the Hog Plum. Historically, Native Americans used the fruits for food and the bark for medicinal purposes.

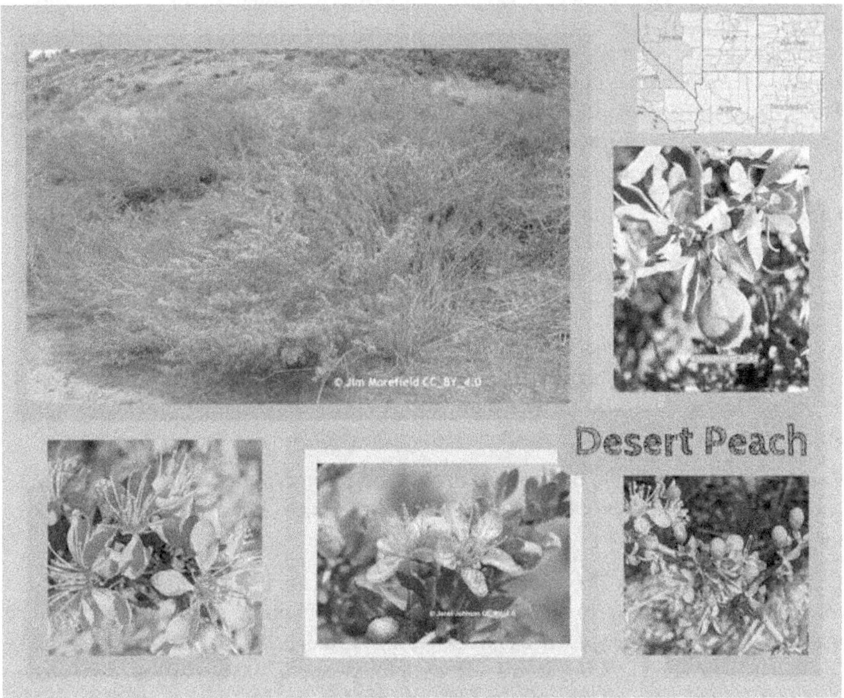

The Desert Peach is native to the western United States and can be found in California, Nevada, and Utah. It is primarily found in arid regions, including deserts, rocky slopes, and canyons. The plant prefers well-drained soils and full sun exposure.

Identification:

GROWTH/SIZE: Small tree or shrub that grows up to 15 feet tall.

BARK/STEM/ROOT: its bark can become rough and grayish-brown, eventually devel- oping fissures or scales. Younger stems have a smoother texture and reddish to purplish hue, often with short, sharp spines. Its deep root system allows it to access water sources far below the soil surface, enabling survival in arid environments. As the roots mature, they may develop a woody texture.

LEAF: The leaves, arranged alternately on the stems, are deciduous and simple. They are usually oblong to elliptic in shape, with a length that varies from 1 to 2.5 inches (2.5 to 6.4 cm). The leaf margins are commonly serrated or toothed, and the upper surface of the leaves is green with a slightly shiny appearance. The underside of the leaves can be paler in color.

FLOWER: The small clusters of flowers emit a strong, pleasant fragrance and are typically pink to rose-colored. Each flower is approximately 1 inch (2.5 cm) across and has five petals and numerous stamens in the center. This plant usually blooms in the spring, typically between March and May, although the exact timing may vary based on factors such as elevation, latitude, and microclimate.

FRUIT/SEED/NUT: The small drupe, resembling a miniature peach or plum, is covered in a dense, short fuzz on its outer skin and can vary in color from reddish to yellowish or even orange when mature. It's important to note that despite its visual appeal, the fruit is not widely considered palatable due to its bitter or astringent taste. The fleshy part of the fruit contains a hard stone or pit, which houses the plant's seed. The timing of fruit maturation can vary depending on local climate and specific conditions, but in its native regions, fruit ripening is typically expected in late summer.

Look-a-like(s): Toxic: **Bitter almond** (*Prunus dulcis var. amara*) produces a fruit with a hard pit. The pit is toxic and contains cyanide. **Wild cherry** (*Prunus avium*) produces a fruit similar in appearance, but its bark, leaves, and seeds contain cyanide and are toxic.

Non-toxic: **Apricot** (*Prunus armeniaca*) is a relative of the Desert Peach and produces a similar fruit. The apricot's fruit is slightly larger and more oval-shaped. **Plum** (*Prunus domestica*) has a similar fruit. The plum's fruit is somewhat larger and more round-shaped.

Cautions: When foraging, be cautious of the hard pit inside the fruit, which can cause choking. Additionally, be aware of the potential presence of cyanide in other plants of the same family.

Culinary Preparations: The fruit is sweet and tart, making it an excellent ingredient for making jams, jellies, fruit preserves, pies, tarts, or chutneys and relishes. It can be used in various desserts such as cakes, muffins, and cobblers. You can also make syrup or sauce when looking for a sweet treat for your pancakes, waffles, or ice cream. Add it to fruit salads and other fruits such as strawberries, blueberries, and grapes.

Medicinal Uses: Discover the incredible healing properties of this natural wonder! Brew a soothing tea from the bark and leaves to ease arthritis and inflammation. The fruit has long been used to treat digestive issues like diarrhea and dysentery, thanks to its fiber-rich composition that promotes healthy digestion. For skin troubles, apply a poultice made from the leaves to soothe eczema, rashes, and wounds. Experience the power of nature's medicine today!

Fun/Historical Fact: Did you know that the Desert Peach was named after Charles L. Anderson, a botanist and explorer who studied the plant in the late 1800s?

Dog toxicity: While the fruit of the Desert Peach is not considered toxic to dogs, a hard pit inside the fruit can pose a choking hazard. If a dog does ingest the pit, it can cause intestinal blockages, leading to vomiting, diarrhea, and other gastrointestinal issues.

New Mexico Raspberry

Rubus neomexicanus [ROO-bus nee-oh-mex-ih-KAN-us]

Are you in search of a mouthwatering and extraordinary fruit? Your quest ends here with the New Mexico Raspberry! Belonging to the Rosaceae (rose) family, this plant is commonly called the Western or New Mexican raspberry. Surprisingly, it has no connection to the typical raspberry that many are accustomed to.

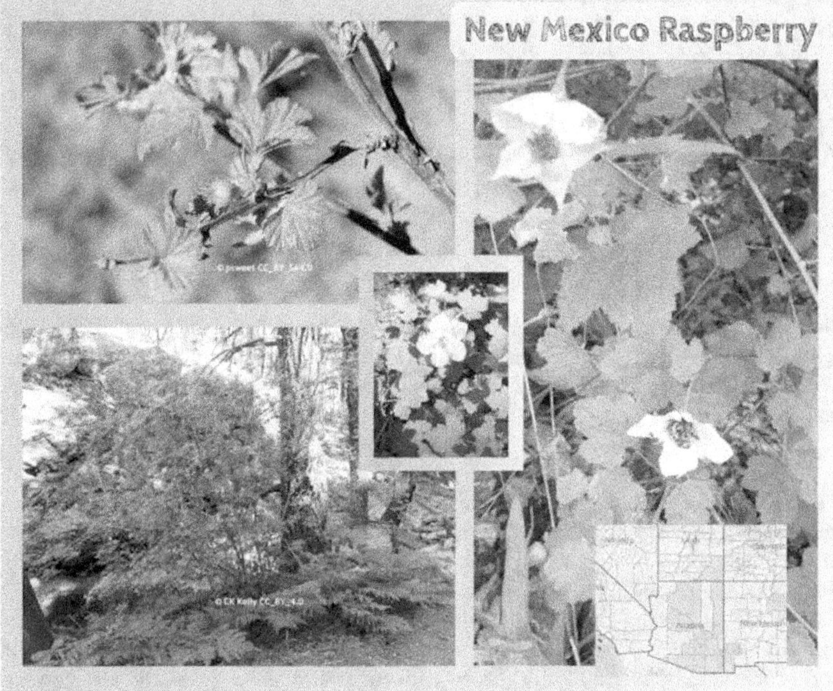

This desert dweller is a true native of the American Southwest, thriving in the wilds of Arizona, New Mexico, Nevada, and Utah. With a preference for arid and rocky terrain, this hardy plant basks in the sun and can often be spotted in areas with ample sunlight.

Identification:

GROWTH / SIZE: A shrub growing up to 6 feet tall.

BARK / STEM / ROOT: The stems, known as Canes, can be biennial, focusing on leaf and branch growth in their first year and fruit production in their second. They start green and mature into brown or reddish-brown, often armed with thorns or prickles. The perennial and woody roots create a dense underground network, allowing the plant to spread and colonize an area effectively. The plant can also send up new shoots, ensuring its survival and expansion through vegetative growth.

LEAF: The leaves consist of three to five leaflets, which are oval to ovate in shape and taper to a point, and they can be up to 6 inches long. The edges of the leaflets are typically serrated or toothed. The upper surface of the leaf is usually green and may have a slightly rough texture, while the underside is often paler and may have a delicate hair-like covering.

FLOWER: The flowers are usually white, occasionally displaying a pale pink hue. They have five broad and rounded petals, often with slightly crinkled or wavy edges. Surrounding a central pistil, you'll find numerous yellowish stamens that protrude outward. The stamens are typically more numerous than the petals and are easily visible. These flowers tend to be in loose clusters. The individual flowers are relatively small and bloom in the late spring or early summer.

Fruit/Seed/Nut: The fruit begins green and ripens to a deep red or nearly black hue, typically possessing a soft and juicy texture when fully matured. Although its size may differ, it is generally smaller than commercially grown raspberries or blackberries. It ripens in the late summer to early autumn.

Look-a-Like(s): Toxic: **Nightshade** (*Solanum spp.*) are typically smaller berries with a more waxy appearance. **Hairy Nightshade** (*Solanum sarrachoides*): the leaves have a hairy texture, and the green berries are clear distinguishing features.

Non-toxic: **Wineberry** (*Rubus phoenicolasius*): Wineberry is an invasive plant with reddish-orange berries. The critical difference lies in the color of the berries. Wineberries are bright, shiny, and red. The leaves are also deeply serrated with three leaflets per leaf.

Cautions: There are no known cautions associated with the New Mexico Raspberry.

Culinary Preparations: Transform these flavorful berries into mouthwatering jams and preserves, craft a heavenly filling by combining them with a touch of sugar, a hint of cinnamon, and a dash of lemon zest, and indulge in the fruity goodness by pouring this delectable mixture into a pie crust or tart shell and baking until it turns a golden brown. Elevate the taste of your fruit salads and add a burst of vibrant color by infusing these juicy berries into them, or create a refreshing and bursting-with-flavor sorbet or gelato by blending the berries with sugar and lemon juice and freezing the mixture. Using these ripe berries, you can add a delightful twist to your water or beverages.

Medicinal Uses: Teas and infusions from the plant's leaves and roots can alleviate indigestion, bloating, and stomach cramps. Additionally, the plant contains anti-inflammatory properties that can reduce inflammation and relieve conditions such as arthritis, joint pain, and muscle soreness. Rubus neomexicanus can also provide respiratory support by easing coughs and sore throats with its expectorant qualities. Its diuretic properties can increase urine production, aiding in flushing toxins and excess fluids from the body.**Fun/Historical Fact:** It is one of the few plants in the rose family with male and female flowers on separate plants.

Dog Toxicity: The New Mexico Raspberry is not toxic to dogs. However, if your dog consumes too much of the fruit, it could cause an upset stomach or diarrhea.

cotillo

Fouquieria splendens [FOO-KWEER-EE-UH SPLEN-DENZ]

Ocotillo, a captivating desert plant from the Fouquieriaceae (ocotillo) family, boasts many names, such as Candlewood, Slimwood, and Coachwhip. This remarkable plant, widely found in the enchanting landscapes of the southwestern United States, actually originates from the vibrant lands of Mexico and various parts of South America.

Native to the sun-drenched lands of Arizona, New Mexico, Nevada, and Utah, this remarkable plant flourishes in the arid embrace of desert environments. Thriving in well-drained, sandy, or rocky soils, the ocotillo plant graces open desert landscapes, adorns rocky hillsides, and adds a touch of beauty to the majestic canyons.

Identification:

GROWTH/SIZE: Grows up to 20 feet tall, but its average height is 10-15 feet.

BARK/ROOT/STEM: The branches grow in a dense cluster, creating a thorny appearance. The bark is grayish-brown, and its stem is long and thin. The root system is shallow but extensive.

LEAF: The leaves are arranged alternately, are small, and have a lanceolate to elliptic shape. They typically measure between 0.5 to 2 inches (1.3 to 5 cm) long. These green leaves create a striking contrast against the plant's long, spiny, and sometimes bare stems. The plant may seem lifeless and devoid of leaves during dry periods, but it can swiftly generate foliage after a good rain.

Flower: The tubular flowers are found in dense clusters at the tips of their long, spiny stems, usually bright red or coral-colored. With a length of about 1 inch (2.5 cm), each flower has a tubular corolla with flared petal-like lobes at the open end. These flowers typically bloom after rainfall, mainly in the spring, but can also bloom sporadically throughout the year with adequate moisture.

Fruit/Seed/Nut: produces an elongated, spindle-shaped capsule measuring approximately 0.5 to 1 inch (1.3 to 2.5 cm) long. These fruits emerge at the branch tips following the pollination and withering of the red tubular flowers. The mature fruit has a dry and slightly rough surface. While initially greenish, it typically develops a brownish hue as it matures. Inside the capsule, numerous small, dark seeds can be found. The fruits ripen in late summer and fall off the plant.

Look-a-Like(s): Toxic: **Red Yucca** (*Hesperaloe parviflora*) leaves are more like tough grass and do not have spines. The flowers form along a tall central spike. **Horse Crippler Cactus** (*Echinocactus texensis*) is round, low to the ground, and doesn't have typical leaves.

Non-Toxic: **Candelilla** (*Euphorbia antisyphilitica*) The stems are shorter and grow more closely together. It has a waxy coating on its stems. **Agave** (*Agave spp.*) The leaves grow rosette from a central point and are often shorter. Agaves usually have a large, tall, flower stalk that extends from the center.

Cautions: There are no known associated issues with the ocotillo plant.

Culinary Preparations: Ocotillo is not commonly used in culinary preparations. However, here are a few creative ways to incorporate it into your cooking. *Ocotillo Syrup:* You can create a unique syrup from the flowers to add a touch of desert flavor to your culinary creations. Boil the flowers in water, sugar, or honey until it thickens into a syrup-like consistency. The syrup can be drizzled over pancakes, waffles, or desserts. *Ocotillo Spice Rub:* Grind dried Ocotillo flowers, leaves, or stems into a fine powder and combine it with other spices such as chili powder, cumin, and garlic powder. Use this homemade spice rub to season meats, vegetables, or roasted dishes, adding a touch of desert flavor.

Medicinal Uses: The plant is traditionally used topically to reduce inflammation in wounds, cuts, and skin irritations. Direct application of the sap or a poultice to the affected area helps soothe and heal. It has a longstanding history of use for respiratory ailments, effectively relieving symptoms of conditions like coughs, bronchitis, and sore throat. Infusions or tinctures from the bark and leaves are commonly consumed to alleviate discomfort. Additionally, it aids digestion by alleviating symptoms such as indigestion, bloating, and stomach discomfort. Consumption of extracts or teas derived from the bark and leaves promotes digestive health.

Fun/Historical Fact: The ocotillo plant is also known as "old man's bones" due to its skeleton-like appearance during periods of drought.

Dog Toxicity: Ocotillo is not toxic to dogs. However, the plant's thorny branches can cause injuries to dogs if they come into contact with them.

ayless Greenthread

Thelesperma megapotamicum [THUH-LESS-PER-MUH MEG-UH-PUH-TAM-IH-KUM]

If you have a fondness for wildflowers, then the Rayless Greenthread is a must-know for you! This captivating plant, a member of the Asteraceae (aster/daisy) family, it goes by the names apricot-colored dogweed and copper-colored dogweed owing to its vibrant orange-yellow flowerheads. It's also been called Navajo tea or Hopi tea greenthread. It boasts stunning hues and its potent fragrance also serves as a natural insect repellent, keeping pesky mosquitoes and flies at bay.

This captivating wildflower thrives in the enchanting landscapes of the southwestern United States, gracing the arid regions of Arizona, New Mexico, Nevada, and Utah. Its delicate petals can be discovered in the most unexpected places, adorning the dry expanses of deserts, the vastness of grasslands, and the rugged slopes of rocky terrains.

Identification:

GROWTH: Grows up to 2 feet tall and spread up to 1 foot wide.

BARK/STEM/ROOT: This plant's slender and erect stems are typically somewhat woody at the base and may exhibit a reddish-to-greenish hue. These stems often branch out and can have a slightly rough texture. Unlike trees, as a herbaceous plant, it lacks a typical "bark," but its outer covering can have a slight texture. A taproot that enables it to thrive in arid native environments. The taproot is specifically adapted to penetrate deep into the soil, allowing the plant to access water sources.

LEAF: The leaves have a linear to lanceolate shape, being long, narrow, and tapering to a point at both ends. They are arranged in an opposite pattern on the stems. The leaves can be divided (pinnately compound), with the divisions occasionally being further divided, resulting in a somewhat feathery appearance. The leaf margins are usually entire, lacking any teeth or serrations. The leaves are green, often with a slightly grayish or whitish tint due to a covering of fine hairs, which can give them a somewhat rough texture.

FLOWER: The flowers have a vibrant yellow color and resemble daisies. They usually have both ray and disk florets. The ray florets are slim and elongated, which gives the flower a unique and somewhat fragile look. The central disk florets are tubular and also yellow. It typically blossoms from March to October.

FRUIT/SEED/NUT: It usually yields a compact, arid fruit known as an achene. Achenes are single-seeded fruits that do not burst open when they reach maturity. The seed is enclosed within the achene. It may also possess a pappus, which consists of hair-like structures that assist in the dispersal of seeds by the wind. Typically, fruiting occurs during the late summer to early fall season.

Look-a-Like(s): Toxic: **Locoweed** (*Astragalus and Oxytropis spp.*) has purple flowers and fuzzy leaves, and **Poison Hemlock** (*Conium maculatum*) has white, umbrella-shaped flowers and purple-spotted stems.

Non-toxic: **Desert Marigold** (*Baileya multiradiata*) has bright yellow flowers, and

Blackfoot Daisy (*Melampodium leucanthum*) has white flowers with a yellow center.

Cautions: There are no significant cautions associated with the Rayless Greenthread.

Culinary Preparations: It has a slightly sweet and earthy flavor that can be enjoyed in various culinary preparations. Here are some ideas:

- Use the leaves and flowers to make tea
- Add the flowers to salads or soups
- Dry and crush the leaves to use as a seasoning for meat dishes

Medicinal Uses: Native Americans traditionally used it to treat stomach and digestive issues, coughs, and colds. Recent research has also shown that the plant contains compounds with anti-inflammatory and antimicrobial properties, which could have potential medical applications.

Fun/Historical Fact: The Rayless Greenthread gets its name because it lacks ray flowers, the small, petal-like structures found in the outer ring of many other plant plants in the aster family. Traditionally, the flowers were used to make a natural dye for fabrics.

Dog Toxicity: The Rayless Greenthread is not considered toxic to dogs.

Stretchberry

Forestiera pubescens [FOR-ES-TEE-AIR-UH PEW-BES-SENZ]

Stretchberry, a captivating Oleaceae (Olive) family member, is enchanted with its intriguing characteristics. Known by various names such as desert olive, downy forestiera, New Mexico Privet, and elbowbush, this remarkable plant has its roots firmly planted in North America, specifically in the eastern regions.

Stretchberry thrives in the landscapes of California, Nevada, Utah, Colorado, New Mexico, Arizona, and Texas and even stretches into the northern regions of Mexico. Its roots dig deep into the fertile soil, allowing it to flourish along the meandering streams, in the lush valleys, on the gentle slopes of hillsides, and atop the majestic mesas. This resilient plant embraces elevations ranging from 3,000 to 7,000 feet.

Identification:

GROWTH/SIZE: Grows up to 30 feet tall but can sometimes reach up to 50 feet. It has a narrow, upright growth habit and can grow as a single-stemmed or multi-stemmed shrub or tree.

BARK/STEM/ROOT: When young, the bark is smooth and shiny but becomes rough and dark gray as the plant ages. The stem is typically reddish-brown, and the roots are shallow and fibrous.

LEAF: The leaves are arranged opposite and typically have an elliptical to lanceolate shape. They are generally small to medium, usually measuring about 1 to 3 inches (2.5 to 7.5 cm) in length. The edges are smooth, lacking any teeth or serrations. The species name "pubescens" indicates a slightly hairy or downy texture. This results in the leaves (especially when young) and often the stems having a soft, fine pubescence or fuzziness. The leaves are green, typically a medium to dark green, but may turn yellowish in the autumn before they fall.

FLOWER: The inconspicuous flowers, with their small size and lack of bright color, may easily go unnoticed. They often grow in clusters along the stems. It's dioecious, meaning that individual plants are either male or female. The small, yellowish-green flowers lack petals but display small greenish-yellow sepals. Their more noticeable stamens distinguish male flowers, while female flowers possess a central ovary. It typically blooms in early spring, preceding the emergence of its leaves.

FRUIT/SEED/NUT: The fruit is a diminutive drupe, usually around 1/4 inch (approximately 0.6 cm) in size. Its drupes ripen into a deep blue or black hue, exhibiting a subtle sheen. Typically found in clusters, the fruit may occasionally possess a slightly elongated or oval form. Enclosed within the drupe resides a solitary, sturdy seed. The fruit ripens in late summer and early fall.

Look-a-Like(s): Toxic: **Carolina Laurel cherry** (*Prunus caroliniana*) is an evergreen shrub or small tree that can resemble a Stretchberry due to its glossy green leaves. However, it contains toxic compounds, particularly in its seeds and leaves.

Non-toxic: **Privet** (*Ligustrum spp.*) is a shrub commonly used in landscaping and can resemble Stretchberry in appearance. While Privet is not highly toxic, its berries can cause stomach discomfort if ingested in large quantities.

Cautions: The seeds and leaves contain hydrocyanic acid, which can cause nausea and vomiting if consumed in large quantities.

Culinary Preparations: Harvest the leaves, dry them, and then either make tea or grind them into a fine powder. Combine the powdered leaves with other dried herbs and spices to create a distinctive seasoning blend. Sprinkle this blend over grilled meats or roasted vegetables, or use it as a rub for poultry or fish. You can infuse the leaves or flowers into a sugar syrup or fruit mixture to create a delicious flavored syrup or jam.

Medicinal Uses: The plant's roots have been utilized in traditional remedies as anti-inflammatory agents and other plant parts. A poultice made from the plant has been applied to the skin to alleviate various conditions or irritations. Additionally, certain Native American tribes have employed the plant to treat rheumatism.

Fun/Historical Fact: It has been used by Native Americans for hundreds of years for both medicinal and culinary purposes. The fruit was used to make pemmican, a food stored for long periods and used during travels.

Dog Toxicity: Stretchberry is not known to be toxic to dogs. However, the seeds and leaves contain hydrocyanic acid, which can cause gastrointestinal upset if consumed in large quantities. If your dog eats Stretchberry, monitor them closely for any symptoms of illness, such as vomiting or diarrhea.

Valley Bladderpod

Lesquerella arizonica [LESS-KER-EL-UH AIR-UH-ZON-IH-KUH]

Valley Bladderpod, a delightful little flowering plant, belongs to the esteemed Brassicaceae (mustard) family, renowned for its members like broccoli, kale, and mustard. This charming plant is also known as Arizona bladderpod and Arizona mustard.

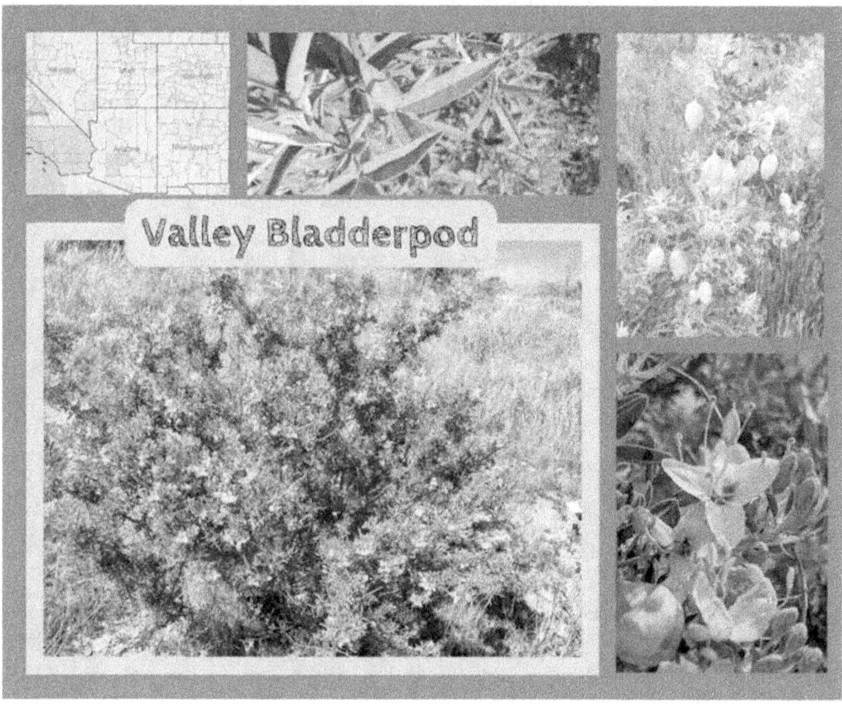

This unique plant has perfectly adapted to survive in arid environments, particularly in Arizona. This resilient plant flourishes in soils that drain well, including gravelly or sandy soils. Its natural habitat spans elevations ranging from approximately 1,300 to 7,900 feet (400 to 2,400 meters), showcasing its remarkable ability to thrive in diverse conditions.

Identification:

GROWTH/SIZE: Typically grows up to 12 inches tall and 24 inches wide. BARK/STEM/ROOT: The stems of this plant are hairy and green. The roots are taproots.

LEAF: The plant features a basal rosette, with circularly arranged leaves growing from the base. While some leaves may also grow on the stems, the basal rosette is the most prominent. The leaves are typically spatulate or oblanceolate in shape, meaning they can be spoon-shaped or taper from a rounded base to a pointed tip with the widest portion below the middle. The margins are usually smooth and not serrated or lobed.

The leaves are generally small to medium-sized and may have a slightly hairy or pubescent surface, giving the plant a silvery or grayish appearance. While typically green, the leaves may have a grayish tint due to fine hairs.

FLOWER: The mustard family is known for its bright yellow flowers ranging from 0.25 to 0.5 inches (roughly 0.6 to 1.2 cm) in diameter, with four petals arranged in a cross or "X" shape. The flowers usually contain six stamens, four long and two short, and appear in clusters, forming a raceme. As the fruits mature, the slender stalks (or pedicels) elongate. The plant is low-growing with a rosette-like appearance, featuring basal leaves and flowering stalks emerging from the center. They bloom in the spring, typically from March to June.

FRUIT/SEED/NUT: The fruit is a capsule that splits open when mature. The capsules are rounded and inflated, resembling small bladders, hence the name "bladderpod." The outer surface of the capsule is smooth and can range in color from green to brown or tan. Inside the capsule, multiple small seeds can be found. The seeds are flat and can be round to oval, often brownish. The pods are typically found from June to August.

Look-a-Like(s): Toxic: **Jimsonweed** (*Datura stramonium*) has white or pink trumpet-shaped flowers and large, spiky seed pods. **Poison Hemlock** (*Conium maculatum*) has small, white flowers and fern-like leaves.

Non-toxic: **Desert Marigold** (*Baileya multiradiata*) has yellow-orange flowers and finely divided leaves. **Mexican Gold Poppy** (*Eschscholzia mexicana*) has bright yellow flowers and feathery leaves.

Cautions: There are no known associated issues with Valley Bladderpod.

Culinary Preparations: The seeds can be roasted and ground into a nutty-tasting flour. The leaves and stems can be used as a salad green or cooked like spinach. The flowers can be used to make tea or as a garnish.

Medicinal Uses: It has been traditionally used by Native Americans to treat various ailments such as coughs, fever, and arthritis. Recent studies have shown that the plant may have anti-inflammatory and antioxidant properties.

Fun/Historical Fact: Valley Bladderpod was once used by Native Americans to make a yellow dye for textiles.

Dog toxicity: No information is available about whether Valley Bladderpod is toxic to dogs.

Wax Currant

Ribes cereum [RYE-BEES SEER-EE-UM]

The Wax Currant, also known as Squaw Currant or Skunk Currant, belongs to the Grossulariaceae (gooseberry) family. This beautiful plant is native to the western United States and thrives in elevations ranging from 3,000 to 10,000 feet. It's a common sight in the mountainous regions, where it grows wild and adds to the landscape's natural beauty.

The plant thrives in the most challenging environments, where the soil is dry and rocky, like the majestic mountain slopes and breathtaking canyons. Its resilience knows no bounds as it proudly calls four states its home: Arizona, New Mexico, Nevada, and Utah.

Identification:

GROWTH/SIZE: A small to medium-sized shrub that can grow up to 5 feet tall and wide.

BARK/STEM/ROOT: The bark is smooth and grayish-brown. The stems are slender, flexible, and reddish-brown.

LEAF: The simple leaves are typically palmately lobed, with 3 to 5 main lobes radiating from a central point, resembling the shape of a hand. They measure 1 to 3 inches

(2.5 to 7.5 cm) across. They have a slightly wrinkled or puckered surface, and their texture can be described as somewhat leathery or thick. They may be smooth or slightly hairy. The edges are toothed or serrated, particularly towards the tips of the lobes. They are usually green on the upper surface, while the underside is paler, sometimes even whitish or glaucous. The veins are prominent and typically follow the lobes of the leaves.

FLOWER: The flowers usually have a tubular or funnel-shaped structure arranged in branch racemes. These flowers are typically pale to deep pink, although occasionally, they may appear whitish. They are relatively small, usually measuring less than half an inch (around 1 cm) in length. Each flower typically consists of five petals slightly bent backward (reflexed), exposing a longer tube. Within this tubular structure are five stamens and a central pistil that may occasionally protrude slightly from the mouth of the flower. The flowers bloom in early to mid-summer.

FRUIT/SEED/NUT: Produces small, edible berries around 0.25 inches in diameter. When ripe, the berries are red or black and ready for harvest in late summer.

Look-a-Like(s): Toxic: **Death Camas** (*Toxicoscordion venenosum*) have white flowers and grow in wet areas. **Water Hemlock** (*Cicuta douglasii*) has small, white flowers and grows in wetlands and marshes.

Non-toxic: **Oregon Grape** (*Mahonia aquifolium*) has yellow flowers and dark blue berries. **Golden Currant** (*Ribes aureum*) has yellow flowers and produces bright yellow berries.

Cautions: There are no significant cautions associated with the Wax Currant.

Culinary Preparations: The Wax Currant is edible and offers a delightful combination of sweetness and a hint of tartness in its berries. To fully enjoy this fruit, here are a few suggestions for preparing it: Incorporate the berries into pancakes or muffins for a delightful fruity twist. Transform the berries into jelly or jam for a delectable spread. Combine the berries with other fruits in a refreshing fruit salad. Create a flavorful salsa by mixing the berries with cilantro and onion. Enhance the taste of ice cream or sorbet by infusing it with the berries. Craft a delectable syrup using the berries to drizzle over waffles or pancakes as a delightful topping.

Medicinal Uses: The Wax Currant possesses both traditional and modern therapeutic applications. Its berries are rich in vitamin C, which aids in strengthening the immune system. Moreover, the leaves and bark of this plant contain compounds that possess anti-inflammatory and pain-relieving properties. Throughout history, Native Americans have relied on it to address digestive issues, respiratory infections, and skin irritations.

Fun/Historical Fact: The Wax Currant plays a vital role in the ecosystems it inhabits, serving as a crucial plant. Its berries are a vital food source for birds and other wildlife, while its nectar attracts essential pollinators like bees and butterflies. Additionally, Native American tribes have long utilized the Wax Currant in traditional ceremonies and as a natural dye for basket weaving and clothing.

Dog toxicity: The Wax Currant is not toxic to dogs; its berries can be a healthy treat. A dog eating a lot of berries may experience diarrhea or an upset stomach.

PART FOUR
HERBS & GRASSES

Arrowleaf Balsamroot

Balsamorhiza sagittata [BAL-SUH-MUH-RYE-ZUH SAJ-IH-TAH-TUH]

Arrowleaf Balsamroot is a flowering plant belonging to the Asteraceae (aster/daisy) family and is known by several other common names, such as Arrowleaf Sunflower, Balsamroot, and Wild Sunflower. The plant has a rich history of traditional use by indigenous people for food and medicine.

It's a native plant found in Arizona, New Mexico, Nevada, and Utah. It grows wild in various habitats such as sagebrush steppe, pinyon-juniper woodland, and mountain meadows.

Identification:

GROWTH/SIZE: Grows up to 3 feet tall and 2 feet wide.

BARK/STEM/ROOT: The stem is stout and covered in fine hairs. The root is a taproot. When crushed, the roots give off a balsamic scent, reflected in the name "balsamroot."

LEAF: The basal leaves of this plant are often large, sometimes exceeding a foot (30 cm) long. They have an arrowhead or broadly lanceolate shape, tapering to a point at the tip and featuring wide, rounded bases. They are slightly hairy, making them textured and somewhat grayish or silvery. Their edges are smooth. A prominent central vein runs the length of each leaf, with lateral veins branching off from it, resembling the shaft and vanes of an arrow. The leaf stalk, if present, is very short or absent, causing the leaf blade to attach directly to the plant's base.

FLOWER: boasts large flower heads measuring 2 to 4 inches (5 to 10 cm) in diameter. The bright yellow petals, known as ray florets, radiate outward from the flower's center. The center, known as disc florets, is a darker yellow or sometimes brownish and is filled with numerous tiny individual flowers. Typically, these flowers are singly atop a tall, erect stem that can reach heights up to 3 feet (90 cm).

FRUIT/SEED/NUT: The seeds are small and have a bristly pappus that allows them to be easily dispersed by wind. The seeds mature in July and August.

Look-a-Like(s): Toxic: **Sneezeweed** *(Helenium spp.)* has daisy-like flowers with dark centers. The leaves are typically narrow and not shaped like arrows. **Western Pasqueflower** *(Anemone occidentalis)* has distinct fluffy seed heads and pale lavender or white flowers. The leaves are also more divided and fern-like rather than arrow-shaped.

Non-toxic: **Sunflowers** *(Helianthus annuus)* are generally taller, with bigger flower heads. The leaves are more heart-shaped and slightly serrated. **Mule's Ears** *(Wyethia spp.)* have larger and somewhat glossy leaves that can resemble the ears of a mule. While they have similar yellow flowers, their leaves tend to be more elongated, and the plant is generally more robust and taller.

Cautions: There are no significant cautions associated with Arrowleaf Balsamroot.

Culinary Preparations: The roots of this plant can be slow-roasted and peeled, resulting in a starchy and slightly sweet flavor similar to roasted potatoes or turnips. Some Native American tribes have also ground the seeds to create flour, which can be used in bread-making or as a thickener in soups and stews. The large leaves can also be used as a natural wrap for cooking small pieces of meat or fish, while the young shoots can be cooked and served as greens. These shoots can be steamed or sautéed, making a fresh, earthy addition to salads or as a side dish.

Medicinal Uses: *Cough and Cold Treatment:* People boil the roots and leaves of the plant to create a tea or tonic. Drinking this could help soothe the throat and clear up congestion. The plant has special chemicals to break down mucus and ease irritation. *Wound Healing:* They can be ground into a paste and applied directly to the skin. *Digestive Aid:* Prepare a tonic from the roots and drink it to help calm an upset stomach. *Pain Relief:* It's been used to relieve muscle and joint pain. This could be done by either drinking tea made from the plant or applying a paste from the roots directly to the painful area. *Skin Care:* By grinding the roots into a powder and mixing it with water to make a paste, it can be applied to the skin. This paste helps to moisturize the skin and reduce itching or irritation.

Fun/Historical Fact: Arrowleaf Balsamroot is known for its deep taproot, reaching up to 15 feet long. This root allows the plant to survive in dry habitats with little water.

Dog Toxicity: Arrowleaf Balsamroot has no known toxic effects on dogs.

B itterroot

Lewisia rediviva [LOO-ISS-EE-UH REE-DIH-VY-VUH]

Meriwether Lewis of the Lewis and Clark Expedition named Bitterroot a flowering plant from the Montiaceae (purslane) family. It is also known as Rock Rose and Resurrection Flower.

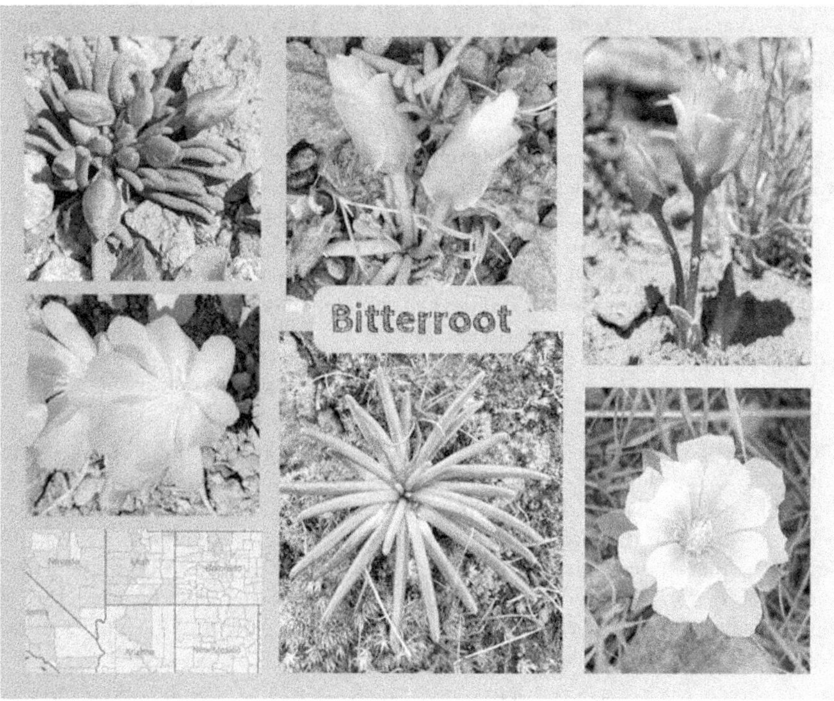

It's native to the western United States and commonly observed in Arizona, New Mexico, Nevada, and Utah. It thrives in arid and rocky regions, displaying its adaptability by flourishing at elevations ranging from 1,000 to 12,000 feet.

Identification:

GROWTH/SIZE: Grows to be around 4-8 inches in height and can spread up to 10-12 inches in diameter.

BARK/STEM/ROOT: It has a thick taproot with multiple stems and narrow leaves. The bark is rough and brownish.

LEAF: basal rosette leaves that grow at ground level. They are narrow and linear to lanceolate in shape and can have a slightly fleshy or succulent texture. They are 1 to 3 inches (2.5 to 7.5 cm) long and often have a slightly rolled inward appearance, giving them a cylindrical or semi-cylindrical shape. While the leaves are primarily green, they may develop a reddish tint, particularly as they dry out. The leaves emerge early in the spring and wither away when the plant starts to flower or shortly after.

FLOWER: displays various colors, from deep pink to almost white. Its narrow-based, wide-out petals are somewhat spatulate, with 5-9 petals per flower reaching up to 2 inches (5 cm) in diameter. The center of the flower contains numerous stamens with yellow anthers surrounding the central pistil. It blooms in the spring, from April to June, and appears on a leafless stem rising from a rosette of fleshy, linear leaves that usually wither by flowering time.

FRUIT/SEED/NUT: The fruit is a dry, dehiscent capsule that contains numerous seeds.

Look-a-Like(s): Toxic: **Death Camas** (*Zigadenus spp.)* has a similar size and shape and typically has white or cream-colored flowers. The leaves are usually grass-like. **White Locoweed** *(Oxytropis sericea)* often has clusters of white flowers. The leaves are compound and pinnate.

Non-toxic: **Stonecrop** *(Sedum spp.)* Many types of Stonecrop are edible, with a slightly sour or peppery taste. The leaves can be eaten raw in salads or cooked. The leaves are usually more plump and juicy than bitterroot's fleshy leaves. Its flowers can vary in color but are often yellow or red. **Spring Beauty** *(Claytonia lanceolata)* The entire plant is edible, including the leaves, flowers, and corms (a bulb-like stem). The taste is mild and can be eaten raw or cooked. It often has delicate white or pink flowers with pink veins, which might resemble bitterroot. However, the leaves of Spring Beauty are thin and lance-shaped.

Cautions: There are no significant cautions associated with Bitterroot.

Culinary Preparations: *Salad:* The roots can be cleaned, soaked to remove some of the bitterness, and then chopped into small pieces. Then, mix with greens and other vegetables to create a salad. *Mashed:* The roots can be boiled until soft and mashed like potatoes. *Soup:* The roots can be added to soups and stews, giving them a unique flavor. The roots absorb flavors from other ingredients. *Fried:* the roots can be sliced thinly and fried in oil until crispy. They can be seasoned with salt and spices, turning them into a unique snack or appetizer. This crunchy treat showcases the root's natural flavors differently.

Medicinal Uses: Tea was believed by some tribes to have a soothing effect on sore throats, while those with digestive issues used root preparations to ease discomfort. Bitterroot was applied topically to wounds and sores, as it was thought to promote healing and reduce inflammation. Additionally, some Native American tribes used Bitterroot tea to remedy headaches, believing it could alleviate pain and pressure.

Fun/Historical Fact: The Bitterroot flower is significant in Montana as the state flower and shares a deep-rooted history with the Shoshone-Bannock tribes. This plant played a crucial role in their culture, serving as a source of sustenance, healing remedies, and spiritual connections.

Dog toxicity: Bitterroot is not toxic to dogs.

Buffalo Grass

Bouteloua dactyloides [BOO-TUH-LOO-UH DAK-TY-LOY-DEEZ]

Buffalo Grass, a resilient perennial grass from the Poaceae (grass) family, is also known as St. Augustine grass and curly mesquite.

Buffalo Grass, native to the Great Plains region, thrives in prairies, meadows, and open fields across the United States, particularly in dry and hot climates.

Identification:

GROWTH/SIZE: grows to 3-6 inches tall and can spread to 2-3 feet wide.

BARK/STEM/ROOT: The stems are thin and wiry, while the roots are long and deep, making them highly drought-resistant.

LEAF: short, ranging from 2 to 12 inches (5 to 30 cm) long, and narrow, about 1/8 inch (about 3 mm) wide. They have a flat or slightly rolled blade with a fine texture and are typically blue-green to gray-green. In drought conditions, the leaves may turn yellowish or brownish. The grass grows in low, dense mats or tufts, giving a landscape a soft, fine-textured appearance. The base of the leaf blade may be slightly hairy, while the edges are typically smooth.

FLOWER: The spikelets are arranged in comb-like racemes, resembling fingers, which extend outward from the main stem, resulting in a horizontally oriented inflorescence. Each raceme consists of multiple small, slender spikelets. While the color of the spikelets may differ, they generally exhibit a greenish to straw hue, which darkens to a brownish shade as they mature. They bloom in summer.

FRUIT/SEED/NUT: The seeds typically have a greenish-tan color and a flattened shape. They are found on short, curved seed heads resembling miniature brushes or combs. As the seeds mature, they appear straw-like, usually during late summer or early fall. These seeds are pretty small, often measuring only about 1/8 inch long. Although Buffalo Grass is primarily utilized as a ground cover, its seeds can be gathered in autumn when they become dry and brittle.

Look-a-Like(s): Toxic: **Foxglove** *(Digitalis purpurea)* has tubular, bell-shaped flowers and tall stalks. The leaves might be confused with grass, but a closer look reveals a different texture and shape. **Hemlock** *(Conium maculatum)* has finely divided, feathery leaves, which might resemble grasses but typically grow much taller. Its stem is often spotted or streaked with red or purple.

Non-toxic: **Rye Grass** *(Lolium spp.)* Rye Grass seeds are sometimes used as a grain in cereals or bread, providing fiber and nutrients. The young leaves can also be eaten. It typically has longer, more slender leaves, and its seed heads are often larger and more distinct. It's generally found in cooler climates, while Buffalo Grass prefers warmer areas. **Barley** *(Hordeum vulgare)* is a nutritious grain commonly used in soups, stews, bread, and beverages. It's rich in fiber, vitamins, and minerals. Barley grows much taller and has distinct, bushy seed heads. It's usually cultivated as a crop, while Buffalo Grass grows wild.

Cautions: There are no known cautions associated with Buffalo Grass.

Culinary Preparations: The grass seeds can be used to make flour for baking. Buffalo Grass can be brewed into tea.

Medicinal Uses: Buffalo Grass has been traditionally used as a medicinal plant by Native American tribes for various ailments, including fever, stomach issues, and sore throat. Modern research has shown that the plant contains antioxidant and anti-inflammatory properties that may help improve overall health and prevent chronic diseases.

Fun/Historical Fact: Buffalo Grass was the primary source of forage for millions of bison that once roamed the Great Plains. Native Americans also used it to make homes, clothing, and baskets.

Dog toxicity: Buffalo Grass is not toxic to dogs, and there are no known associated symptoms if ingested.

anadian Goldenrod

Solidago canadensis [SUH-LID-UH-GOH KAN-UH-DEN-SIS]

Canadian Goldenrod, a breathtaking wildflower from the Asteraceae (aster/daisy) family. Also known as Aaron's Rod, woundwort, and blue mountain tea, this remarkable flower is not indigenous to Canada but hails from North America. Its roots can be traced back to the eastern and central regions of the continent.

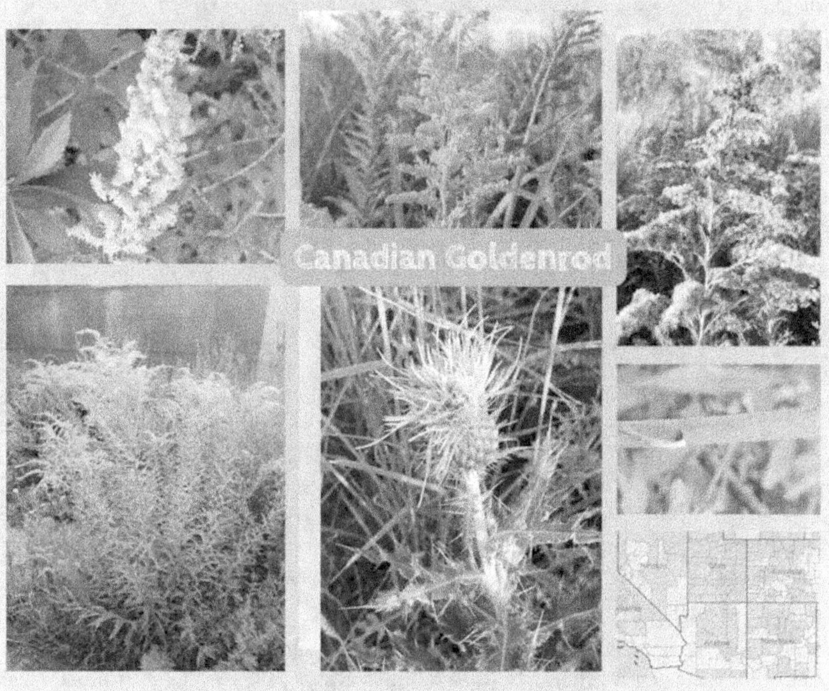

Goldenrod is a native plant to Arizona, New Mexico, Nevada, and Utah and can also be found in other regions across North America. It can be found in moist environments near rivers, streams, ponds, and lakes and thrives in open fields with well-draining soil. Additionally, the edges of woodlands, where there is a transition between forested areas and open fields, can be a good location.

Identification:

GROWTH/SIZE: It can reach 2-4 feet tall and grow 18 inches wide.

BARK/STEM/ROOT: It has a sturdy, erect stem with small ridges and a light brown color.

LEAF: serrated and shaped like a lanceolate to narrowly ovate, arranged in an alternating pattern, measuring 2 to 6 inches (5 to 15 cm). The upper surface has a coarse texture, and the underside may be fuzzy. The veins are pinnate, extending in parallel from the midrib to the leaf's margin. The leaves are a medium to dark green color.

FLOWER: bright golden-yellow flowers arranged in a plume-like, elongated cluster that can sometimes take on a pyramidal shape. The cluster comprises numerous tiny flower heads containing ray florets (8-12) and disk florets. The flower-bearing stems are usually erect and unbranched, reaching several feet tall. This species typically blooms from late summer to fall.

FRUIT/SEED/NUT: The fruits are tiny achenes, with each seed equipped with a pappus of fine hairs, aiding in their distribution.

LOOK-A-LIKE(S): Toxic: **Dogbane** (*Apocynum spp.*) has clusters of small, yellowish flowers and opposite leaves. Dogbane also has milky sap, which can be toxic if ingested. **Tansy Ragwort** (*Senecio jacobaea*) has similar yellow flowers, deeply lobed leaves with a fern-like appearance and a bitter taste.

Non-toxic: **Early Goldenrod** (*Solidago juncea*) has more elongated and cylindrical flower clusters and narrower leaves with smooth edges. **Lance-leaved Goldenrod** (*Solidago graminifolia*) has long, narrow leaves resembling grass blades and tends to have more elongated flower clusters.

Cautions: Goldenrod is generally safe for humans and animals to consume, but some people with allergies may experience mild irritation if they come into contact with the plant.

Culinary Preparations: For *Herbal Tea*, simply steep a tablespoon of dried goldenrod in a cup of hot water for approximately 10 minutes. It's perfect for relaxation and savoring. To create *Infused Honey*, place the flowers in a clean jar. Pour raw honey over the flowers, ensuring they are completely submerged. Allow the mixture to infuse for a few weeks, gently shaking the jar occasionally. For a *Pesto*, blend fresh goldenrod leaves, garlic, pine nuts (or any preferred nuts), Parmesan cheese, olive oil, and a pinch of salt. Lastly, boil equal parts water and sugar until the sugar dissolves for a Flower Syrup. Add the goldenrod flowers to the syrup and let it simmer for 10 minutes. Strain the mixture and allow it to cool before use.

Medicinal Uses: The leaves and flowers of this plant can be utilized as a potent anti-septic for wounds when applied directly to cuts and scrapes in the form of a salve or poultice. It has been traditionally used to aid digestion, offering relief from stomach aches and indigestion when consumed as a tea or tincture, potentially calming the digestive system. It's also been known to provide respiratory relief, as teas or syrups made from it can help soothe the throat and alleviate symptoms associated with respi-ratory issues such as colds, coughs, or bronchitis. Apply topically to the skin to address conditions like eczema or rashes, as its anti-inflammatory and antiseptic prop-erties may effectively soothe irritated skin. Lastly, despite being mistakenly associated with allergies, this plant may assist in relieving allergy symptoms. Some herbalists even recommend Goldenrod tea to reduce symptoms like a runny nose or watery eyes.

Fun/Historical Fact: Goldenrod became a popular alternative to tea in colonial times after the Boston Tea Party. Additionally, Native Americans utilized it as a natural dye for textiles.

Dog Toxicity: Goldenrod is not toxic to dogs; they can safely consume the plant without experiencing any adverse effects.

C **heatgrass**

Bromus tectorum [BROH-MUS TEK-TOR-UM]

Cheatgrass, scientifically classified as a Poaceae (grass) family member, is commonly called Downy Brome. This grass species, which shares lineage with wheat and corn, was initially found in Europe and Asia but has since spread to various regions across the globe, including North America.

Cheatgrass, a non-native plant, thrives in the Southwest, encompassing Arizona, New Mexico, Nevada, and Utah. It also extends its presence to numerous US, Canada, and Mexico states. This plant dominates disturbed environments such as fields, roadsides, and construction sites.

Identification:

GROWTH/SIZE: Typically grows 6-24 inches tall but can sometimes reach 3 feet.

BARK/STEM/ROOT: It has thin, wiry stems and shallow roots.

LEAF: The stem bears leaves that are arranged alternately. These leaves are long, linear, and usually narrower than other types of grass. When young, they have a soft and downy texture and are bright green. As the plant matures, the leaves may turn reddish-brown or purplish. The leaf sheath is closed and covered in soft hairs, while the ligule is short and membranous. Although the leaf blades can grow up to 25 cm long, they are often shorter.

FLOWER: Each panicle is loose and nodding with multiple spikelets. The spikelets are elongated and somewhat flat, with bristle-like structures called awns that can be 1-2 cm long. When the flowers first emerge, they can have a green to purplish tint, adding a touch of color to the grass. They turn a tan or straw-like color as they mature and dry out. The grass can grow 12 to 30 inches (30 to 76 cm).

FRUIT/SEED/NUT: The fruit is a seed about 1/4 inch in size and has a bristly appearance. It typically matures in the summer.

Look-a-Like(s): Toxic: No toxic plants closely resemble Cheatgrass.

Non-toxic: **Wheat** *(Triticum spp.)* Wheat is a significant food source worldwide, used to make bread, pasta, cereals, and more. The grains are nutritious and provide a lot of energy. While Cheatgrass and wheat have similar feathery seed heads, wheat's stalks are generally sturdier and thicker. Wheat also tends to grow taller, with more substantial seed heads. **Barley** *(Hordeum vulgare)* is another edible grain rich in nutrients. It's often used in soups, stews, and as a base for fermented products like beer. Though similar in appearance to Cheatgrass, barley's seed heads are usually more dense and thick, especially at a young stage. Cheatgrass's awns (bristle-like parts) are also typically longer and more slender than barley's. **Rye** *(Secale cereale)* makes rye bread, crackers, and alcoholic beverages. It's known for its unique, robust flavor and health benefits, such as providing fiber and essential nutrients. Ryegrass can look similar to Cheatgrass but has a more vigorous growth pattern with thicker stems. Cheatgrass often turns reddish-brown as it matures, while rye maintains a more consistent green color.

Cautions: Cheatgrass is not toxic but can be a problem for livestock and wildlife. The bristly seeds can get stuck in the noses and throats of animals, causing respiratory problems.

Culinary Preparations: Cheatgrass is not typically used as a food source for humans, but it can be fed to livestock as hay or forage.

Medicinal Uses: Cheatgrass has traditionally been used in herbal medicine to treat various ailments, including urinary tract infections and arthritis. Modern research has shown that it has antioxidant properties and may help treat inflammation and other conditions.

Fun/Historical Fact: Cheatgrass was introduced to North America in the late 1800s and quickly became a problem in many parts of the continent. It is now considered an invasive species in many areas and is a common sight in disturbed habitats like construction sites and abandoned fields.

Dog Toxicity: Cheatgrass is not toxic to dogs. However, the bristly seeds can get stuck in their fur and can cause discomfort and irritation. If a dog ingests a large amount of Cheatgrass, it may cause gastrointestinal upset.

Desert Agave

Agave deserti [UH-GAH-VEE DIH-ZUR-TEE]

The Desert Agave is a succulent plant that belongs to the Asparagaceae (asparagus) family. It is commonly known as the Century Plant, but it does not take 100 years to bloom as its name suggests. It has a long history of use by Native American tribes for food, medicine, and fiber.

It's native to Arizona, California, Nevada, New Mexico, and Utah, where it can grow in the wild in arid regions and rocky slopes. It is also commonly cultivated in gardens and landscapes.

Identification:

GROWTH/SIZE: Grows 3 to 5 feet tall and 4 to 6 feet wide.

BARK/STEM/ROOT: The stem is woody and usually not visible. The root system is fibrous and shallow, allowing the plant to absorb water quickly after rain.

LEAF: The leaves are thick and fleshy, with sharp spines on the edges and a pointed tip. They can be up to 2 feet long and 6 inches wide, and their color ranges from blue-green to gray-green.

FLOWER: It produces a tall flower stalk, which can reach up to 20 feet in height, with yellowish-green flowers that bloom in the summer. The flowers are tubular and about 2 inches long.

FRUIT/SEED/NUT: It produces a large cluster of oval-shaped fruits, about 1 inch long, and contains black seeds. The fruit ripens in the fall.

Look-a-Like(s): Toxic: **Sotol** *(Dasylirion spp.)* The leaves are not typically toxic but very sharp and can cause physical harm if not handled carefully. Sotol has a similar rosette shape but tends to have longer, more slender leaves. Unlike Agave, which flowers once and then dies, Sotol can flower multiple times throughout its life. **Spanish Bayonet** *(Yucca aloifolia)* Similar to other Yuccas, Spanish Bayonet has very sharp leaves that can cause injury. The plant's sap can also cause skin irritation in some people. This plant grows more upright with stiffer leaves compared to the broader leaves of Agave deserti. The white or purplish flowers also differ from the yellowish flowers of Agave.

Non-toxic: **Yucca** *(Yucca spp.)* The flowers and fruit are edible and can be cooked and eaten. The roots of some species can be used to make soap. Yucca plants often have longer, narrower leaves. While both have a central flower stalk, Yucca's stalk is typically branched. **Aloe Vera** *(Aloe barbadensis miller)* is renowned for its edible gel found inside the leaves, often used in beverages and for its medicinal properties. Aloe Vera leaves are usually more fleshy and filled with a clear gel, unlike the solid and fibrous leaves of Agave deserti. Aloe's leaves are also typically more spotted.

Cautions: The Desert Agave has no significant cautions associated with its use.

Culinary Preparations: Syrup: The sap from the core of the agave plant can be extracted, filtered, and heated to create agave syrup or nectar. It's a sweetener that can be used instead of sugar in recipes, drizzled on pancakes, or used in beverages like tea. **Hearts** can be roasted and eaten. This was a traditional practice among indigenous peoples. The heart is dug up, roasted in a pit, and has a sweet, molasses-like flavor. **Candy**: The roasted heart of the agave plant can be further processed into sweet candy. It's a traditional treat in some parts of Mexico. **Drinks**: The sap can be fermented to make a traditional alcoholic beverage called pulque. This milky, sour drink has been consumed in Mexico for centuries. Different types of agave, like Agave tequilana, are used to make tequila.

Medicinal Uses: Below are some potential medicinal uses for Agave deserti based on historical and traditional contexts, which modern science may not support. **Wound Healing**: The sap or juice from the leaves has been applied to cuts and wounds in traditional practices. It was believed to help clean the wound and promote healing. **Toothache Relief**: The leaves have been used to alleviate toothaches in some traditional methods. Chewing on the plant's fibers might have provided temporary relief. **Soothing Skin Irritations**: The sap has been used to soothe skin irritations such as rashes or insect bites. Applying the sap to the affected area might have helped reduce itching and inflammation.

Fun/Historical Fact: It played a role in the production of mezcal, a type of alcoholic beverage that is still popular in Mexico today. The word "agave" comes from the Greek word "agavos," which means "noble."

Dog toxicity: The Desert Agave is not toxic to dogs, but its spiny leaves can cause injury if ingested or touched. Symptoms may include mouth irritation, vomiting, and diarrhea.

# Desert Bitterbrush

Purshia glandulosa [PUR-SHI-UH GLAN-DYOO-LOH-SUH]

Desert Bitterbrush, a resilient plant from the Asteraceae (aster/daisy) family, is often known as tarbush, tarweed, or desert resin bush. Initially documented by the German botanist Frederick Traugott Pursh in 1814, this plant derives its name from the fruit's key-like appearance within a membrane.

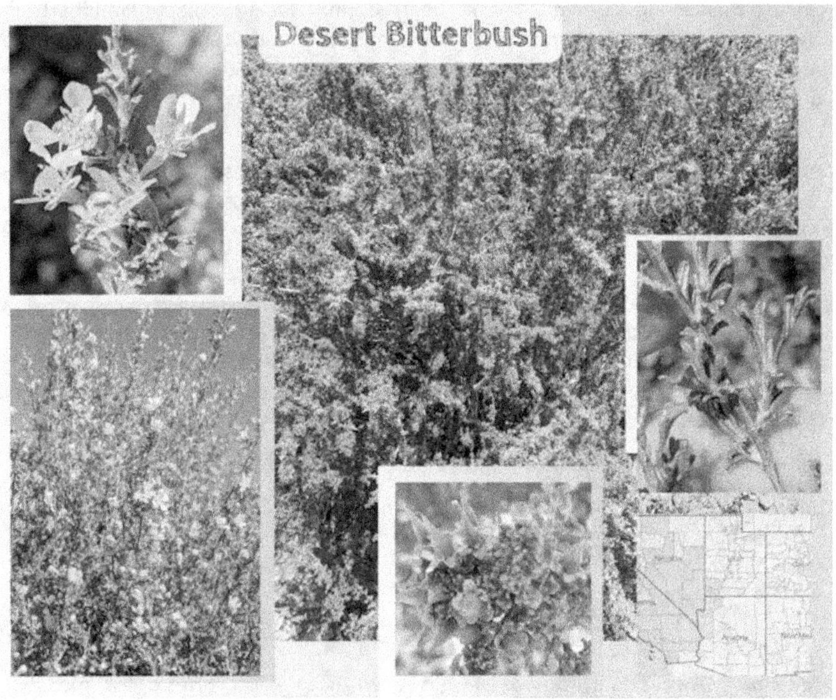

It's indigenous to the southwestern United States and can be spotted in Arizona, New Mexico, Nevada, and Utah. It thrives in desert areas, particularly on stony slopes and sandy streams.

Identification:

GROWTH/SIZE: Grows up to 6 feet tall and 5 feet wide.

BARK/STEM/ROOT: The bark is gray-brown, and the stem and roots are thick and woody.

LEAF: The leaves are arranged alternately on the branches and are simple, ranging from wedge-shaped to oblong, with a narrowed or tapered base. They are generally small, 1 to 3 cm (0.4 to 1.2 inches) long. They are usually smooth but may have a few shallow teeth or lobes towards the tip. The upper surface is dark green and somewhat shiny, while the undersides are lighter and may have glandular hairs that give them a slightly sticky feel. Crushing the leaves may release a distinct aroma due to the presence of these hairs.

FLOWER: The flowers are usually pale yellow to creamy white, with relatively small size. They resemble rose flowers and often grow in clusters at the branch tips. Blooming occurs in late spring to early summer. The center of the flower showcases numerous stamens, which are usually prominent and noticeable, resulting in a slightly bushy appearance.

FRUIT/SEED/NUT: The fruit is classified as achene, a small, dry, and hard fruit that remains closed and does not release its seed (indehiscent). Glandular bitterbrush achenes are frequently accompanied by a feathery or plumose structure that disperses their wind. This feathered attachment gives the seeds a unique appearance, resembling a small plume or tuft of hair. The achene, not including the feathery portion, is typically less than one centimeter.

Look-a-Like(s): Toxic: **Rabbitbrush** (*Chrysothamnus spp.*) has bright yellow flowers. The leaves are more needle-like. **Death Camas** (*Zigadenus spp.*) typically has more prominent white or greenish flowers clusters. Its leaves are generally more slender and grass-like.

Non-toxic: **Sagebrush** (*Artemisia tridentata*) Some Native American tribes have used sagebrush for medicinal purposes, but it's not typically consumed as food. Its leaves can be used in small quantities for flavoring. While sagebrush and Bitterbrush both have three-tipped leaves, sagebrush leaves are usually silvery-gray and give off a robust sage-like aroma, unlike the darker green leaves of Bitterbrush.

Cautions: There are no significant cautions associated with Desert Bitterbush.

Culinary Preparations: Desert Bitterbush can be used as an herb in cooking, or the leaves can be brewed into tea. Here are some ways to prepare it: Use the leaves as a seasoning for roasted meats or vegetables. Steep the leaves in hot water for a calming tea.

Dry the leaves and use them to make a smudge stick for cleansing.

Medicinal Uses: Desert Bitterbush has been used for centuries for medicinal purposes. Native Americans have used the plant to treat various ailments, including stomachaches, headaches, and infections. Modern research has shown that Desert Bitterbush has anti-inflammatory and antioxidant properties.

Fun/Historical Fact: Desert Bitterbush is a tough and resilient plant that can survive in extreme conditions. During the 1950s, the United States government used Desert Bitterbush as a soil stabilizer for road construction in the Mojave Desert.

Dog Toxicity: Desert Bitterbush is not toxic to dogs.

Purplenerve Spring Parsley

Cymopterus multinervatus [SIGH-MOP-TUH-RUS MYOO-TEE-NER-VAY-TUS]

Purplenerve Spring Parsley is a fascinating plant with a rich history and numerous uses. It belongs to the Apiaceae (carrot/parsley) family, which includes many well-known herbs and spices, such as parsley, dill, and coriander. Other common names are Purplenerve Mitrewort and Streambank Mitrewort.

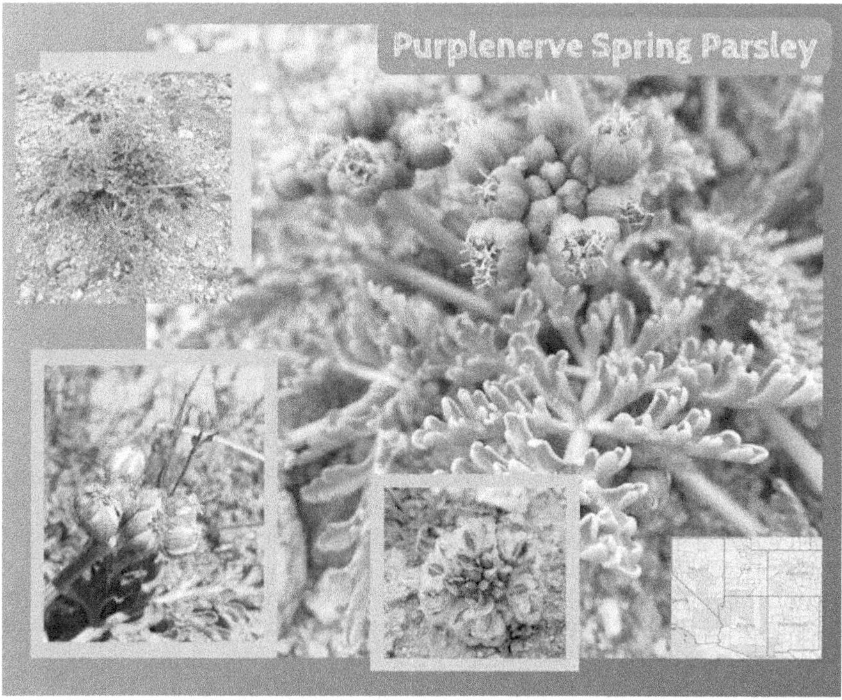

It's native to the southwestern United States, including Arizona, New Mexico, Nevada, and Utah. It grows wild in various habitats, including deserts, woodlands, and rocky slopes.

Identification:

GROWTH/SIZE: It typically grows about 6-12 inches tall.

BARK/STEM/ROOT: The bark is thin, smooth, and light brown. The stem is slender and erect, growing up to a foot tall, and it has a greenish hue with ridges running along its length. The roots are fibrous and spread underground, helping the plant anchor itself in the soil and absorb water and nutrients.

LEAF: is narrow and divided into smaller leaflets. The leaflets are often deeply lobed or toothed, giving them a feathery appearance. The leaves grow in a rosette shape close to the ground, giving the plant attractive and distinctive features.

FLOWER: small and clustered together in an umbrella-like shape called an umbel. They have delicate, white to pale yellow petals with a vibrant yellow center, creating a beautiful contrast. These flowers bloom in the spring, usually between April and June, adding a splash of color to the landscape during that time of year.

FRUIT/SEED/NUT: produces small, rounded fruits that resemble tiny seeds or nuts. These fruits are typically green when immature and turn brown as they ripen. They have a round shape and are relatively small in size. The fruits can be harvested in late summer or early fall when they have reached maturity and have a dry, papery texture. Inside each fruit, you can find small seeds or nuts that are often dark brown and can be used for propagation or culinary purposes.

Look-a-Like(s): Toxic: **Poison Hemlock** (*Conium maculatum*) has small white flowers arranged in umbrella-shaped clusters. The leaves are larger and have a fern-like appearance. **Spotted Cowbane** (*Cicuta maculata*) is a tall perennial plant that can grow up to 8 feet tall. The flowers are small and white and grow in clusters at the end of the stem.

Non-toxic: **Common Cinquefoil** (*Potentilla simplex*) is a plant that produces similar small white or pink flowers and has lobed leaves. The flowers typically have five petals, and the plant grows in various habitats, including meadows, rocky slopes, and forests. **Foamflower** (*Tiarella cordifolia*) is another small plant that grows in shady areas and produces delicate, white, or pink flowers in the spring. The leaves of Foamflower are also lobed, with a heart-shaped base, and grow in a basal rosette.

Cautions: There are no significant cautions associated with this plant.

Culinary Preparations: Their delicate texture and mild, slightly tangy flavor can enhance your salad's overall taste and visual appeal. *Infused oil or vinegar:* Simply steep a handful of leaves in your preferred oil or vinegar for a couple of weeks, then strain and use the infused liquid to add a delightful herbal twist to your culinary creations. *Herbal tea:* The leaves can be dried and brewed into an herbal tea. This aromatic infusion can be enjoyed independently or blended with other herbs to create a personalized tea blend. *Herb butter:* Blend finely chopped leaves into softened butter to create a flavorful herb butter.

Medicinal Uses: The plant's leaves or roots can make tea or infusions for digestive troubles. Drinking a decoction or herbal tea made from the leaves or roots of Cymopterus multinervatus may provide respiratory relief. Applying a poultice or salve made from the plant's leaves or roots to minor cuts, scrapes, or skin irritations may assist in wound healing.

Fun/Historical Fact: The Purplenerve Spring Parsley has a long history of use by Native American tribes, who used it for food and medicine.

Dog Toxicity: While the Purplenerve Spring Parsley is not considered toxic to dogs, if your dog consumes a large amount of this plant, it may experience digestive upset or vomiting.

Quackgrass

Elymus repens [EH-LY-MUS REE-PENZ]

Quackgrass is a perennial grass that belongs to the Poaceae (grass) family. It is commonly called couch grass, quick grass, or twitch grass. Quackgrass originated in Europe but has been introduced to many regions worldwide, including the United States.

Quackgrass is non-native to the southwest region, including Arizona, New Mexico, Nevada, and Utah. It can be found in every state in the United States except for Hawaii. Quackgrass grows in many habitats, including roadsides, meadows, pastures, and disturbed areas.

Identification:

GROWTH/SIZE: grows up to 3-4 feet tall, with a spread of up to 2 feet.

BARK/STEM/ROOT: The stem is erect and smooth, with nodes that bear leaves. The root system consists of long, white rhizomes.

LEAF: The leaves are flat, long, and narrow, with a rough texture. They are typically light green but can turn yellowish-brown in the fall.

FLOWER: It produces spike-like flower clusters in the late spring or early summer. The flowers are small and greenish, with a purplish tint.

FRUIT/SEED/NUT: The seed heads are narrow, with tiny, reddish-brown seeds. They mature in the late summer.

Look-a-Like(s): Toxic: **Darnel Ryegrass** (*Lolium temulentum*) contains alkaloids that can cause symptoms like dizziness, vomiting, and even convulsions if ingested in large quantities. While both types of grass have similar-looking leaves, Darnel Ryegrass usually grows taller, and its seeds are more compact. Quackgrass often has creeping underground stems called rhizomes, while darnel does not. **Wall Barley or False Barley** (*Hordeum murinum*) can irritate the skin and mucous membranes. Its sharp awns (bristle-like structures) can injure the eyes and mouths of grazing animals. It has a distinctive "spiky" appearance with long, sharp awns extending from the seed heads, unlike quackgrass's more compact seed heads.

Non-toxic: **Rye Grass** (*Lolium spp.*) is sometimes grown for its seeds, which are used to make rye flour for bread and other baked goods. The young leaves can be grazed by livestock but are not commonly consumed by humans. It tends to grow in tufts with a more upright growth pattern compared to the creeping habit of Quackgrass. Rye Grass's seed heads are more substantial and noticeable. **Oats** (*Avena sativa*) are well-known for their nutritious seeds for making oatmeal, granola, and other healthy foods. Oats have a unique seed head structure, often drooping, setting them apart from the more rigid appearance of Quackgrass. Oats also tend to grow taller, with more substantial stems.

Cautions: There are no significant cautions associated with quackgrass.

Culinary Preparations: *Livestock Feed:* While not directly a culinary use for humans, Quackgrass is sometimes used as a forage for livestock. The animals eat the grass, which becomes part of their diet, indirectly contributing to the food chain.

Medicinal Uses: Quackgrass is a common grass used in traditional herbal medicine for various purposes. While it may look like ordinary grass, it has some interesting medicinal uses. *Urinary Tract Infections (UTIs) & Kidney Stones:* It's been used as an herbal remedy for UTIs. Its diuretic properties can aid in flushing out the bacteria causing the infection. By promoting increased urine production, it may also aid in preventing or treating kidney stones. It can help flush out small stones and mineral deposits within the kidneys. *Gout:* Its diuretic properties might also help treat gout, a painful joint condition. Increasing urine production could help the body eliminate excess uric acid, contributing to gout. *Sore Throat and Coughs:* Some traditional practitioners have used it as a tea to soothe sore throats and calm coughs. Its mild anti-inflammatory properties may help ease irritation in the throat. *Skin Conditions:* It's been applied topically to help treat minor wounds, burns, and irritations. It might provide a soothing effect on the affected area.

Fun/Historical fact: Quackgrass is known for its tenacity and ability to spread quickly, which has earned it the nickname "the devil's grass" in some regions.

Dog toxicity: Quackgrass is not toxic to dogs. However, dogs may experience gastrointestinal upset if they consume large amounts. Symptoms may include vomiting, diarrhea, and abdominal pain.

Russian Thistle

Salsola tragus [SAL-SOH-LUH TRAY-GUS]

Russian Thistle, also known as tumbleweed, is a plant that belongs to the Amaranthaceae (amaranth) family. This invasive plant is native to the Eurasian Steppe and was introduced to the United States in the late 19th century. It's an annual plant reproducing through seeds, commonly found in arid and semiarid regions worldwide.

Russian Thistle is a non-native plant in the Southwest region, including Arizona, New Mexico, Nevada, and Utah. It can be found in these states' disturbed areas, fields, and roadsides.

Identification:

GROWTH/SIZE: It grows to 3 feet tall and 2-3 feet wide.

BARK/STEM/ROOT: The stems are green to reddish-brown and have sharp spines. The roots are shallow and fibrous.

LEAF: The leaves are small, narrow, and succulent. They are green to gray-green.

FLOWER: The flowers are small, greenish-white, and bloom in late summer to early fall.

FRUIT/SEED/NUT: It produces small, thorny fruit that contains one seed. The fruit turns brown as it dries and detaches from the stem, allowing it to disperse by the wind.

Look-a-Like(s): Toxic: **Barilla** *(Halogeton glomeratus)* contains high levels of oxalates, which can be toxic to livestock and potentially humans if ingested in large quantities. It can cause kidney damage and other health problems. Although similar in appearance, Barilla usually has more succulent, thicker leaves, and its seeds are encased in a bladder-like structure, unlike the Russian Thistle. **Jimsonweed** *(Datura wrightii)* is highly toxic, containing substances called alkaloids that can cause hallucinations, seizures, and even death if ingested. It's one of the more dangerous plants that could be confused with the Russian Thistle. Though it may grow in similar environments, Jimsonweed has broader leaves and trumpet-shaped flowers, making it more distinguishable from Russian Thistle on closer inspection.

Non-toxic: **Lambsquarters** *(Chenopodium album)* is considered a nutritious wild edible. Its young leaves can be eaten raw in salads or cooked like spinach. The seeds can be ground into flour. Unlike the spiky leaves of Russian Thistle, Lambsquarters has soft, toothed leaves. While both are in the same family, Lambsquarters is generally more tender and lacks tumbling behavior. **Saltwort** *(Salsola soda)* is cultivated in some places as a vegetable. Its young shoots can be boiled or steamed and are known for their salty flavor. Though related to Russian Thistle, Saltwort has a more delicate appearance with softer leaves. It's usually found in salt marshes, unlike Russian Thistle, which often grows in drier areas.

Cautions: Russian Thistle is not toxic to humans or animals.

Culinary Preparations: Russian Thistle can be prepared as food in various ways, including as a vegetable. The young, tender shoots can be cooked and eaten like spinach. They can be steamed, sautéed, or boiled and have a somewhat salty flavor. *Salads and Garnishes:* When picked young and tender, the leaves can be added to salads for a unique, wild, foraged touch. They offer a mild, earthy taste. *Soups and Stews:* It can be added to soups and stews for flavor and texture. Its subtle saltiness might help season the dish and add greens to the meal. *Bread and Pancakes:* The seeds can be harvested, ground into flour, and used in bread, pancakes, or other baked goods. This can add a rustic and unique flavor.

Medicinal Uses: While it's mainly recognized for its ability to tumble across landscapes, it has also been associated with some traditional medicinal uses. Here's a list of those uses. *Digestive Aid:* In some traditional practices, it has been used to help digestion. A tea made from the plant might help with stomach aches, bloating, or indigestion by soothing the digestive tract. *Respiratory Relief:* It has been used in folk medicine to relieve respiratory problems like coughs and colds. Inhalation of steam from a brew made from the plant might help ease congestion. *Blood Pressure Regulation:* Some claims have been that it can help regulate blood pressure. Drinking tea made from the plant might assist in managing high blood pressure, although this use is not widely recognized. *Laxative Effect:* Some people have used it as a mild laxative to help constipation.

Fun/Historical Fact: The tumbleweed is a familiar symbol of the American West, appearing in countless movies and TV shows. However, it's not a native plant.

Russian Thistle was brought to the United States in the late 19th century and quickly became a nuisance due to its ability to spread rapidly and disrupt agriculture.

Dog Toxicity: Russian Thistle is not toxic to dogs.

S and Dropseed

Sporobolus cryptandrus [SPOH-ROH-BUH-LUS KRIP-TAN-DRUS]

Sand Dropseed belongs to the Poaceae (grass) family. This hardy plant is also called Sand Lovegrass or Sand Muhly and is native to North America, particularly in the western United States.

It's native to Arizona, New Mexico, Nevada, and Utah. It can grow in sandy or gravelly soil in desert areas, including sagebrush, pinyon-juniper woodlands, and mesas.

Identification:

GROWTH/SIZE: Grows to a 1 to 3 feet tall height. BARK/STEM/ROOT: It has fibrous, narrow stems and roots.

LEAF: The narrow leaves range from 1 to 6 inches long and 1/16 to 1/4 inch wide. They are typically green but can sometimes have a blue-green hue.

FLOWER: The flowers are tiny and can range from green to purple. They bloom in late summer or early fall and are about 1/8 inch long.

FRUIT/SEED/NUT: It produces small, brownish seeds about 1/8 inch long. The seeds are typically mature in late fall to early winter.

Look-a-Like(s): Toxic: **Darnel** (*Lolium temulentum*) contains alkaloids that can be harmful if ingested. Consuming it can lead to symptoms such as dizziness, digestive problems, and even hallucinations. While they might look similar at a glance, Darnel tends to have a more slender appearance, with the seed heads closely aligned with the stems. **Yellow Bristle Grass** (*Setaria pumila*) can be contaminated with toxic fungi, making it hazardous for consumption. If ingested, It may cause nausea, vomiting, and abdominal pain. It has a more bristly appearance with seed heads that are densely packed and often have a yellowish tint.

Non-toxic: **Big Sandgrass** (*Sporobolus giganteus*) is closely related to Sand Dropseed, and its seeds can be collected and ground into a nutritious flour. It tends to be taller and more robust with a thicker stalk. While both are part of the same genus, they often grow in different environments. **Indian Ricegrass** (*Achnatherum hymenoides*) has edible seeds that were historically an essential food source for Native American tribes. The seeds can be ground into flour or cooked as a grain. Though similar in appearance, Indian Ricegrass has a more open and branched seed head compared to the tighter cluster of Sand Dropseed. The leaves are also often more curled or twisted.

Cautions: There are no significant cautions associated with Sand Dropseed.

Culinary Preparations: *Seed Flour:* The tiny seeds can be collected and ground into flour. This flour can be mixed with other flour to make bread, muffins, or pancakes, adding a nutty and earthy flavor. *Grain Substitute:* The seeds can be cooked whole as a grain substitute. They can be boiled and used in dishes like salads, stews, or side dishes like quinoa or rice to add texture and a unique taste. *Porridge:* You can create a nourishing porridge by simmering the ground or whole seeds in water or milk. Sweeten with honey or sugar, and add fruits or nuts for a wholesome breakfast. *Sprouting:* the seeds can be sprouted and used in salads, sandwiches, or garnish. Sprouting the seeds may enhance their nutritional content and provide a fresh, green flavor. *Seed Roasting:* The seeds can be roasted to create a crunchy snack or a topping for various dishes. Roasting will intensify their flavor, and they can be seasoned with salt, spices, or herbs for additional taste.

Medicinal Uses: While it's mostly known for stabilizing soil and providing food for wildlife, there is limited information on its medicinal uses. Traditional practices mention a few potential applications, such as *Digestive Aid:* Some Native American tribes may have used Sand Dropseed as a mild digestive aid. Consuming tea made from seeds or leaves might help soothe stomachaches or indigestion. *Wound Healing:* The plant might have been used in poultices applied to cuts, scrapes, or minor wounds. Its potential antiseptic properties could help clean and heal the affected area. *Respiratory Relief:* Inhalation of steam from a brew made from the plant might have been used to ease congestion or symptoms of a cold. This could act as a natural expectorant, helping to clear mucus. *Skin Conditions:* A preparation might have been applied to alleviate conditions like rashes or eczema. Its possible anti-inflammatory effects could reduce irritation and itchiness.

Fun/Historical Fact: Sand Dropseed has a unique property. It can absorb and retain large amounts of water, making it useful for erosion control and as a plant for reclamation projects.

Dog Toxicity: Sand Dropseed has no known toxic effects on dogs.

all Tumblemustard

Sisymbrium altissimum [SIS-SIM-BREE-UM AL-TISS-IH-MUM]

Tall Tumblemustard is a fascinating plant that you may have seen around the southwest region of the United States. It's a Brassicaceae (mustard) family member, known by several other common names, such as Tall Tumbleweed Mustard, Tumbleweed Mustard, and Tumble Mustard. This plant has a long history, and it's believed to have originated in Europe and Asia.

It's a non-native plant in the southwest region of the United States. It can be found in states such as Arizona, Nevada, Utah, and New Mexico, where it thrives in various habitats like sandy washes, desert slopes, and disturbed areas.

Identification:

GROWTH/SIZE: This plant can grow up to 3-6 feet tall.

BARK/STEM/ROOT: The thick stem can be green or purple. The root is long and can grow up to 6 feet deep.

LEAF: The leaves are alternate, lobed, and can be up to 6 inches long. The color can range from green to blue-green.

FLOWER: The flowers are small, yellow, and are arranged in clusters. They can be up to 1/4 inch in diameter and bloom from late spring to early summer.

FRUIT/SEED/NUT: The fruit is a long, thin pod that contains several seeds. It's about 2- 3 inches long and can be green or brown. The seed can be 1/8 inch long and is brown.

Look-a-Like(s): Toxic: **White Snakeroot** (*Ageratina altissima*) contains a toxin called tremetol, which can harm humans and animals if ingested. It can cause symptoms such as trembling, vomiting, and heart failure. White Snakeroot has broader leaves and white, fluffy flowers, rather than the yellow flowers of Tumble Mustard. **Field Pennycress** (*Thlaspi arvense*) is not highly toxic but can be problematic in large amounts, especially for livestock. It contains substances that might taint the flavor of milk in dairy animals and can cause digestive issues. Its leaves are generally broader, and its flowers are white. The seed pods are flat and round.

Non-toxic: **London Rocket** (*Sisymbrium irio*) is a relative of Tumble Mustard and has edible young leaves that can be used in salads or cooked. The seeds can be ground into a spicy mustard-like paste. London Rocket tends to be shorter and bushier, with more lobed and serrated leaves. The flowers are similar but often arranged differently on the stalk. **Shepherd's Purse** (*Capsella bursa-pastoris*) has edible leaves that can be eaten raw or cooked. The young seed pods can also be consumed, and they have a peppery flavor. While similar in leaf shape, Shepherd's Purse has distinctive heart-shaped seed pods, unlike Tumble Mustard's long, slender pods. The flowers are also typically smaller.

Cautions: There aren't any associated issues with Tall Tumblemustard.

Culinary Preparations: While it's not typically found in mainstream culinary uses, it has been used by foragers and those interested in wild edibles. *Salads:* The young leaves can be picked and added to salads. They have a mild mustard flavor that adds a tangy kick to a fresh green salad. *Cooked Greens:* The more mature leaves can be a bit tough, so cooking them down in a sauté with garlic, olive oil, and some lemon juice can make a tasty side dish. Think of them as an alternative to spinach or kale. *Homemade Mustard:* The seeds can be collected and ground into a paste, mixed with vinegar, salt, and other spices to create a homemade mustard. It's a project for those interested in making condiments from scratch. *Stir-Fries:* The young leaves and flowers can be tossed into a stir-fry with the vegetables and protein of your choice. The mustard flavor adds an exciting twist to a familiar dish. *Pickled Pods:* The young seed pods can be pickled in a mixture of vinegar, sugar, and salt, much like you would pickle other vegetables. They add a crunchy, tangy element to dishes or can be eaten independently. *Soup Greens:* The leaves can be chopped and added if you're making a soup or stew and looking for extra greens. They'll contribute a unique flavor and extra nutrition.

Medicinal Uses: Tall Tumblemustard has been used traditionally to treat various ailments, such as digestive issues, respiratory problems, skin diseases, rheumatism, and fever. There is ongoing research to investigate the medicinal properties of Tall Tumblemustard.

Fun/Historical Fact: Did you know that Tall Tumblemustard is also known as the "Russian Thistle" and is considered an invasive species in some areas?

Dog Toxicity: Tall Tumblemustard isn't toxic to dogs. However, the plant can cause mechanical injury if the dog ingests spiny fruit or seeds. The symptoms can include vomiting, diarrhea, and abdominal discomfort.

White Horehound

Marrubium vulgare [MUH-ROO-bee-um vuhl-GAIR-ee]

White Horehound is a member of the Lamiaceae (mint) family. It is also known as Common Horehound, Houndsbane, and Eye of the Star. Its origins can be traced to the Mediterranean region, but it has since been introduced to many parts of the world.

It's a non-native wild plant in Arizona, New Mexico, Nevada, and Utah. It grows in various habitats, including roadsides, fields, and disturbed areas.

Identification:

GROWTH/SIZE: Grows up to 2 feet tall and 1 foot wide.

BARK/STEM/ROOT: It has a square, woody stem with fine hair covering its surface. The roots are also woody and extend deep into the soil.

LEAF: The leaves are round to oval-shaped, with a wrinkled texture and toothed edges. They can grow up to 1 inch long and are a grayish-green color.

FLOWER: The flowers are small and white, arranged in whorls around the stem. They bloom from May to October.

FRUIT/SEED: The fruit is a small nutlet that is brown. It matures in late summer or early fall.

Look-a-Like(s): Toxic: **White Deadnettle** (*Lamium album*) Though not highly toxic, it can cause digestive issues if consumed in large quantities. White Deadnettle has larger and brighter white flowers, and its leaves are often heart-shaped. **Henbane** (*Hyoscyamus niger*) is a toxic plant and can be harmful if ingested, causing symptoms like dry mouth, blurred vision, hallucinations, seizures, and even death in severe cases. While Henbane may have similar hairy leaves, its flowers are yellow with purple veins, and the plant generally has a more spreading habit.

Non-Toxic: **Lemon Balm** (*Melissa officinalis*) leaves have a delightful lemony scent and taste. Although Lemon Balm belongs to the same family, its leaves are usually more rounded and emit a lemon fragrance when crushed, while horehound has a more pungent and slightly bitter taste. **Spearmint** (*Mentha spicata*) is widely used for culinary purposes. It's famous for its sweet and minty taste. The leaves are typically bright green, and the plant emits an unmistakable minty fragrance when the leaves are crushed.

Cautions: There are no associated cautions with White Horehound.

Culinary Preparations: This herb has been used for various purposes, including in the kitchen. Its flavor is quite strong, with a bitter, minty taste. Here are some culinary uses for horehound: *Candy:* Probably the most famous use for horehound is in making hard candies. By boiling the leaves with sugar and other ingredients, you can create a unique candy enjoyed for generations, especially for soothing sore throats. *Flavoring for Baked Goods:* In small quantities, it can be added to cookies or muffins for a unique, earthy flavor. It pairs well with other herbs like rosemary or thyme. *Beer:* Historically, it has been used to flavor certain traditional beers or ales. Its bitter flavor could complement the different tastes in the brew. *Seasoning for Meat Dishes:* It can be mixed with herbs and spices to create a robust marinade or rub for meats like lamb or pork. *Syrups:* A syrup from Horehound can be drizzled over desserts or sweetened and used to flavor beverages. The syrup is often combined with honey or other sweeteners to reduce its bitterness. *Herbal Vinegar and Salad Dressings:* Horehound-infused vinegar can be a base for salad dressings. The sharp, bitter taste could add a different dimension to salads, especially when mixed with olive oil, mustard, and other seasonings.

Medicinal Uses: White Horehound has a long history of use in traditional medicine. Here are some medicinal uses. *Cough and Cold Remedy:* It's been used as a natural cough suppressant. Its extracts are often found in cough syrups and lozenges. It may help soothe sore throats and reduce coughing by helping to loosen phlegm in the lungs. *Respiratory Support:* Beyond its use for coughs, it's been used to support overall respiratory health. It might help treat bronchitis, asthma, or other respiratory conditions by relaxing the muscles around the airways and improving breathing. *Digestive Aid:* Traditionally, horehound has been used to support digestion, stimulate appetite, ease indigestion, and reduce bloating or gas. People might consume it as tea or include it in food to achieve these effects. *Menstrual Pain Relief:* Some women have used it to alleviate the discomfort associated with menstrual cramps. Its potential muscle-relaxing properties might ease uterine muscle spasms.

Fun/Historical Fact: White Horehound was considered a sacred plant believed to have magical properties in ancient times. It was used to ward off evil spirits and protect against witchcraft.

Dog toxicity: White Horehound is not toxic to dogs. However, it is always a good idea to consult a veterinarian before giving your dog any new plant or medication.

Wild Bergamot
Monarda fistulosa [MO-NAR-DA FUH-STUH-LOH-SUH]

Wild Bergamot, also known as Bee Balm, is a beautiful aromatic plant that belongs to the Lamiaceae (mint) family. The plant has several other common names, such as Horse Mint, Wild Oswego Tea, and Bergamot. Interestingly, Wild Bergamot is unrelated to the Bergamot fruit, used to flavor Earl Grey tea.

It is native to several states in the Southwest region, including Arizona, New Mexico, Nevada, and Utah. It can also be found in many other states, such as Texas, Illinois, and Michigan. Wild Bergamot in the Southwest can be found in open woods, fields, and stream banks.

Identification:

GROWTH/SIZE: Grows to a height of 2-4 feet and has a spread of 1-2 feet. BARK/STEM/ROOT: The stem is square-shaped, and the root is long and slender.

LEAF: The leaves are lance-shaped and about 3-4 inches long. They are dark green and have a slightly fuzzy texture.

FLOWER: The flowers are tube-shaped and about 1-2 inches long. They come in shades of pink, lavender, and purple and bloom mid to late summer.

FRUIT/SEED/NUT: The fruit is a small, dry capsule that contains tiny seeds. It matures in late summer and early fall.

Look-a-Like(s): Toxic: **Purple Larkspur** (*Delphinium barbeyi*) is a tall, showy plant that resembles Wild Bergamot. However, all parts of the plant, especially the seeds, contain highly toxic alkaloids to humans and animals. **Poison Hemlock** (*Conium maculatum*) is a tall, branching plant with finely divided leaves that resemble Wild Bergamot. All parts of the plant, especially the leaves and roots, contain a potent toxin called coniine, which can cause respiratory failure and death if ingested.

Non-toxic: **Lavender Hyssop** (*Agastache foeniculum*) is another mint family member. Its flowers are more elongated and narrow than Wild Bergamot flowers. **Purple Coneflower** (*Echinacea purpurea*) - Purple Coneflower produces beautiful purple flowers with a raised cone-shaped center, and its leaves are lance-shaped and hairy. However, Purple Coneflower flowers are more conical in shape than Wild Bergamot flowers.

Cautions: There are no significant cautions associated with Wild Bergamot.

Culinary Preparations: Wild Bergamot has a delightful flavor and can be used in many culinary preparations. *Tea Infusion:* The leaves can be dried to make a minty and aromatic tea. Simply strain the dried leaves in hot water for several minutes before enjoying a comforting cup of wild bergamot tea. *Salads:* The fresh or dried leaves can be chopped and added to salads. Its taste combines oregano and mint, giving various green salads a light and unique twist. A small sprinkle of the leaves can add both color and flavor. *Herbal Vinegar:* It can be used to create flavored vinegar. Placing the fresh leaves in a bottle of vinegar and letting it sit for a few weeks will absorb the herb's flavors. This infused vinegar can then be used in dressings, marinades, or other recipes requiring vinegar. *Garnish:* The bright flowers and leaves can be used as a garnish for various dishes. The flowers have a milder taste than the leaves, and they can add a pop of color and light flavor to dishes like soups, desserts, or meat platters. *Baking Ingredient:* It can be included as an ingredient in baking. The dried and crushed leaves can be added to bread, muffins, or cookies for a hint of minty flavor. Using this herb in baking can give a unique twist to familiar recipes and impress your friends and family.

Medicinal Uses: Wild Bergamot has a long history of medicinal uses. Here are a few: *Treating Cold and Flu Symptoms:* When you have a cold or the flu, drinking tea from this plant can help soothe a sore throat, reduce coughing, and clear up nasal congestion. It's like a natural cold medicine! *Aiding Digestion:* People have used it to make a tea that can calm an upset stomach. It can help with gas, nausea, and cramping. *Antiseptic for Cuts and Wounds:* The oils have antiseptic properties. If you have a cut or scrape, applying a little bit of this plant can help prevent infection. It's like a natural band-aid! *Headache Relief:* People have used it in the form of tea or applied the oil to their temples to help relieve headaches. It's a way to chase those headaches away without always using medicine from the store. *Anxiety and Stress Relief:* Feeling stressed or anxious? Wild Bergamot has been used to make teas to help calm your nerves. Drinking a cup might make you feel more relaxed. Think of it as a natural chill-out drink.

Fun/Historical Fact: Native Americans used wild Bergamot as a natural dye.

Dog Toxicity: Wild Bergamot is not toxic to dogs, and its leaves and flowers are safe for dogs to consume. If a dog were to consume a large amount of Wild Bergamot, it could cause mild gastrointestinal upset, such as vomiting or diarrhea.

Yellow Spine Thistle

Cirsium ochrocentrum [SIR-see-um oh-kroh-SEN-trum]

The Yellow Spine Thistle belongs to the Asteraceae (aster/daisy) family. Other common names for the plant include the Goldspine Thistle, Yellow Centaury, and Yellow Starthistle.

It's a native plant to the southwestern states of Arizona, New Mexico, Nevada, and Utah. This plant often grows in dry and rocky habitats such as canyons, foothills, and mountain slopes. It may also develop in meadows, grasslands, open woodlands, road-sides, old fields, and abandoned mining sites, where it grows in clumps or scattered groups.

Identification:

GROWTH/SIZE: Grows up to three feet tall and two feet wide. BARK/STEM/ROOT: The stem is rigid and hairy. The root is a taproot. LEAF: The leaves are hairy, lance-shaped, and can be up to 8 inches long.

FLOWER: The flowers are yellow and have spiny bracts around the base. The bloom time is from late spring to early summer.

FRUIT/SEED/NUT: The plant produces small seeds dispersed by wind.

Look-a-Like(s): No toxic plants resemble the Yellow Spine Thistle.

Non-toxic: **Blanketflower** (*Gaillardia pulchella*) has yellow and red flowers similar to Yellow Spine Thistle flowers. Blanketflower lacks the spiny bracts and has a more rounded flower head. **Hairy Golden Aster** (*Chrysopsis villosa*) has similar yellow flowers and a more rounded flower head and lacks the spiny bracts of the Yellow Spine Thistle.

Cautions: The Yellow Spine Thistle is not known to have any harmful effects.

Culinary Preparations: There is nothing on this plant you can't eat, making it very versatile. The young leaves are tender and can be boiled or steamed like other leafy greens, such as spinach or kale. They can be eaten as a side dish or added to salads. The roots can be roasted or boiled and used as a substitute for potatoes or other starchy vegetables. They have a nutty, slightly sweet flavor. The unopened flower buds can be harvested before they bloom and boiled or steamed. They are similar in taste to artichokes. The seeds can be ground into flour and used to make bread, pancakes, and other baked goods. The stems can be pickled like other vegetables, such as cucumbers or asparagus. They are crunchy and tangy.

Medicinal Uses: Traditionally, the plant has been used to treat digestive disorders, liver and gallbladder problems, and skin conditions. Modern research shows that the plant has anti-inflammatory and antioxidant properties. The leaves can be dried and used to make tea. Simply steep the dried leaves in hot water for several minutes, strain, and enjoy. The tea has a slightly bitter taste and is believed to have medicinal properties.

Fun/Historical Fact: During the early 20th century, Yellow Spine Thistle became a symbol of resistance for the Industrial Workers of the World (IWW), also known as the Wobblies, a labor union that fought for workers' rights. The IWW adopted the Yellow Spine Thistle as its emblem due to its hardiness and resilience, which they believed represented the working class. They also admired the thistle's sharp spines, which they saw as a symbol of their willingness to defend themselves against oppression and exploitation. Today, it remains a symbol of resistance and strength, and various labor and social justice organizations still use its image. This plant reminds us of the power of nature and the importance of standing up for what we believe in.

Dog Toxicity: The plant is not toxic to dogs.

PART FIVE
TREES & NUTS

Apache Plume

Fallugia paradoxa [FAH-LOO-jee-uh PUH-RAH-dox-uh]

Have you ever heard of the Apache Plume? This exciting plant belongs to the Rosaceae (rose) family. It's also known as Fallugia paradoxa or "Ponil" by the Navajo people.

It's native to Arizona, New Mexico, Nevada, and Utah. It grows in arid environments such as deserts, rocky slopes, and canyons. The plant has also been introduced to other California, Texas, and Mexico regions.

Identification:

GROWTH/SIZE: Grows up to 6 feet tall and spread to 6 feet wide.

BARK/STEM/ROOT: Its bark is gray-brown and shreddy, and the stems are slender and woody.

LEAF: The leaves are small and gray-green, shaped like feathers. They're about 1 inch long and 0.5 inches wide.

FLOWER: The white flowers have five petals and bloom from late spring to early summer. They are about 1 inch in diameter.

FRUIT/SEED/NUT: The fruits are feathery and resemble plumes. They're about 1 inch long and 1/2 inch wide.

Look-a-Like(s): Toxic plants: Apache Plume doesn't have a widely recognized set of toxic look-alikes.

Non-toxic plants: **Rosemary** *(Rosmarinus officinalis)* is often used in cooking. Its needle-like leaves are robust and flavorful and are often used to season meats and bread. Though Rosemary has needle-like leaves like Apache plume, it lacks the feathery seed heads of Fallugia paradoxa. The leaves of Rosemary are also darker green and more rigid. **Lavender** *(Lavandula)* is used in various culinary dishes, such as baked goods or teas. The flowers add a soft, floral flavor to foods and are also used for garnishing. While both plants have woody stems, Lavender's flowers are purple and fragrant. Apache plume's white flowers are followed by feathery seed heads, which are not seen in Lavender.

Cautions: There are no significant cautions to consider with Apache Plume.

Culinary Preparations: The Apache Plume has been traditionally used for food by Native Americans. Here are some ways you can prepare it:

- Use the flowers to make tea
- Roast the seeds for a coffee substitute
- Eat the fruits raw or cooked
- Mix the fruits with sugar to make a jelly

Medicinal Uses: The Apache Plume has been traditionally used to treat various ailments, including diarrhea, coughs, and sore throats. Modern research suggests the plant may have antibacterial properties and help lower blood pressure.

Fun/Historical Fact: The Apache Plume is named after the Apache Indians who used its plumed fruit for decorating their clothing and as a trade item. The plant has also been used for firewood, and its bark has been used to make baskets.

Dog Toxicity: The Apache Plume is not known to be toxic to dogs. However, as with any plant, it's best to keep pets from eating it to avoid any potential stomach upset.

 **rizona Walnut**

Juglans major [JUG-LANZ MAY-JOR]

The Arizona Walnut is a Juglandaceae (walnut) family member, including other walnuts and hickories. Common names, such as the New Mexico Walnut and the Southern California Walnut, also know the plant.

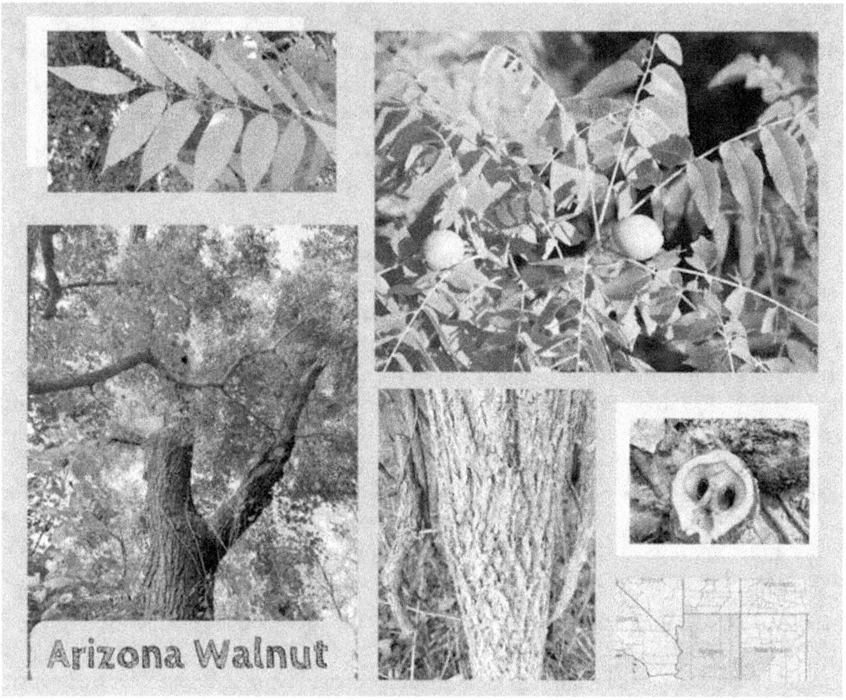

Interestingly, the plant is not native to Arizona but to Mexico and Central America. It can be found in the wild throughout the Southwestern states, growing in various habitats such as canyon bottoms, stream banks, and moist areas in the desert.

Identification:

GROWTH/SIZE: grow to 50 feet tall and 30 feet wide.

BARK/STEM/ROOT: The bark is rough and grey-brown, and the stems and roots are similar in color.

LEAF: The leaves are pinnately compound, with 11-19 leaflets 2-5 inches long and 0.5-

1.5 inches wide. They are a light green color.

FLOWER: The flowers are small and green and bloom in the spring.

FRUIT/SEED/NUT: The nuts are round, 1.5-2 inches in diameter, and have a hard, thick shell. They are ready to harvest in the fall.

Look-a-Like(s): Toxic: **Black Locust** (*Robinia pseudoacacia*). Its bark and leaves contain toxins called lectins, which can cause nausea, vomiting, and diarrhea if ingested. It can be particularly harmful to livestock. While the Black Locust has similar compound leaves, the leaflets are smaller, and the plant has clusters of fragrant white flowers. The fruit is a flat legume, not a round nut-like Juglans major.

Non-Toxic: **Texas Walnut** (*Juglans microcarpa*) produces edible nuts. They can be used like other walnuts, such as baking or snacks. Texas walnut is closely related to Juglans major, but its nuts are smaller and harder to crack. The leaflets may also differ slightly in shape and size. **Mesquite Tree** (*Prosopis spp.*) produces seed pods that can be ground into sweet, nutty flour. This flour is used in baking and adds a unique flavor to bread, muffins, and other treats. While mesquite trees have compound leaves like Juglans major, they have thorns, and the seed pods are quite different from the round walnuts of Juglans major.

Cautions: There are no major cautions associated with the Arizona Walnut.

Culinary Preparations: *Snacks:* The nuts can be eaten raw or toasted with a bit of salt. Toasting brings a richer flavor and a crunchy texture, making it a perfect snack. *Baking Ingredient:* the nuts can be chopped and added to baked goods like muffins, cookies, and brownies. They give a pleasant crunch and a nutty flavor that pairs well with sweet dishes. *Salad Topping:* These walnuts can be sprinkled over salads to add a bit of crunch and taste. Whether in a fruit salad or a green leafy salad, walnuts can enhance the texture and flavor. *Butter:* You can grind the walnuts into a paste to make walnut butter. This can be spread on bread or used as a dip. It's a nutritious and tasty alternative to traditional butter or peanut butter. *Oil:* the walnuts can be pressed to produce walnut oil. This oil has a distinct, rich flavor and can be used in salad dressings or as a finishing oil to drizzle over dishes. *Pesto:* Traditional pesto can be made with walnuts instead of pine nuts. This provides a twist to the classic sauce, adding a new flavor dimension that pairs well with pasta, sandwiches, or a marinade.

Medicinal Uses: *Skin Treatments:* The juice from the green husks can be used to treat fungal infections on the skin, like athlete's foot or ringworm. It's known for its antifungal properties, which can help clear up infections. *Wound Healing:* The leaves can be made into a poultice, a soft, moist substance that relieves soreness and inflammation. When applied to wounds, it may help reduce swelling and promote healing. *Parasite Treatment:* It's been used to treat internal parasites, such as worms in the digestive tract. Consuming preparations made from the bark or husks can help expel these parasites, though this treatment should be used cautiously and under expert guidance. **Dental Care:** The astringent qualities can be used in dental care. Chewing on the bark or using a preparation as a mouth rinse may help tighten gums and alleviate toothache.

Fun/Historical Fact: The Arizona Walnut was an important food source for the native people of the southwestern United States. The nuts were often ground into a paste and used to make bread.

Dog Toxicity: The nuts and leaves of the Arizona Walnut are toxic to dogs. Symptoms of toxicity can include vomiting, diarrhea, and tremors. It's essential to keep your furry friends away from this plant.

Blue Palo Verde

Parkinsonia florida [PAR-KIH-NOW-NEE-UH FLOR-I-DUH]

Blue Palo Verde is a medium-sized tree from the Fabaceae (legume) family. This tree is also called Yellow Palo Verde or Cercidium Floridum. The Blue Palo Verde tree has been growing in the Sonoran Desert for centuries and was used by the Native Americans for medicinal and food purposes. Today, it is grown for ornamental and shade purposes in many parts of the world.

It's native to the Southwest region of the United States and can be found growing in the wild in Arizona, New Mexico, and Nevada. It is also planted in other parts where the climate is hot and dry.

Identification:

GROWTH/SIZE: it can grow up to 30 feet tall and wide.

BARK/STEM/ROOT: The bark is smooth, green, and photosynthetic. The branches are thin and green, and the roots are shallow and spreading.

LEAF: The leaves are small, feathery, and bluish-green, with multiple leaflets.

FLOWER: The flowers are bright yellow, pea-like, and about an inch long. They bloom from late March to early May.

FRUIT/SEED/NUT: The fruit is a small, flat, brownish pod, about 1.5 inches long. The seeds are small, black, and edible.

Look-a-Like(s): Toxic: No known toxic look-a-likes.

Non-Toxic: **Honey Mesquite** *(Prosopis glandulosa),* the pods can also create flour. Its sweet taste makes it suitable for desserts. *Differences:* Though the branches and leaves might look similar, Honey Mesquite usually has larger thorns, and its flowers are yellow or white, while Blue Palo Verde's are yellow. **Catclaw Acacia** *(Senegalia greggii)* sweet pods can be consumed and have been used by indigenous peoples as a food source. *Differences:* Catclaw Acacia has curved thorns resembling a cat's claws (hence its name) and usually bears white or pale yellow flowers, unlike the bright yellow flowers of Blue Palo Verde. **Chilean Mesquite** *(Prosopis chilensis)* Like other Mesquites, its pods can be turned into flour. The flour is gluten-free and has a unique, earthy flavor. *Differences:* Chilean Mesquite has more massive, spreading branches and lacks the bluish-green hue found in Blue Palo Verde's branches and leaves.

Cautions: There are no significant associated issues with the Blue Palo Verde tree.

Culinary Preparations: The Blue Palo Verde tree has edible seeds, and the flowers can make a refreshing tea. Here are some ways to prepare the Blue Palo Verde tree as food:

- Roasted seeds
- Palo Verde flower tea
- Dried and ground seeds as a seasoning
- Seed paste as a dip

Medicinal Uses: The Blue Palo Verde tree has been used for centuries by Native Americans to treat various ailments, such as arthritis, infections, and respiratory issues. Modern research has shown that the Blue Palo Verde tree has anti-inflammatory, antibacterial, and antiviral properties, making it a potential treatment for many diseases.

Fun/Historical Fact: The Blue Palo Verde tree is the state tree of Arizona, and it blooms in the spring, covering the desert in a beautiful yellow blanket.

Dog Toxicity: The Blue Palo Verde tree is non-toxic to dogs. However, the tree seeds can cause gastrointestinal problems, such as vomiting and diarrhea, if ingested in large quantities. It is best to keep the seeds away from dogs.

Desert Almond

Prunus fasciculata [PROO-NUS FAH-SIK-YOO-LAH-TUH]

The Desert Almond belongs to the Rosaceae (rose) family. It is also called the Arizona almond, New Mexican almond, and foothill almond.

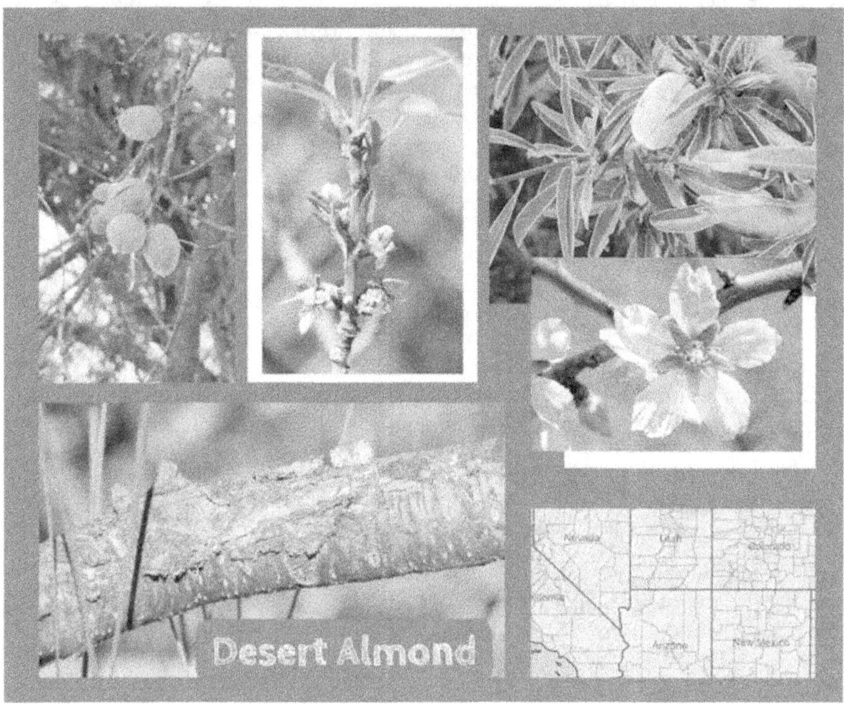

The Desert Almond is a native plant in Arizona, New Mexico, Nevada, and Utah. It grows wild in the Sonoran and Mojave deserts, rocky areas, and canyons.

Identification:

GROWTH/SIZE: it can grow up to 15 feet tall but usually reaches around 8 feet.

BARK/STEM/ROOT: The bark is grayish-brown, and the stems are thin and have small thorns. The root system is shallow and spreads wide.

LEAF: The leaves are narrow, about 1-2 inches long, and light green.

FLOWER: it produces small white or pink flowers in clusters, measuring about 1 inch in diameter. The blooming season is from late winter to early spring.

FRUIT/SEED/NUT: The plant produces small nuts that measure about 1 inch in length. The nuts have a hard outer shell and a bitter taste. They are in season from late summer to early fall.

Look-a-Like(s): Toxic: **Jimsonweed** (*Datura stramonium*) is a highly toxic plant. Ingesting any plant part can cause hallucinations, seizures, and even death. While both plants might be found in desert regions, Jimsonweed has large, trumpet-shaped flowers, unlike the small clusters of Desert Almonds. The leaves are also broader and coarser. **Castor Bean Plant** (*Ricinus communis*) The seeds contain ricin, a highly toxic protein that can be fatal if ingested in large quantities. Castor Bean has large, palmate leaves and distinct spiky seed pods.

Non-toxic: **Mountain Mahogany** (*Cercocarpus montanus*) While not typically used in cooking, some indigenous people have consumed the seeds of Mountain Mahogany. The leaves are typically more elongated and leathery. Additionally, Mountain Mahogany has feathery seed tails not found in Desert Almonds. **Ocean Spray or Cream Bush** (*Holodiscus discolor*) Some Native American tribes have consumed the flowers and seeds. Ocean Spray has clusters of white flowers like Desert Almond, but its leaves are more lobed and serrated. Ocean Spray typically grows in a wider variety of habitats, including coastal regions, unlike the desert-dwelling Desert Almond.

Cautions: There are no known cautions associated with the Desert Almond.

Culinary Preparations: The nuts of the Desert Almond can be roasted and eaten as a snack, used in baking, or made into almond butter. They can also be used as a substitute for regular almonds in recipes.

Medicinal Uses: Desert Almond has been used in traditional medicine to treat various ailments, including coughs, sore throats, and digestive issues. Recent research has shown that the plant may have anti-inflammatory and anti-cancer properties.

Fun/Historical Fact: The Desert Almond has played an important role in the diets of Native American tribes in the southwestern United States for centuries. The nuts were a valuable source of food during times of scarcity.

Dog Toxicity: The Desert Almond is not toxic to dogs. However, the nuts can be a choking hazard and should be given to dogs in small pieces. Symptoms of choking may include difficulty breathing, coughing, and wheezing.

Desert Willow

Chilopsis linearis [KIL-OH-PIS LIN-EE-AIR-IS]

The Desert Willow is a hardy plant native to the southwest region of the United States, belonging to the Bignoniaceae (trumpet vine) family. It's also known as Desert Catalpa or Flowering Willow. Despite its common name, the Desert Willow is unrelated to the willow tree family.

The Desert Willow is well adapted to arid conditions and prefers well-draining soil. Its presence in these regions is a testament to its adaptability in surviving and thriving in the challenging desert environment. Predominantly found throughout the Southwest region, especially in desert washes and canyon bottoms.

Identification:

GROWTH/SIZE: grows up to 30 feet tall.

BARK/STEM/ROOT: The bark is grayish-brown, and the stem is usually thin and flexible. The plant's roots are extensive and can grow up to three times the size of the plant.

LEAF: The leaves are long and narrow, ranging from 4 to 12 inches long. They are green and have a waxy texture that helps the plant retain moisture.

FLOWER: It produces beautiful trumpet-shaped flowers, ranging from 1 to 3 inches long, with various colors like pink, purple, and white. The blooming season for the plant is usually from late spring to early fall.

FRUIT/SEED/NUT: It produces slender pods around 4 to 12 inches long. The pods contain small, flat seeds.

Look-a-Like(s): Toxic: **Oleander** *(Nerium oleander)* All parts are highly poisonous, especially if ingested. The plant contains toxins that can affect the heart. Oleanders have lance-shaped leaves, while Desert Willow has narrower, willow-like leaves. The oleander flowers are usually in shades of pink, red, or white and are more tubular than Desert Willow flowers. **Datura** *(Datura spp.)* All parts are poisonous, especially the seeds and flowers. Consuming them can lead to hallucinations and, in larger quantities, more severe poisoning or even death. Datura has large, trumpet-shaped white or purple flowers. Its leaves are also broader than the Desert Willow.

Non-Toxic: **Texas Mountain Laurel** *(Sophora secundiflora)* Be careful! While the flowers have a sweet grape-like scent, eating the seeds can be toxic. This shrub or small tree has shiny, evergreen leaves. Its purple-blue flowers are packed tightly in upright clusters and smell like grape soda. **Desert Bird of Paradise** *(Caesalpinia gilliesii)* While visually stunning, it's best to admire this plant's beauty rather than its edibility. It is not typically consumed. This shrub showcases bright yellow flowers with long red stamens that look shooting out. It's a very distinct appearance.

Cautions: There are no major associated issues with the Desert Willow plant.

Culinary Preparations: The Desert Willow is not commonly used as food. However, the flowers can be used to make a tea that has a slightly sweet taste.

Medicinal Uses: *Cough and Cold Treatment:* The Desert Willow has been used as a remedy for coughs and colds. Native people would make tea from its bark and leaves to help ease symptoms. *Anti-fungal Properties:* Extracts have shown antifungal actions. This means it can help fight off certain types of fungal infections. *Skin Irritations and Wounds:* The bark or leaves can be made into a poultice and applied to the skin. This helps in soothing minor wounds, cuts, and skin irritations. *Treatment for Bacterial Infections:* Some studies suggest that Desert Willow has antibacterial properties. Traditional uses included brewing tea to fight off internal infections. *Natural Pain Relief:* Pain relief is another traditional use for the Desert Willow. Drinking tea made from its parts, especially the bark, was believed to help reduce pain.

Fun/Historical Fact: The Desert Willow's name is misleading, as it is unrelated to the willow tree family. It got its name due to its willow-like leaves and habitat in desert regions.

Dog Toxicity: The Desert Willow is not toxic to dogs. However, ingesting large quantities of the plant can cause digestive upset, such as vomiting or diarrhea.

One-seed Juniper

Juniperus monosperma [JOO-NI-PUH-RUS MON-OH-SPUR-MUH]

The One-seed Juniper belongs to the Cupressaceae (cypress) family. It is commonly called the New Mexico juniper, desert juniper, or mountain cedar. The plant is native to North America, from southern Canada to Central America.

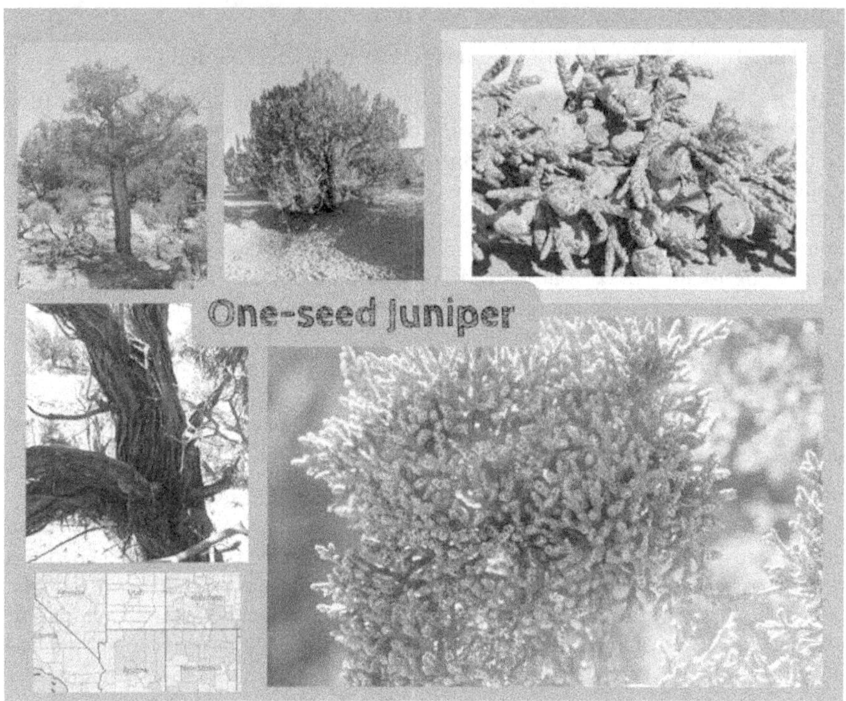

It's native to the southwestern region of the United States, including Arizona, New Mexico, Nevada, and Utah. It can be found in various locations within these states, including deserts, grasslands, and forests.

Identification:

GROWTH/SIZE: Can grow up to 50 feet tall but typically ranges from 10 to 30 feet.

BARK/STEM/ROOT: The bark is reddish-brown, and the stem and roots are woody and tough.

LEAF: The leaves are evergreen, needle-like, and range from 0.2 to 0.6 inches in length. The color of the leaves varies from blue-green to gray-green.

FLOWER: It produces small, yellowish-green flowers that bloom in the spring.

FRUIT/SEED/NUT: The fruit is a small berry-like cone, about 0.4 inches in diameter, and takes up to two years to mature.

Look-a-Like(s): Toxic: **Sacred Datura** *(Datura wrightii)* has large, trumpet-shaped white flowers and spiky seed pods. It doesn't have the blueberries. **Buffalo Bur** *(Solanum rostratum)* has yellow flowers and spiky green fruits.

Non-toxic: **Utah Juniper** *(Juniperus osteosperma)* The berries can be eaten but are often used as a dish flavoring rather than a primary food source. While both are junipers, the Utah Juniper has harder, more shaggy bark, and its berries are slightly larger than those of the One-seed Juniper. **Alligator Juniper** *(Juniperus deppeana)* Like other junipers, its berries can be used for flavoring but are not commonly consumed. The bark looks like an alligator's checkered skin, making it stand out.

Cautions: There are no major associated issues with the One-seed Juniper.

Culinary Preparations: *Spice:* The small berries can be dried and used as a spice. They give dishes a unique, earthy flavor with a hint of pine. *Meat Marinades:* Crushed juniper berries can be added to marinades for meats, especially game meats like venison or elk. They give the meat a woodsy, aromatic taste that complements the strong flavors of wild game. *Flavored Oils:* You can make a fragrant oil by steeping dried juniper berries in olive oil. This oil can be drizzled on salads or used as a base for cooking to add an extra layer of flavor. *Juniper Tea:* Some people brew mild tea using juniper berries. The tea has a slightly tangy, resinous taste and is believed to have some medicinal properties. *Juniper Berry Syrup:* When boiled with sugar and water, juniper berries can make delicious syrup. This syrup can be used on pancakes, in cocktails, or as a glaze for meats. *Flavoring for Sauces:* Crushed juniper berries can be simmered in sauces to impart their unique flavor. They pair well with tomato-based sauces or even fruit sauces.

Medicinal Uses: Native American tribes have traditionally used this tree for medicinal purposes. Here are five examples. *Respiratory Relief:* The berries and leaves make teas or infusions to help with respiratory problems. *Stomach Issues:* A tea made from berries has been traditionally taken to help with an upset stomach. *Antiseptic Uses:* The juniper has natural antiseptic properties. This means it can help clean out wounds and prevent infections. A crushed juniper leaf or berry paste was sometimes applied directly to minor cuts or scrapes. *Joint and Muscle Pain:* A poultice made from juniper can be used to sore muscles or joints. This has been believed to reduce pain and inflammation.

Fun/Historical Fact: Though typical gins are made with common juniper, you can experiment by infusing gin with One-seed Juniper berries to give it a Southwestern twist.

Dog Toxicity: The One-seed Juniper is not toxic to dogs, but ingesting large quantities of the berries can cause mild gastrointestinal upset. Symptoms may include vomiting, diarrhea, and lethargy.

Quaking Aspen

Populus tremuloides [PUH-PUH-lus TREM-YOO-LOY-DEEZ]

The Quaking Aspen belongs to the Salicaceae (willow) family. It is also commonly called trembling aspen, white poplar, and golden aspen. The Quaking Aspen is native to the cooler regions of North America, from Alaska to Newfoundland and even down to the mountains of Mexico.

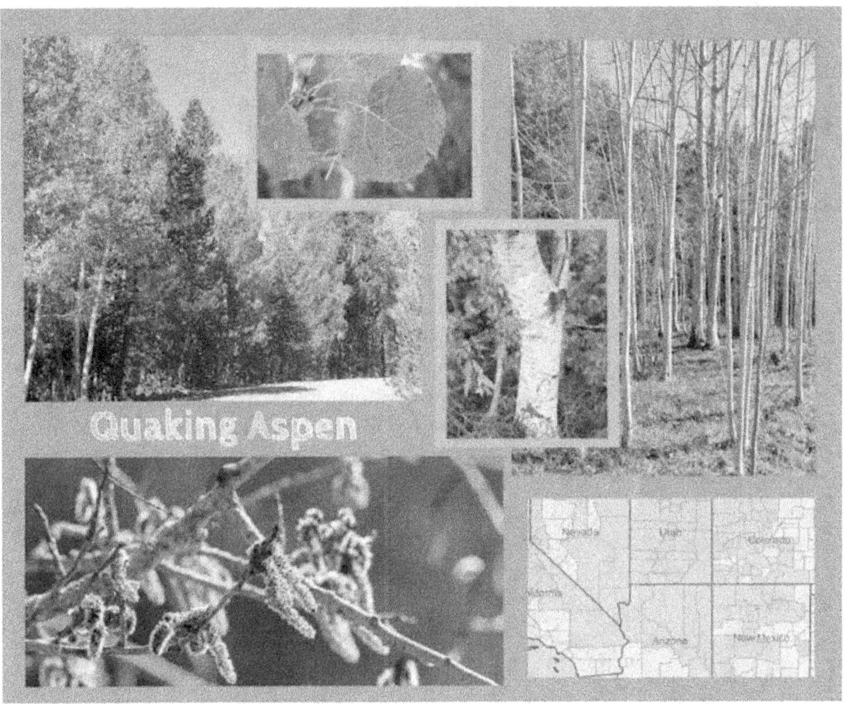

The Quaking Aspen is native to Arizona, New Mexico, Nevada, and Utah. It is often found in areas with a lot of sunlight and water, such as near streams or wetlands.

Identification:

GROWTH/SIZE: It's a deciduous tree that can grow up to 20-60 feet tall and 5-20 inches in diameter.

BARK/STEM/ROOT: When young, the bark is usually smooth and greenish-white, becoming gray and furrowed. The stem is generally straight and slender, while the root system is extensive, often growing from root sprouts to form large colonies.

LEAF: The leaves are circular to oval-shaped, measuring 1-4 inches long and 1-3 inches wide. They are green on the top and lighter on the bottom, with small teeth on the edge.

FLOWER: The flowers are greenish-yellow and grow in drooping clusters. They bloom in early spring before the leaves appear.

FRUIT/SEED/NUT: The fruit is a small capsule that contains many small seeds, each with a tuft of cottony hairs that helps it to disperse in the wind. The capsules ripen in late spring or early summer.

Look-a-Like(s): Toxic: **Chinaberry Tree** (*Melia azedarach*) The berries are very toxic if eaten. They can cause upset stomach, breathing problems, and more. *Differences:* The Chinaberry tree has leaves that are more divided and lacy. Its berries are small, yellowish, and can be found in clusters.

Non-Toxic: **Cottonwood Trees** (*Populus deltoides*) The young, green seed pods are edible. *Differences:* Cottonwood trees have broader leaves, and the bark is often more deeply furrowed. They also produce cotton-like seeds in the spring, which can cover the ground. **Manzanita** (*Arctostaphylos spp.*) Manzanitas produce edible red or orange berries. These berries can be consumed fresh, dried, or made into cider. *Differences:* They have a distinctively smooth, red-brown bark. The leaves are also more rigid and leathery than the Quaking Aspen's fluttery leaves.

Cautions: There are no significant cautions associated with the Quaking Aspen.

Culinary Preparations: Quaking Aspen is more than just a pretty tree! It has been used for food for a long time. Some culinary ways people use this tree include *Aspen Tea:* You can make a mild tea by steeping the inner bark or young leaves. This tea has a unique, somewhat earthy flavor and has been traditionally used for its potential health benefits. *Aspen Sap Syrup:* Like maple trees, the Quaking Aspen can be tapped for its sap. This sap can then be boiled down to create syrup. The syrup has a mild sweetness, different from maple syrup, but still tasty on pancakes or waffles. *Aspen Leaf Salad:* Young, tender leaves can be added to salads. They offer a mild, slightly bitter flavor and can be a unique addition to your greens. *Aspen Bark Soup Thickener:* When boiled, the ground's inner bark can be a natural thickener for soups or stews. It gives the dish a slightly woody taste and can be an emergency substitute if you run out of regular thickeners.

Medicinal Uses: Quaking Aspen has been used for medicinal purposes by Native Americans and other traditional herbalists. Here's a list of some of its medicinal uses. *Pain Reliever & Fever Reducer:* The bark contains a natural chemical called salicin. This chemical works similarly to modern-day aspirin and can help relieve pain, such as headaches or muscle aches joints, and helps to reduce fever. *Skin Issues:* A poultice made from the bark can be applied to the skin. It can help with skin irritations, wounds, and burns by reducing inflammation and promoting healing. *Antiseptic Uses:* The bark has properties that can help in preventing infections. It can be used to clean wounds or to prevent wounds from becoming infected. *Stomach Issues:* A tea made from the bark can calm an upset stomach and reduce discomfort. It can help with mild stomachaches or digestive problems.

Fun/Historical Fact: The Quaking Aspen is North America's most widely distributed tree. It is often referred to as the "lungs of the West" because of its ability to take in carbon dioxide and release oxygen.

Dog Toxicity: The Quaking Aspen is not toxic to dogs.

S crewbean Mesquite

Prosopis pubescens [PRO-SOH-PIS PYOO-BES-SENS]

It is a unique plant with an intriguing history. This plant is part of the Fabaceae (legume) family, the same as beans and peas! Some folks might know it by its more common name, Tornillo.

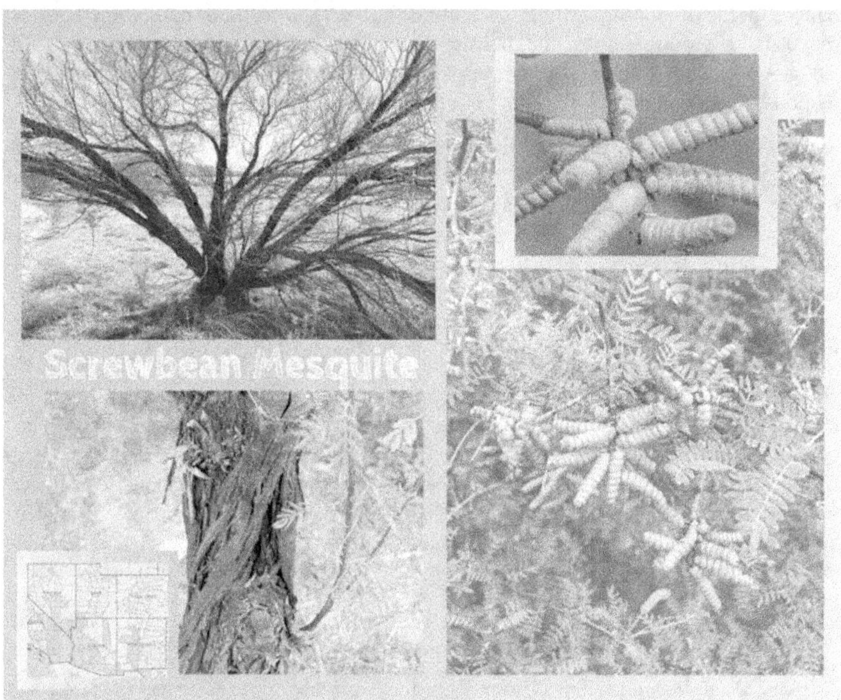

It loves to grow in the southwestern regions of the U.S. If you're from Arizona, California, Nevada, New Mexico, or Texas, you might have seen it around since it calls these states its native home. It enjoys the desert and riparian habitats, so watch out next time you're on a desert hike!

Identification:

GROWTH/SIZE: a small tree or shrub growing up to 15 to 25 feet tall. Its growth pattern is often spread out, with multiple branches creating a vast canopy.

BARK/STEM/ROOT: Its bark is dark brown to grayish, often cracked or deeply grooved. The stems carry a similar brownish color and can twist and turn in various directions, giving way to the plant's iconic spiral-shaped seed pods. The roots can grow surprisingly deep, sometimes reaching 50 feet to find water!

LEAF: The leaf is a bright green color. These leaves are small and pinnately compound, like the feathers on an arrow. Each leaflet is oval or oblong and can be about half an inch long. They grow in pairs opposite each other, giving the tree a full and bushy appearance.

FLOWER: pale yellow to greenish-yellow, forming small, dense, and fluffy clusters. Each flower is tiny, but together, they create a noticeable and attractive display. These flowers typically bloom in the spring, from April to May.

FRUIT/SEED/NUT: has a spiral or screw-shaped pod, which is how the tree got its "screwbean" name. The pods are about 1 to 2 inches long and are brownish when mature. Inside these unique pods, you'll find the seeds, which are small and hard. The tree usually produces these fascinating screw-like pods in the summer, typically between June and August. If you're thinking of harvesting them, it's best to wait until the pods turn green to brown, indicating they are ripe and ready.

Look-a-likes: Toxic: **Castor Bean Plant** *(Ricinus communis)* The seeds of this plant are highly poisonous due to a toxin called ricin. Even a few seeds can be deadly if ingested. *Differences:* Though it has a similar bushy appearance, its large, star-shaped leaves and red or green spiky seed pods distinguish it from the Screwbean Mesquite. **Russian Olive** *(Elaeagnus angustifolia)* While not highly toxic, the Russian Olive's berries can cause stomach upset if consumed in large quantities. *Differences:* This tree has silver-grey leaves, giving it a distinctive look. Its fruit is a small, yellow to reddish-brown berry, very different from the screw-shaped pods of the Screwbean Mesquite.

Non-Toxic: **Velvet Mesquite** *(Prosopis velutina)* pods can be ground into flour. The beans inside the pods can be eaten directly, too. *Differences:* The Velvet Mesquite has long and straight pods with a velvety texture on its leaves, unlike the spiral pods of the Screwbean Mesquite. **Catclaw Acacia** *(Senegalia greggii)* The beans inside the pods can be cooked and eaten, and its gum has been used as a food source by Native Americans. *Differences:* While it has similar-looking pods, Catclaw Acacia gets its name from its claw-like thorns that can "grab" onto you, unlike the generally thornless Screwbean Mesquite.

Cautions: There are no significant cautions associated with the Screwbean Mesquite.

Culinary Uses: *Mesquite Flour:* The pods of the Screwbean Mesquite can be dried and ground into a sweet, nutty flour. This flour can be mixed with other flour to make bread, muffins, and even pancakes! *Sweetener:* When young and green, the pods can be boiled to make a sweet syrup. This syrup can be a natural sweetener in various dishes or drinks. *Mesquite Jelly:* Ripe Screwbean Mesquite pods can make sweet and tangy jelly. This jelly pairs well with toast, muffins, or as a glaze for certain meats. *Roasted Seeds:* The seeds inside the pods can be burned to make a crunchy snack. They're somewhat like sunflower seeds in taste.

Medicinal Uses: *Sore Throat Soother:* A tea made from the bark or leaves of the tree has been used to soothe sore throats. Its calming properties can provide relief from irritation. *Skin Treatment:* The gum, which oozes out from the tree naturally, has been applied to the skin to treat wounds, sores, and infections. It acts as a protective layer and can help with healing. *Dental Care:* Some tribes chewed the tree's twigs to clean their teeth and keep their gums healthy. The twig's fibers would act like a natural toothbrush!

Fun/Historical Fact: The "screwbean" name comes from the plant's seed pods, which are spirally twisted, kind of like a corkscrew! The wood from the Screwbean Mesquite was used to make tools and furniture.

Dog Toxicity: No concrete evidence suggests that Screwbean Mesquite is toxic to dogs.

Two-needle Pinon Pine

Pinus edulis [PY-NUS EH-DYOO-LIS]

The Two-needle Pinon Pine is believed to have been present in the southwestern United States for thousands of years, and its historical usage dates back to the indigenous peoples of the region. It's a member of the Pinaceae (pine) family name, and it's commonly referred to as Pinon Pine, Pinon, Pinyon Pine, or Two-needle Pinyon.

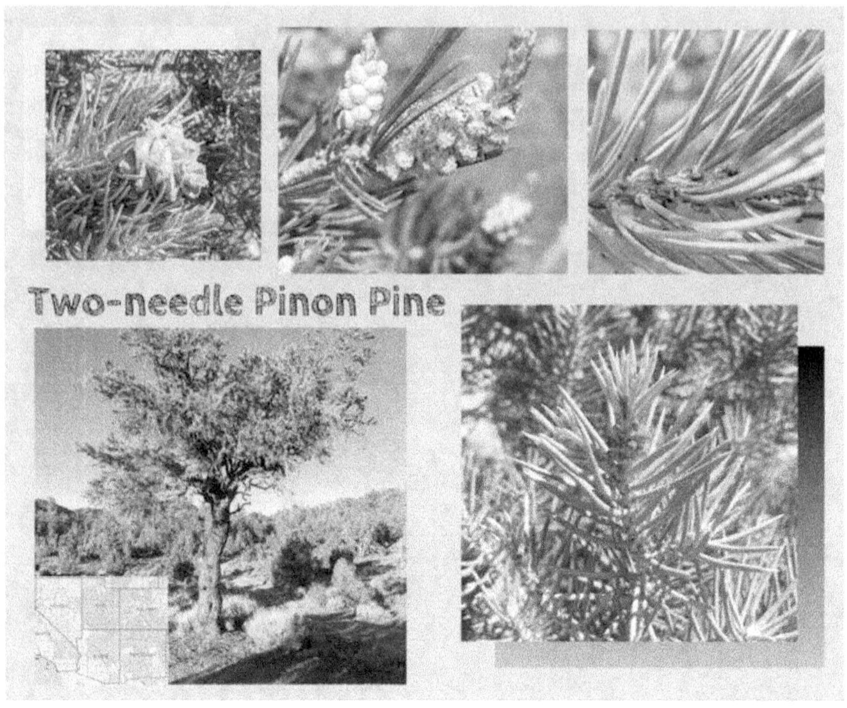

It's native to Arizona, New Mexico, Nevada, and Utah. It can be found in the wild throughout these states, typically in higher elevations, such as mountainous areas.

Identification:

GROWTH/SIZE: it's a slow-growing tree that can reach heights of up to 50 feet and have a spread of up to 25 feet.

BARK/STEM/ROOT: The bark is thick and scaly, typically gray or brown. The stem is straight and can have a diameter of up to 18 inches. The root system is shallow and widespread.

LEAF: The needles are 2-3 inches long and come in pairs. They are typically a bluish-green color.

FLOWER: it produces small brown cones that can grow up to three inches long. The cones typically appear in the fall and can take up to three years to mature.

FRUIT/SEED/NUT: The cones contain edible seeds called piñon nuts. The seeds are typically 1-2 inches long and are brown. They mature in the late summer and fall.

Look-a-Like(s): Toxic: **Yew Trees** *(Taxus species)* All parts of the yew tree, especially the seeds inside the berries, are highly toxic when ingested. They can cause dizziness, abdominal pain, difficulty breathing, and even heart failure. *Differences:* Yew trees have flat, needle-like leaves that are darker and shinier than Pinyon Pine. While Pinyon Pine produces brown cones, yews have red, berry-like fruits with a seed inside.

Non-toxic: **Ponderosa Pine** *(Pinus ponderosa)* The young inner bark (cambium) of the Ponderosa Pine can be eaten. Its nuts are also edible, although smaller and less flavorful than Pinyon Pine nuts. *Differences:* Ponderosa Pines are much taller than Pinyon Pines and have longer needles, usually in bundles of three. The bark of mature Ponderosa Pines can have a yellow-orange hue and emits a pleasant vanilla scent, especially when warmed by the sun. **Limber Pine** *(Pinus flexilis)* Limber Pine also produces edible nuts, which can be eaten raw or roasted. *Differences:* Limber Pines are often found at higher elevations. They have flexible branches (called "limber"), and their needles usually come in bundles of five.

Cautions: There are no associated cautions with the Two-needle Pinon Pine.

Culinary Preparations: *Pinyon Pine Nuts:* The most popular culinary use! The seeds inside the cones are what we call pine nuts. They're creamy and rich; you can eat them raw or roasted. They're perfect for snacking or sprinkling on salads. *Pine Nut Butter:* Think peanut butter but with pine nuts! You can blend roasted nuts until they're smooth and spreadable. *Pine Nut Pesto:* Pesto isn't just for basil. You can combine Pinyon Pine nuts with garlic, olive oil, parmesan cheese, and some herbs to make a rich and tasty sauce. It's perfect for pasta or as a spread on bread. *Pine-Infused Oil and Dressing:* You can capture a unique pine flavor by infusing cooking oil with Pinyon Pine needles. This oil is excellent for dressings or drizzling over dishes to add a unique twist. Blend Pinyon Pine nuts with vinegar, olive oil, and your favorite herbs to make a creamy, tangy salad dressing.

Medicinal Uses: *Respiratory Relief:* The resin from Pinyon Pine can be used to make balms or salves. Applying or inhaling them can help clear the sinuses and support respiratory health, especially when feeling stuffy or congested. *Wound Healing:* The sap or resin contains antiseptic properties. This means it can help clean wounds and prevent infections. In the past, people might have applied the sap directly to cuts or scrapes to promote healing. *Soothing Skin:* Oils or creams can moisturize and help with dry skin, chapped lips, and conditions like eczema. *Pain Relief:* Balms can be applied to sore muscles or joints. They have properties that can help reduce pain and inflammation. *Relaxation:* The aroma can be calming. Inhaling the scent, whether from the tree or products made from it, can help reduce stress and promote relaxation.

Fun/Historical Fact: These trees can live a super long time. Some Pinyon Pines can live for over 1,000 years! New Mexico loves the Pinyon Pine so much that they chose it as their state tree.

Dog Toxicity: The Two-needle Pinon Pine is not toxic to dogs. However, consuming large quantities of piñon nuts could lead to digestive upset or other issues.

PAY IT FORWARD!

Picture this: someone's standing in the middle of a Southwest wilderness, surrounded by the raw beauty of nature. But there's a tiny hiccup - they're a tad unsure which of the green wonders before them might serve as a delicious snack or which might send them on an unplanned trip to the ER. Now, what if YOUR review could be the deciding factor that guides them on this green gastronomic journey?

Food for Thought: How many times have we relied on the experiences of others before diving into a new adventure? Countless, right? How gratifying does it feel when we can be that guiding light for someone else?

Leaving a review isn't just a simple clickety-clack of your keyboard. Nope! It's a chance to share your wisdom, your "Ah-ha!" moments, and even your "Oops, shouldn't have eaten that" tales. By jotting down your thoughts, you're crafting a lighthouse for fellow plant enthusiasts, helping them navigate the vast ocean of edible greens in the Southwest.

Why We Need YOU!

In this digital age, there's an overabundance of information, but what's truly precious? Genuine experiences. Your insights are invaluable. By leaving an honest review, you ensure others get the most out of their edible journey without the pitfalls. Remember, your words could be the compass someone else is desperately seeking.

The 'Ask'

We're reaching out with a heartfelt plea: could you spare a few moments to leave an honest review of "Wild Edible Plants of the Southwest"? Your words will be the torch that lights up another enthusiast's path.

How to Review:

Scan the QR code below.

Pour your heart out! Let us know what you loved, what you learned, and any tips you might have.

Hit "Submit". Voilà!

The Ripple Effect

Every keystroke, every word, creates a ripple. By sharing your experiences, you're not just adding to a digital platform but making a real, tangible impact in someone's life. Your review could catalyze someone's passion or even help a novice avoid a potentially prickly situation.

With gratitude and a green thumbs-up, Shannon Warner

PART SIX
MUSHROOMS & FUNGI

The experience of mushroom foraging can be rewarding and fun. However, it is essential to correctly identify mushrooms before consuming them. Learning how to identify mushrooms by using field guides, taking foraging classes, or observing experienced foragers is critical. You should pay close attention to the cap, stem, and gills' shape, color, and texture. It is also crucial to consider the mushroom's habitat and the plants and trees it grows near.

Many poisonous mushrooms can cause severe illness or even death if ingested. Whenever you are foraging, stay away from mushrooms with white gills. Additionally, many poisonous mushrooms have red pigmentation on their cap or stem.

Whenever possible, be cautious and only consume mushrooms that an expert has positively identified. It would be best never to eat raw mushrooms because some toxic mushrooms can cause severe reactions. It is also important to remember that even though the mushroom is edible, some people will still experience allergic reactions. Therefore, starting small is essential when trying a new mushroom species.

It is generally recommended that dogs not be allowed to eat wild mushrooms, as it can be challenging to identify toxic species, and even a tiny amount of a poisonous mushroom can be harmful to a dog. It is best to err on the side of caution and keep your dog away from wild mushrooms.

Black Trumpet

Craterellus cornucopioides [KRAH-TUH-RELL-US KOR-NUH-KOH-PEE-OY-DEEZ]

This fascinating fungus isn't just a treat to find but has been a part of various cuisines for years. It belongs to the Cantharellaceae (chanterelle) family. Some nicknames include "Black Trumpet" and "Horn of Plenty."

While they're more commonly associated with other parts of the U.S., there have been sightings in the oak woodlands of Arizona and New Mexico.

Identification:

GROWTH/SIZE: Typically, they reach about 2 to 5 inches tall, with the funnel opening around 2 to 3 inches wide. They grow individually or in small groups, often hiding among fallen leaves on the forest floor.

CAP: has a unique shape that resembles a hollow horn or funnel.

HYMENIUM: smooth and slightly wrinkled, almost like the surface of your brain. This area is usually dark gray to black, matching the overall color of the mushroom. The size matches the size of the mushroom itself, usually 2 to 5 inches tall and 2 to 3 inches wide.

STIPE: The color of the stipe is dark, usually a deep gray to black. It can be anywhere from 2 to 5 inches tall, depending on the overall size of the mushroom.

SPORE PRINT: a light creamy color, almost like a pale yellow or buff.

ECOLOGY & SEASON: These mushrooms prefer to grow in moist, deciduous forests, often making close friends with oak trees. It can get nutrients from the tree's roots while giving it some minerals. The Black Trumpet tends to pop up during the summer and fall when the weather cools down after a good rain.

Look-a-like(s): Toxic: **Black Elfin Saddle** (*Helvella lacunosa*) They contain toxins that can cause stomach problems when eaten. *Difference:* This mushroom has a more wrinkled and irregular appearance than the Black Trumpet. Also, the stem has a unique, spongy look. **Earthfan** (*Thelephora terrestris*) is not deadly but can cause serious tummy troubles if eaten! *Difference:* They fan out more than the trumpet shape and have a rough, almost hairy texture.

Non-Toxic: **Chanterelle Mushrooms** *(Cantharellus species)* These are quite tasty and have a fruity aroma, like apricots. *Differences:* While they might resemble Black Trumpets, Chanterelles are usually a vibrant orange or yellow. They also have wrinkly ridges underneath, not gills. **Wood Ear** *(Auricularia auricula-judae)* These mushrooms are often used in Asian cuisines, especially in soups. They have a unique, gelatinous texture. *Differences:* While they're somewhat trumpet-shaped, Wood Ears are more floppy and ear-like. They're usually brown and have a jelly-like feel.

Cautions: Remember, safety first! It's always good to double-check with someone knowledgeable before considering it for your next meal.

Culinary Uses: These mushrooms aren't just fun to find; they're super delicious, too. Let's explore ways to use them in your kitchen: *Black Trumpet Risotto:* Imagine creamy rice flavored with garlic, onion, and a sprinkle of parmesan, combined with finely chopped Black Trumpets. *Black Trumpet Soup:* Start with a base of vegetable or chicken broth. Add in your Black Trumpets, some potatoes for thickness, and your favorite herbs. *Pasta with Black Trumpet Sauce:* Sauté your mushrooms with garlic, onions, and a touch of cream. Pour this luscious sauce over spaghetti or fettuccine. A sprinkle of fresh parsley on top. *Black Trumpet Pizza:* Upgrade your homemade pizza by adding sliced Black Trumpets, mozzarella cheese, and perhaps some caramelized onions. *Black Trumpet Omelette:* Whisk some eggs, toss in Black Trumpets, cheddar cheese, and maybe a dash of herbs. Cook until fluffy. *Black Trumpet and Goat Cheese Crostini:* Toast some bread slices until golden. Top them with a spread of creamy goat cheese, followed by sautéed Black Trumpets. *Black Trumpet-Stuffed Chicken:* Mix chicken breasts with Black Trumpets, breadcrumbs, and herbs. Bake until golden.

Medicinal Uses: *Antioxidant Properties:* Like many mushrooms, Black Trumpet has compounds that may help fight off free radicals in the body. *Support Immune System:* Some studies suggest this mushroom might boost the immune system. *Anti-inflammatory Effects:* Some compounds in Black Trumpet may help reduce excessive inflammation. *Anti-tumor Properties:* Preliminary research suggests Black Trumpet might contain compounds that can slow down the growth of some tumors. *Supporting Digestive Health:* Mushrooms often contain dietary fiber and other compounds to maintain a healthy digestive system. *Supporting Brain Health:* Some studies on mushrooms indicate potential neuroprotective effects. This means they might help protect brain cells from damage, which is crucial for maintaining cognitive functions.

Fun Fact: Despite its name, the Black Trumpet isn't always black. It can come in shades of dark gray, brown, or even purplish. The name "Black Trumpet" sounds more mysterious, though!

# hicken of the Woods

Laetiporus sulphureus [LAY-TIP-OH-RUS SUL-FYUR-EE-US]

This fantastic fungus is often called the Chicken of the Woods because, believe it or not, its taste and texture are somewhat similar to chicken meat. Belonging to the Polyporaceae (shelf/bracket) family, this mushroom is not just known by its chicken-y nickname. Some folks also call it the Sulphur Shelf.

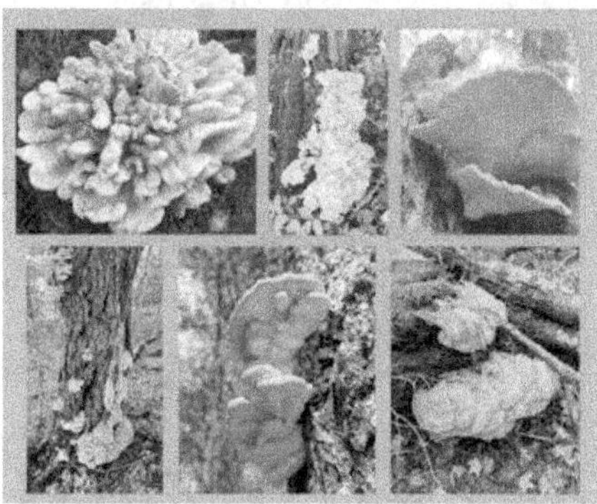

You can often find it in Texas, Arizona, and New Mexico. This mushroom prefers to grow on decaying hardwood trees, especially oak trees.

Identification:

GROWTH/SIZE: grows in bright yellow and orange tree shelves or layers. These fungi can become quite large, with some shelves reaching up to 20 inches across.

CAP: Unlike typical mushroom caps, it's fan-shaped and grows in layers or shelves on trees.

HYMENIUM: Instead of gills like some mushrooms, this fungus has tiny tubes or pores where the spores develop and drop from. The underside is smooth and yellow, covered in tiny pores.

STIPE: it usually has no distinct stem. Instead, it grows directly from the wood in layered, shelf-like formations.

SPORE PRINT: the spore print is white to pale yellow.

ECOLOGY & SEASON: It mainly grows on dead or dying hardwood trees, especially oaks, helping to break down the wood over time. This process makes it a decomposer, a helpful worker in the forest's recycling team. By breaking down the wood, this mushroom returns nutrients to the soil, supporting other plants and trees. Prime harvest time is late spring through fall.

Look-a-like(s): Toxic: **Jack-O-Lantern** *(Omphalotus olearius)* This mushroom is toxic and can cause stomach problems if eaten. *Differences:* While Jack-O-Lanterns can have a similar bright orange color, they grow on the ground, often in clusters, and have gills on the underside instead of tiny pores. **Spectacular Rustgill** *(Gymnopilus junonius)* This mushroom contains compounds that can cause hallucinations and stomach upsets. *Differences*: It typically grows on wood, just like Chicken of the Woods, but it has gills underneath its cap and is usually more of a rusty-orange or brownish color.

Non-Toxic: **Berkeley's Polypore** *(Bondarzewia berkeleyi)* This mushroom is also large and grows in shelf-like clusters, but its taste isn't as favored as Chicken of the Woods. *Differences*: It's typically paler, often white to tan, and more irregular. Plus, it grows at the base of trees rather than on the trunks. **Hen of the Woods** *(Grifola fron- dosa)* has a rich, earthy flavor. *Differences*: This mushroom is more grayish-brown than bright yellow or orange. It grows in a large, rosette-like cluster at the base of trees, especially oaks.

Cautions: While Chicken of the Woods loves growing on hardwoods, be cautious if you find it on eucalyptus, cedar, or pine trees. Mushrooms from these trees might upset your stomach. If it's your first time trying Chicken of the Woods, eat a small amount to start. Some folks might be sensitive or allergic.

Culinary Uses: *Fried "Chicken" Mushroom:* Cut the mushroom into thin slices or strips. After dipping them in a seasoned batter, fry them until they're golden and crispy. *Mushroom Soup:* Cook the mushroom pieces in a pot with onions, garlic, broth, and herbs. Blend it all for a creamy soup that's both hearty and flavorful. *Mushroom Risotto:* This classic creamy rice dish gets even better with chunks of Chicken of the Woods. For a creamy, delightful risotto, cook the mushroom with Arborio rice, broth, onions, and Parmesan cheese. *Mushroom Sandwich:* Think of a grilled cheese sand- wich, but better. Place sautéed Chicken of the Woods between two slices of bread with cheese, then grill until golden. This sandwich is both melty and packed with mush- room goodness!

Medicinal Uses: *Natural Antibiotic:* Some studies suggest that Chicken of the Woods has compounds that can fight against certain bacteria. *Supporting Digestive Health:* Some folks believe Chicken of the Woods can help digestion. This means it might assist the body in breaking down food and absorbing nutrients. *Anti-tumor Properties:* Early research hints that this mushroom might have compounds that can slow down or prevent the growth of certain tumors. More studies are needed, but it's an exciting area of research. *Skin Health:* Some people use this mushroom to treat skin conditions thanks to its anti-inflammatory properties. Its compounds might help soothe irritated skin and promote healing.

Fun/Historical Fact(s): Long before modern medicine, some Native American tribes believed this mushroom had healing properties. They used it for various ailments, showcasing its historical medicinal value.

Elm Oyster

Hypsizygus ulmarius [HIP-SI-ZY-GUS UL-MAR-EE-US]

It belongs to the Tricholomataceae family. Despite its name, it's not a true oyster mushroom, but it looks similar!

Are you venturing around the Southwest Region? Keep your eyes open for the Elm Oyster, especially on dying Elm trees or deadwood. These mushrooms love elm trees, which is how they got their name! States like Texas, Arizona, and New Mexico have reported sightings, making it native to this beautiful region.

Identification:

GROWTH/SIZE: grows about 2-8 inches in diameter and has a 3-8 inches height. CAP: The cap is fan-shaped and ranges in color from white to light brown.

HYMENIUM: The underside of the mushroom cap contains small, closely spaced, white or cream-colored gills.

STIPE: The stipe is short and stout, typically measuring 1-2 inches long and about 1/2 inch in diameter. It is usually off-center and has a whitish color.

SPORE PRINT: The spore print is white.

ECOLOGY AND SEASON: They grow on dead or dying hardwood trees, particularly elm trees. Harvest season is generally in the fall, but depending on the local climate, it can sometimes be found from late summer to early winter.

Look-a-Like(s): Toxic: **Deadly Galerina** (*Galerina marginata*) This mushroom contains potent toxins that can be deadly if eaten. Seriously, just a small bite can be harmful! *Differences:* They are smaller than Elm Oysters and often grow on decaying wood. The gills run down the stem a little, often with a small ring on the stem. **Angel Wings** (*Pleurocybella porrigens*) Once considered edible, there have been recent reports of it causing brain issues and sometimes even death when consumed in large quanti- ties. *Differences:* They're typically white, thin, and delicate, and they usually grow on conifer logs. They are a bit more translucent and wavy than the Elm Oyster.

Non-Toxic: **True Oyster Mushroom** (*Pleurotus ostreatus*) This mushroom is popular in many dishes because of its tender texture and mild, savory flavor. *Differences:* While it grows on wood and has a similar shape, the true oyster often has a more pronounced "oyster" or shell-like appearance. Its gills usually extend right to where the stem joins the cap, which differs from the Elm Oyster. **Summer Oyster** (*Pleurotus pulmonarius*) Another tasty treat, the Summer Oyster, has a somewhat lighter, almost fruity taste. *Differences:* As the name suggests, this mushroom prefers the warmer months. It's a bit paler than the Elm Oyster and often has a more delicate appearance.

Cautions: While they love elm trees, you might occasionally find them on other trees. Always note the tree type, as it can help in accurate identification.

Culinary Uses: *Stir-Fries:* Toss the sliced mushrooms into your favorite stir-fry recipe. The mushrooms will absorb the flavors of the sauce and other ingredients, like bell peppers, onions, and chicken. They give the dish a meaty texture and an earthy flavor. *Grilled Skewers:* Marinate the mushrooms in a mixture of olive oil, garlic, lemon juice, and herbs. Then, thread them onto skewers and grill them until they're slightly charred and tender. *Risotto:* This is a creamy rice dish cooked with broth. Adding the sliced mushroom gives the risotto a delightful texture and earthy flavor. *Stuffed*: For a fancy appetizer, you can stuff large caps with a mixture of breadcrumbs, cheese, garlic, and herbs. Bake them until they're golden and the cheese is melty.

Medicinal Uses: *Vitamins and Minerals*: Mushrooms can be a good source of vitamins like Vitamin D and B vitamins. They also have important minerals like selenium and potassium that our body needs. *Digestive Health*: Some mushrooms contain fibers that are good for our stomach and intestines. This can help us digest food better and keep our tummy happy. *Anti-inflammatory*: This means that mushrooms might help reduce swelling inside our body. When parts of our body get swollen, it can lead to pain or other problems. *Lowering Cholesterol*: Cholesterol is a fat-like substance in our blood. Some mushrooms might help reduce the bad kind of cholesterol, which is good for our heart. *Potential Anti-Cancer Properties*: Some studies on mushrooms have shown that they might help in fighting against certain types of cancer. However, more research is needed to be sure.

Fun/Historical Fact: Did you know that the Elm Oyster mushroom was first discovered in Japan in the 1800s and named after the elm trees it commonly grows on?

Hedgehog

Hydnum repandum [HIH-DNUM REH-PAN-DUM]

It's often known as the "Wood Hedgehog." The reason it's called that? Instead of the typical mushroom gills, it has excellent spiky teeth underneath its cap!

This mushroom belongs to the Hydnaceae family. That's a big word, but think of it as a big family where mushrooms have teeth instead of gills. It's also got other fun names, like "Sweet Tooth."

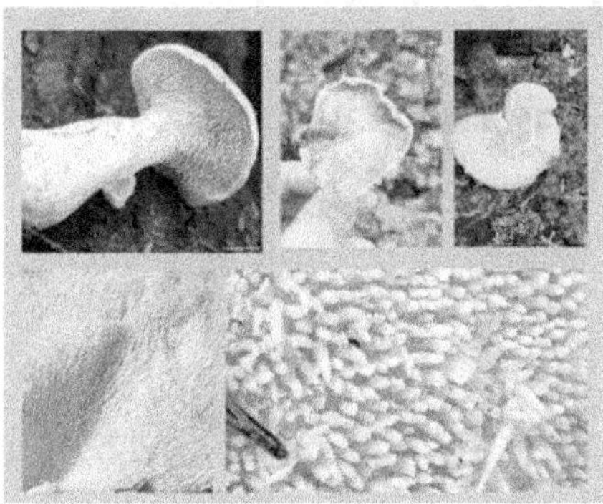

In the Southwest region, it's native to areas with higher elevations and cooler climates, especially after good rainfall. The states that can proudly call this mushroom native include parts of Arizona and New Mexico. But remember, while the Southwest can be pretty dry, our friend the Hedgehog Mushroom prefers those wetter spots.

Identification:

GROWTH/SIZE: grows uniquely with little spiky "teeth" underneath its cap instead of the usual mushroom gills. This mushroom usually has a cap that's between 2 to 6 inches wide. When fully grown, it can be about the size of an adult's hand or sometimes even bigger!

CAP: kind of like an umbrella. It's primarily flat or a little wavy, and its color can be a mix of orange, tan, or pale yellow.

HYMENIUM: Instead of the typical gills or pores you might find on other mushrooms, this one has spiky teeth hanging down from its cap. These teeth are where the mush- room produces its spores.

STIPE: This is usually creamy white or light orange and can be either straight or a bit curvy. The texture is pretty smooth, and it's firm to the touch.

SPORE PRINT: pale orange to salmon

ECOLOGY & SEASON: They're a bit picky about where they live, preferring moist and cool environments, especially in areas with a good mix of rain and shade. If you're walking in a forest after a rainfall, you might spot these mushrooms hanging out with the trees! The prime time to spot Hedgehog Mushrooms is in late summer through the fall and sometimes into early winter.

Look-a-Like(s): Toxic: **False Hedgehog** (*Sarcodon spp.*) Some species of Sarcodon mushrooms can be toxic if eaten, causing stomach problems and other health issues. *Difference:* These mushrooms might also have teeth-like structures but are often more irregular, and the spines might be longer or differently colored. **Fibrous Hedgehog** (*Hydnum rufescens*) It's not exactly toxic, but some people can have stomach discomfort after eating it. *Difference:* This mushroom might look similar to the Hedgehog Mushroom, but its cap is often more fibrous or scaly.

Non-toxic: **Bear's Head Tooth** (*Hericium americanum*) This one's edible and has a seafood-like taste, often compared to crab or lobster. *Differences:* Bear's Head Tooth mushrooms have longer, more pronounced "teeth" or spines hanging down. They look like they have a beard made of icicles! **Bleeding Tooth** (*Hydnellum peckii*) While not toxic, it's often considered inedible because of its bitter taste. *Differences:* This mushroom is named for the red, liquid-like droplets on its surface. It looks like it's "bleeding." It also has spiky "teeth" underneath, but the bleeding look is a big giveaway that it's not the Hedgehog.

Cautions: No known cautions.

Culinary Uses: Like other mushrooms, these beauties can be added to anything from soup to pizza; let your imagination run wild. Always ensure they are clean and debris-free, no matter how you cook them.

Medicinal Uses: Mushrooms are full of vitamins and minerals and contribute to a healthier overall lifestyle.

Fun/Historical Fact: Finding a Hedgehog Mushroom in the wild is a sign that the forest is healthy! They prefer places that aren't polluted, so their presence indicates a clean environment. While many mushrooms prefer the warmer months, Hedgehog Mushrooms are tough cookies. They can often be found during the colder months, even through the snow! The Hedgehog Mushroom is considered a good one to recognize for people just starting to learn about foraging mushrooms. Its unique "teeth" make it stand out, and there aren't many toxic look-alikes.

Honey

Armillaria mellea [AHR-MIH-LAIR-ee-uh mel-EE-uh]

Some folks call it the Honey Fungus because of its lovely golden-brown color. It looks a bit like honey dripping from the side of trees. It's part of the Physalacriaceae family and also goes by boot-lace fungus.

They love hanging out in forests and woodlands, especially around older trees and stumps. They are in Arizona, New Mexico, Utah, and Nevada. The Honey Fungus loves this part of the world and has made its home here.

Identification:

GROWTH/SIZE: grows in clusters at the base of trees or on tree roots, creating a network of thin, black, root-like structures called rhizomorphs.

CAP: usually golden-brown and has a smooth, shiny appearance that can make you think of honey glistening in the sun. The cap is often round when young and becomes flatter as it matures, ranging in size from 1.5 to 6 inches across.

HYMENIUM: found on the gills that are located under the cap of the mushroom, which look like thin, soft ridges running down from the center. These gills are usually cream or pale yellow.

STIPE: usually long and slender, with a creamy white to yellowish color, strikingly contrasting with the honey-colored cap on top. As the fungus matures, you might

notice a skirt-like ring near the top of the stipe, a remnant of a protective covering that once shielded the gills.

SPORE PRINT: white to cream-colored

ECOLOGY & SEASON: This fungus grows mainly on trees and woody shrubs, where it acts as a parasite, drawing nutrients from its host and often causing root rot diseases, which can weaken or even kill the plants it inhabits. However, it's also a decomposer, which helps break down dead plants and return nutrients to the soil.

They typically start to appear in late summer to fall. That's usually from August through November.

Look-a-like(s): Toxic: **Deadly Galerina** (*Galerina marginata*) This mushroom contains potent toxins called amatoxins, which can cause severe liver and kidney damage. *Differences*: Galerina marginata tends to be smaller than *Armillaria mellea*, and its spore print is brown, while Honey Fungus has a white spore print. **Western Jack- O-Lantern** (*Omphalotus olivascens*) While not deadly, eating this mushroom can cause severe cramps, vomiting, and diarrhea. *Differences*: Omphalotus olivascens glows in the dark (bioluminescent) and has a brighter orange color. Unlike the clustered growth of Honey Fungus, it often grows singularly or in small groups.

Non-Toxic: **Chestnut Bolete** (*Pholiota adiposa*) This mushroom is known for its meaty and satisfying texture. It has a nutty, mild flavor, making it a delicious addition to various dishes. *Differences:* The Chestnut Bolete has a scaly cap and stem, which starkly contrasts the smooth cap of the Honey Fungus. It also tends to grow on the ground near trees rather than directly on the wood. **Enoki or Velvet Foot** (*Flammulina velutipes*) Enoki mushrooms are popular in Asian cuisine. They have long, slender stems and small, white caps. They are crunchy and have a mild, delicate flavor. *Differences:* Enoki mushrooms are usually much smaller and more delicate than Honey Fungus. They grow in clusters and have a distinctive velvety appearance on their stems, which is quite different from the fibrous stem of the Honey Fungus.

Caution(s): Even if something looks tasty, like our honey-colored friend, not all fungi are safe to eat. Some can be pretty harmful if eaten, so always be sure.

Culinary Uses: It's important to cook this mushroom well before eating, as it can be tough to digest when raw. Like other mushrooms, these beauties can be added to anything from soup to pizza; here are a few examples. *Grilled Honey Fungus:* Marinate the cleaned mushrooms in a mix of olive oil, garlic, and your favorite herbs (like rosemary or thyme). Then, grill them until they're tender and have those lovely grill marks. They make a fantastic side dish at a BBQ! *Pickled Honey Fungus:* For a tangy treat, clean and boil your Honey Fungus, then submerge them in a mix of vinegar, water, salt, and your choice of herbs and spices. After a few days in the fridge, they'll be a crunchy and zesty addition to salads or sandwiches.

Medicinal Uses: Honey fungi haven't been extensively studied for potential health benefits and are more known for their negative impact on trees.

Fun/Historical Fact(s): Did you know that a colony of Honey Fungus in Oregon is considered one of the largest living organisms on Earth? It covers 2,385 acres of soil—that's almost 1,800 football fields!

Lobster

Hypomyces lactifluorum [HY-POH-MY-seez lak-ti-FLOOR-uhm]

The Lobster Mushroom is a parasitic fungus that grows on other mushrooms, particularly the Russula and Lactarius genus. It belongs to the Hypocreales family and is known as the "Russula-Lactarius Parasite" or "Lobster Fungus." The Lobster Mushroom is not an actual mushroom but a parasitic mold that grows on top of another mushroom, completely altering its appearance and taste.

Lobster Mushrooms love to grow in forests, especially with plenty of conifer trees. They might appear in various states in the Southwest Region, but you'll have a good chance of finding them in Arizona and New Mexico.

Identification:

GROWTH/SIZE: grows up to 8 inches in diameter and 6 inches in height.

CAP: has an irregular, lobed shape and is usually bright red or orange. The cap can be 2-8 inches in diameter.

HYMENIUM: The underside is covered with tiny, white, or cream-colored pores.

STIPE: has a short, stubby stipe that is often covered in the remains of the host mushroom. The stipe can be up to 1 inch long and is usually the same color as the cap.

SPORE PRINT: Lobster Mushrooms are a fungus that grows over the host mushroom, so they don't produce their own spore prints like other mushrooms. Instead, the spore

print you might get from a Lobster Mushroom will be from the mushroom it has grown on, often a *Russula* or *Lactarius* species.

ECOLOGY & SEASON: Lobster Mushrooms are most at home in the forest, especially under conifer trees like pines and spruces. They like to pop up on the forest floor, with plenty of leaves and wood to grow on. If you plan to hunt for Lobster Mushrooms, mark your calendar for late summer through fall.

Look-a-Like(s): Toxic: **Jack-O'-Lantern** *(Omphalotus olearius)* This mushroom contains illudin, which can cause severe stomach cramps, vomiting, and diarrhea. *Differences:*

Jack-O'-Lanterns are bright orange, which might be confused with the Lobster Mushroom's red-orange color. However, they have gills that glow in the dark and usually grow in clusters on wood, not on the ground or other mushrooms. **Brick Caps** (*Hypholoma species*) Some species in this group can cause stomach issues, such as nausea, vomiting, and diarrhea. *Differences:* They often have an orange or brownish color that could be mistaken for a Lobster Mushroom, but they typically have gills that are yellow-brown and a spore print that is dark brown. They grow on wood and not as a parasite on other mushrooms.

Non-Toxic: **Russula** Many Russula mushrooms are edible and have a mild, nutty flavor. They are crisp and can be used in salads or cooked dishes. However, some can be peppery, so it's good to taste a tiny bit before using them in a meal. *Differences:* Russula mushrooms come in various colors but are usually not the bright red-orange that Lobster Mushrooms have. They also lack the rough, bumpy texture that Lobster Mushrooms develop when they grow on them. **Saffron Milkcap** (*Lactarius deliciosus*) This mushroom is considered a delicacy in some countries. It has a rich, slightly fruity flavor and is often used in soups, stews, and sautés. *Differences:* When you cut or break a Saffron Milkcap, it "bleeds" a bright orange milk-like substance, which is not a characteristic of Lobster Mushrooms. They also have gills underneath the cap, while Lobster Mushrooms have a distinctive rough surface.

Cautions: There are no major associated issues with the Lobster Mushroom.

Culinary Preparations: The Lobster Mushroom has a firm, meaty texture and a nutty, sweet flavor. It is excellent in soups, stews, and risotto. It can also be sautéed and served as a side dish or mixed with other mushrooms for a flavorful stir-fry. The Lobster Mushroom can be dried and rehydrated for later use, making it an excellent addition to a mushroom powder.

Medicinal Uses: The Lobster Mushroom has been used in traditional medicine to treat various ailments, such as inflammation, indigestion, and sore throat. It is currently being researched for its potential anti-inflammatory and antioxidant properties.

Fun/Historical Fact: The Lobster Mushroom got its name due to its bright red color and the shape of the lobes on its cap, which resemble the legs of a lobster. Interestingly, the Lobster Mushroom was first recorded in North America in 1822 by a Swiss naturalist, but it was not until the 1980s that it became popular in the culinary world.

ion's Mane

Hericium erinaceus [HUH-RIH-SEE-UHM AIR-IN-AY-SEE-US]

The Lion's Mane mushroom is a type of fungi that belongs to the Hericaceae family. This mushroom is known by names like Bearded Tooth Mushroom, Pom Pom Mushroom, and Satyr's Beard. It has been used for centuries in traditional Chinese medicine for its health benefits. The mushroom is believed to have originated in Asia and Europe, but it is now widely cultivated worldwide.

The Lion's Mane mushroom is a non-native species to the southwest region of the United States, including Arizona, New Mexico, Nevada, and Utah. It grows in the wild throughout North America, Europe, and Asia.

Identification:

GROWTH/SIZE: grows about 6-10 inches in diameter and has a 6-10 inches height.

CAP: The cap is made up of long, shaggy spines that resemble a lion's mane. The color of the cap ranges from creamy white to light brown.

HYMENIUM: The underside of the mushroom cap is made up of tiny, tooth-like structures that are white.

STIPE: has no stipe or stem but grows directly on the tree it is attached to. SPORE PRINT: The spore print is white.

ECOLOGY & SEASON: It grows on the bark of living or dead hardwood trees, especially oak and maple trees, and can be found during the late summer and fall.

Look-a-Like(s): Toxic: **White Coral** *(Ramaria stricta)* The White Coral mushrooms have a complex, branched structure that could be mistaken for Lion's Mane at a glance. Some Ramaria species cause gastrointestinal distress (nausea, vomiting, and diarrhea) in people. The critical difference is that the Lion's Mane has long, soft spines, while White Coral has stiff, brittle branches.

Non-Toxic: **Bear's Head Tooth Fungus** *(Hericium americanum)* is also an edible mushroom. It is tender, succulent, and has a seafood-like taste, often compared to crab or lobster. *Differences*: the Bear's Head Tooth tends to have a more branching structure. The spines are generally longer than those of the Lion's Mane. **Pom-Pom Mushroom** *(Hericium coralloides)* Like Hericium erinaceus, Hericium coralloides is an edible mushroom. It has a similar seafood-like flavor, often compared to lobster. *Differences*: Pompom has more intricate and branching spines, giving it a more coral-like appearance compared to the more waterfall-like tendrils of Hericium erinaceus.

Cautions: No major cautions are associated with the consumption of Lion's Mane mushrooms.

Culinary Uses: Always cook it thoroughly, as this helps to bring out its best flavor and texture; here are a few examples you can make, but remember, let your imagination run wild. There is nothing that wouldn't be made better with a bit of wild mushroom added to it. *Lion's Mane "Crab" Cakes:* you can chop Lion's Mane into small pieces and mix it with breadcrumbs, mayonnaise, spices, and egg, just like you would for a traditional crab cake. Pan-fry them until they are golden and crisp. *Grilled Lion's Mane Steak:* Cut the Lion's Mane into thick slabs and marinate it in your favorite steak marinade. Grill it like a piece of meat until it has nice grill marks and a tender, juicy interior. *Lion's Mane Mushroom "Rice":* Finely chop Lion's Mane mushrooms and sauté them until it release water and starts to brown. Use it in place of or alongside rice in dishes.

Medicinal Uses: Lion's Mane Mushroom has been used for centuries, particularly in traditional Chinese medicine. It is believed to have various health benefits. Here are a few examples. *Memory and Brain Health:* Some studies suggest that Lion's Mane may help support brain health by promoting the growth of nerve cells. This could potentially help improve memory and cognitive function, making it a topic of interest for research on conditions like Alzheimer's disease. *Mental Health Support:* There is some evidence that Lion's Mane may benefit mental health. Some research suggests that it may help to reduce symptoms of anxiety and depression. *Nerve Damage Repair:* Research suggests that Lion's Mane might help repair nerve damage, making it useful for conditions like peripheral neuropathy. It is believed to promote the growth of nerve cells, which could help damaged nerves fix themselves. *Cancer Prevention:* Studies have found that Lion's Mane mushroom has anti-cancer properties. It's thought that certain compounds in the mushroom may help to slow the growth of cancer cells, although much more research is needed before it can be considered a treatment.

Fun/Historical Fact: Did you know that the Lion's Mane mushroom is considered a gourmet mushroom and is highly prized for its flavor and texture? It has a sweet, nutty flavor and texture similar to crab or lobster meat.

Oyster

Pleurotus ostreatus [PLEH-ROH-TUS OS-TREE-AH-TUS]

The Oyster mushroom is an edible fungus belonging to the Pleurotaceae family. The Oyster mushroom gets its name from its resemblance to an oyster's shape and texture. Aside from "Oyster Mushroom," this fungus is known by several other charming names, including "Tree Oyster" and "Pearl Oyster."

You can find them in higher elevation areas, with more moisture and cooler temperatures. Think of places like the forests of Arizona and New Mexico. While the Southwest is generally arid, these mushrooms are resourceful and make their home on various hardwood trees in the region's more temperate areas. It grows in the wild throughout the country and is commonly cultivated in many states, including California, Pennsylvania, and Florida.

Identification:

GROWTH/SIZE: grows in clusters and can reach up to 8 inches in diameter and 4 inches in height.

CAP: The cap is shaped like a fan and ranges in color from grayish-brown to light beige. It is smooth and can have a slightly velvety texture.

HYMENIUM: The underside contains closely spaced, white gills that run down the length of the stem.

STIPE: The stipe is short and thick, measuring about 1 inch and 1/4 inch in diameter. It is typically off-center, and its color matches that of the cap.

SPORE PRINT: The spore print is white.

ECOLOGY AND SEASON: they grow in various habitats, including dead and dying trees, logs, and stumps. They are commonly found in the fall and spring but can grow year-round if the temperature and moisture levels are right.

Look-a-Like(s): Toxic: **Angel Wings** *(Pleurocybella porrigens)* Previously considered edible, this mushroom has been associated with severe neurological issues and has led to multiple deaths in Japan. *Differences*: Angel Wings are white and often thinner and more delicate. Angel Wings are strikingly white. **Ghost Fungus** *(Omphalotus nidiformis)* Although beautiful and bioluminescent, it is unsafe to eat and can cause gastrointestinal upset. *Differences*: It tends to be paler, often white or cream-colored, and can emit a soft greenish glow in the dark. It has a more traditional mushroom shape, with a cap and stem.

Non-Toxic: **Phoenix Oyster** *(Pleurotus pulmonarius)* are edible and delicious. They have a mild, savory flavor and a tender texture. *Differences*: They are closely related and are almost identical in appearance. One way to tell them apart is by noting where and when they grow. Phoenix Oysters prefer warmer temperatures and often appear during the warmer months. **Lentinus** *(Lentinus tigrinus)* This mushroom is edible but not popular due to its tougher texture. It is best when cooked thoroughly, often in broths or stews where it can soften. *Differences*: It's often smaller and has a scaly, rough cap, giving it a 'tiger-striped' appearance. Lentinus species are usually more textured.

Cautions: No major cautions are associated with Oyster mushrooms.

Culinary Uses: Oyster Mushrooms are not just tasty; they are also low in calories and a great source of nutrients, including fiber, vitamins, and minerals. They can transform a simple dish into something special with their tender texture and savory, umami flavor. Let your imagination run wild; these fantastic mushrooms can be eaten alone or added to anything that needs extra flavor.

Medicinal Uses: While they have been used in various traditional medicines worldwide, it's important to remember that more research is needed to confirm these effects. *Anti-inflammatory Effects:* Research has indicated that they may have anti-inflammatory properties. This means they might help to reduce redness, swelling, and pain in the body, which can be especially helpful for people with conditions like arthritis or asthma. *Support Brain Health:* Some studies suggest that antioxidants like ergothioneine may help protect neurons (brain cells) from damage. This could potentially help to preserve memory and cognitive function as we age. *Blood Sugar Regulation:* Some evidence suggests that they might help lower blood sugar levels and improve insulin sensitivity. This could make them a beneficial food for people trying to manage diabetes.

Fun/Historical Fact: Did you know that Oyster mushrooms have been cultivated for thousands of years in Asia? They were considered a delicacy by the ancient Greeks and Romans and have been used in traditional Chinese medicine.

Red Chanterelle

Cantharellus cinnabarinus [KAN-THUH-REL-US SIN-UH-BAR-IN-US]

The Red Chanterelle is a member of the Cantharellaceae family. It's also commonly called the Chanterelle, Cinnabar Red Chanterelle, and Red Trumpet Chanterelle. It originates from Asia, Europe, and North America.

Red Chanterelles can be found in western North America, including Arizona, New Mexico, Nevada, and Utah. They prefer moist and cool habitats like coniferous forests and mossy areas.

Identification:

GROWTH/SIZE: grows up to 4 inches tall and 3 inches wide.

CAP: They have a trumpet-like shape with a wavy, irregular margin. It is bright red and smooth, with a distinct yellowish margin.

HYMENIUM: The gills are thick, wavy, and run down the stem. They're a creamy yellow color.

STIPE: The stem is stout, cylindrical, and can be up to 2 inches long. It's a similar color to the cap, with a slightly paler base.

SPORE PRINT: The spore print of the Red Chanterelle is a creamy yellow color.

ECOLOGY & SEASON: loves to grow in wooded areas, often forming a special partner- ship with certain trees; the mushroom and the tree work together in a win-win situa- tion: the mushroom helps the tree absorb water and nutrients, and the tree provides the mushroom with the sugars it produces through photosynthesis. They typically appear in late spring to early fall, but their peak harvest season is during summer's warm and rainy months.

Look-a-Like(s): Toxic: **False Chanterelle** (*Hygrophoropsis aurantiaca*) can cause stomach upset and should be avoided. *Differences*: It usually has a more orange-brown cap, and its gills are like straight lines running down the stem. **Fibrous Chanterelle** (*Cantharellus fibrillosus*) can cause mild to severe gastrointestinal distress, including nausea, vomiting, and diarrhea. *Differences*: Fibrous Chanterelles are usually darker and browner. The gills under the cap are much finer and more like ridges.

Cautions: There are no major concerns associated with consuming the Red Chanterelle.

Culinary Uses: This mushroom is cherished for its delicate, slightly peppery flavor. Remember to clean the mushrooms properly and cook them thoroughly. Mushrooms should never be eaten raw. Cooking them helps to break down tough cell walls and makes them easier to digest and more flavorful. Here are a few simple ideas on how to utilize your fresh mushrooms. *Sautéed Cinnabar Chanterelles:* Sauté these mushrooms in a little butter or olive oil with some salt and pepper until golden and tender. This method highlights the natural flavor of the mushrooms and makes a delicious side dish to any meal. *Mushroom Gravy:* Sauté the mushrooms, then add flour, butter, and broth to create a thick and flavorful sauce. This gravy is perfect for drizzling over mashed potatoes or meat dishes.

Medicinal Uses: Red Chanterelles have mostly been used for culinary purposes, but traditionally, they were used to treat various health conditions such as joint pain, inflammation, and respiratory problems. Recent studies have also shown that they contain compounds with antioxidant and anti-inflammatory properties.

Fun/Historical Fact: In Japanese folklore, the Red Chanterelle is believed to be the favorite mushroom of the Tengu, a mythical creature that's half-bird and half-human.

Red-Capped Saber Stalk

Leccinum aurantiacum [LEK-SEE-num aw-ran-tee-AH-kum]

This mushroom has been a known character in the world of fungi for a long time. It belongs to the Boletaceae family, a fungus known for its unique sponge-like appearance underneath the cap, instead of the usual gills in many other mushrooms. It's also known by the colorful name Orange Oak Bolete.

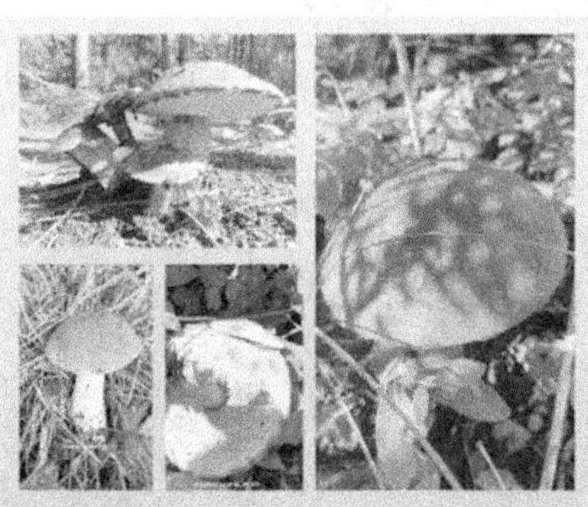

It's considered native in states with higher, cooler areas, such as the mountain regions of Arizona and New Mexico and parts of Utah. It's typically found in higher elevations, where conditions are slightly cooler and wetter than the desert lowlands. It often grows near birch trees, which is part of the reason for its common name.

Identification:

GROWTH/SIZE: grows about 2-6 inches tall and 1-2 inches in diameter.

CAP: can range from 2 to 6 inches wide, creating an umbrella-like shield over a stalk.

HYMENIUM: it has pores. These pores look like a soft, spongy surface under the cap, full of tiny holes. The pore surface starts as white or pale grey when the mushroom is young. As it matures, this area may slowly turn a bit yellowish or brownish, reflecting its age. When the pores are cut or bruised, they will turn blue.

STIPE: usually stands from 4 to 7 inches tall and is typically 1 to 1.5 inches thick. One of the coolest features of this stipe is its "scabers" — these are small, rough, dark, and raised dots or scales that give the stalk a somewhat bumpy texture. It's often whitish to gray when the mushroom is young, but it may turn more brown as it matures. At the base, it's generally a bit swollen or bulb-like.

SPORE PRINT: generally brownish to snuff-brown, a subtle and earthy tone that mirrors the colors of the forest floor.

ECOLOGY AND SEASON: forms a special, beneficial relationship with trees called a "myc- orrhizal association." In this partnership, the mushroom helps the tree absorb water and nutrients from the soil while it shares some of its sugars with the mushroom. The harvest season typically falls from late spring to early autumn, when the weather is just right—not too hot or cold.

Look-a-Like(s): Toxic: **Deadly Galerina** (*Galerina marginata*) contains a highly toxic compound called alpha-amanitin, which can cause severe liver and kidney damage and is often deadly if consumed. *Differences*: it typically has a smaller, brown cap and does not have the scab-like scales on its stem. It also lacks the orange cap color. **Red-stemmed Bolete** (*Boletus sensibilis*) causes gastrointestinal distress if consumed, including nausea, vomiting, and diarrhea. *Differences*: It has a reddish stem and usually a brownish cap. It lacks the scab-like scales on the stem.

Non-Toxic: **King Bolete** (*Boletus edulis*) is known as one of the most delicious wild mushrooms. It has a rich, deep, and earthy flavor. The cap is brown, and the stalk is thick and swollen. *Differences:* Boletus edulis typically has a brown cap. The stem of the King Bolete is usually thicker and lacks distinctive scab-like scales. **Butter Bolete** (*Boletus regius*) This mushroom is known for its pleasant, mild taste and is great for cooking. It has a vibrant red or pink cap and a yellow pore surface that does not change significantly when bruised. *Differences:* It has a red or pink cap, and the stem lacks dark, scab-like scales.

Cautions: While many consider it a good edible mushroom, some people have had mild to severe gastrointestinal upset after eating it.

Culinary Preparations: Like the rest of the mushrooms in this section, these need to be washed and cooked thoroughly. They can be added to any dish you feel needs to be spiced up. Here are a few examples. *Grilled Mushroom Caps:* Clean the mushrooms and remove the stems. Brush the caps with oil and season with salt and pepper. Grill them on a barbecue or stovetop until they are tender and charred. *Pickled Mushrooms:* Clean and slice the mushrooms, then boil them briefly in a mixture of water, vinegar, and salt. Pack them into jars with herbs and spices (like garlic, dill, and peppercorns), then seal and store. These pickled mushrooms can be a tangy snack or a great salad addition.

Medicinal Uses: There are no known medicinal uses for the Red-capped Saber Stalk.

Fun/Historical Fact: Did you know that the Red-capped Saber Stalk is also known as the Brick Cap mushroom because of its reddish-brown cap color?

S ummer Oyster

Pleurotus pulmonarius [PLEH-ROH-TUHS PUHL-MUH-NAIR-EE-UHS]

This mushroom is a delicious and nutritious member of the Pleurotaceae family. Also known by more friendly names such as the "Phoenix Mushroom" or "Indian Oyster," it has been enjoyed by people worldwide. It's a close relative of the popular oyster mushroom, and they share much in common.

While *it* isn't native to the Southwest, it has been introduced and cultivated in various parts of the U.S., including some areas within Arizona, New Mexico, Texas, and Oklahoma. It typically grows on dead or dying hardwood trees, particularly after a rainy period.

Identification:

GROWTH/SIZE: typically grows to be 2-6 inches in diameter and has a height of 2-6 inches.

CAP: The cap is fan-shaped and ranges in color from light brown to grayish-white. HYMENIUM: is smooth or slightly wrinkled, and it's usually white or cream.

STIPE: is quite short and might even be hard to notice because it often blends in with the cap. In many cases, it is off-center, which gives the mushroom its distinct, fan-like appearance. The stipe is usually firm and white or pale, matching nicely with the lighter shade of the cap.

SPORE PRINT: the spore print is typically white to lilac-gray.

ECOLOGY AND SEASON: Summer Oyster Mushrooms grow on dead or dying wood, particularly hardwood trees. It's most commonly found from late spring to early fall, but the exact timing can vary based on the local climate. You might even find it in some warmer regions in the winter months!

Look-a-Like(s): Toxic: **Western Jack O'Lantern** (*Omphalotus olivascens*) is toxic and can cause stomach problems if eaten. *Differences:* While they can have a similar bright orange color, they grow on the ground, often in clusters, and have gills on the underside instead of tiny pores. **Ghost Fungus** (*Omphalotus nidiformis*) People who have consumed this mushroom report severe cramps, vomiting, and diarrhea. The compounds responsible for these nasty effects are called illudins. *Differences:* One of the standout features is its ability to glow in the dark. It typically has a pale, white-to-brownish cap, which can sometimes resemble the colors of oyster mushrooms, but it often has a more watery appearance.

Non-Toxic: **Elm Oyster** *(Hypsizygus ulmarius)* is delicious and safe, with a mild, pleasant taste and a texture that holds up well when cooked. It's excellent in stir-fries, soups, and stews. *Differences:* It usually has a more rounded cap and does not grow in the tight clusters characteristic of true oyster mushrooms. Additionally, the gills of the Elm Oyster do not run down the stem. **Late Fall Oyster** *(Panellus serotinus)* is a safe and tasty dinner table choice. It has a chewy, satisfying texture and a slightly nutty flavor. *Differences:* it tends to appear later in the year. Its caps are generally smaller and more brownish-yellow. Additionally, it has a stiffer, less delicate texture.

Cautions: Some people may have allergic reactions to mushrooms, even if they are considered edible. Always try a small amount first to see how your body reacts.

Culinary Uses: They are not just tasty but also low in calories and a great source of nutrients, including fiber, vitamins, and minerals. They have a sweet odor, just like licorice. Let your imagination run wild; these fantastic mushrooms can be eaten alone or added to anything that needs extra flavor.

Medicinal Uses: It is not just a culinary delight but also celebrated for its potential medicinal properties. Various species of oyster mushrooms have been used in traditional medicine in different parts of the world for centuries. They have been thought to have health-boosting properties, and modern research is starting to explore these potential benefits scientifically. Here are a few potential uses: *Cholesterol Management:* Some studies have shown that it can help lower bad cholesterol levels in the blood. This is likely due to its content of special fibers called beta-glucans, which are known to reduce cholesterol levels. *Digestive Health:* rich in fibers, especially beta-glucans. The human body does not digest these fibers but instead serves as food for beneficial bacteria in our gut. *Potential Anti-Cancer Properties:* Some research suggests that extracts of *Pleurotus pulmonarius* have anti-cancer effects. While the research is still in the early stages, it's thought that the mushroom may help stop the growth of cancer cells and could be used as part of a future treatment strategy for certain types of cancer.

Fun/Historical Fact: Some studies have shown that *Pleurotus pulmonarius* can parasitize certain nematodes (tiny roundworms) and other pests. This means that the mushroom might have a future role in agriculture's natural and sustainable pest control strategies.

Woodchip Morel

Morchella rufobrunnea [MOHR-KEL-UH ROO-FOH-BROO-NEE-UH]

It is a unique-looking mushroom with a cone-shaped cap covered in pits and ridges. It's commonly known as the Reddish-brown Morel or Blushing Morel and is a member of the Morchellaceae family.

The Woodchip Morel is native to the southwestern region of the United States, including Arizona, New Mexico, Nevada, and Utah. It can grow wild in parks, gardens, and other areas with wood chips or mulch.

Identification:

GROWTH/SIZE: typically grows around 2-4 inches in height and 1-2 inches in diameter.

CAP: The cap is cone-shaped and covered in pits and ridges that give it a unique appearance. The color of the cap can range from tan to dark brown.

HYMENIUM: The underside of the cap contains small, closely spaced ridges that are light in color when young but darken as the mushroom matures.

STIPE: The stipe is usually shorter than the cap and can range in color from light brown to dark brown.

SPORE PRINT: The spore print is yellowish-brown.

ECOLOGY AND SEASON: It grows in wood chips and other organic materials and is typically found in the spring and early summer.

Look-a-Like(s): Toxic: **False Morel** *(Gyromitra esculenta)* contains a compound called hydrazine, which can be highly toxic and potentially deadly if ingested. It affects the central nervous system and the liver. *Differences:* False Morels have irregular, wavy, and lobed caps. The inside of a False Morel is not entirely hollow like a true Morel. **Elfin Saddle** *(Helvella lacunosa)* Consuming this mushroom, especially when raw or in large quantities, can lead to stomach issues like cramps, nausea, and vomiting. Elfin Saddles have a strange and irregularly shaped cap that looks more like a saddle or a deflated balloon than a honeycomb. They tend to be more grey or black.

Non-Toxic: **Yellow Morel** *(Morchella esculentoides)* are highly prized and sought after for their nutty and meaty flavor. Like all morels, they must be cooked before eating. *Differences:* They are typically lighter in color, ranging from pale yellow to tan. The ridges and pits on the cap are usually more defined and regular compared to the more irregular surface of the Reddish-brown Morel. **Blonde Morel** *(Morchella rufobrunnea)* Like its close relatives, it is a beloved edible mushroom known for its rich and earthy flavor. It must be cooked before consumption. *Differences:* It tends to be lighter in color, often appearing golden or blonde. The two are closely related and can be challenging to differentiate, but the color is a key distinguishing factor.

Cautions: The Woodchip Morel is generally safe to consume, but it is essential to be cautious when foraging for wild mushrooms and to be able to identify them to avoid any toxic look-a-likes properly.

Culinary Preparations: They have a nutty and earthy flavor and can be prepared in many ways. Like other mushrooms, they can be added to anything from soup to pizza; here are a few examples. *Morel Cream Sauce:* Imagine a velvety, rich cream sauce with the deep flavor of morels. You can make this by sautéing chopped morels in butter until tender, then adding cream and letting it reduce until thick. This sauce is perfect for drizzling over steaks, chicken, or pasta. *Pan-Fried Morels:* Morels can be dipped in a light batter and pan-fried until crispy and golden. This method lets the morels' natural flavor shine and makes for a delicious appetizer or snack. *Morel and Leek Quiche:* Consider a morel and leek quiche for a hearty and delicious breakfast or brunch. The earthy flavors of the morels pair wonderfully with the sweet, mild flavor of leeks. Mix them with eggs, cream, and cheese, pour into a pie crust, and bake until set and golden.

Medicinal Uses: The Woodchip Morel has been used in traditional medicine for its anti-inflammatory and anti-tumor properties. Modern research is still ongoing to explore its potential medicinal benefits.

Fun/Historical Fact: Did you know that the Woodchip Morel is one of the easiest types of mushrooms to grow at home? They can be cultivated in wood chips or other organic materials, making them a great option for growing mushrooms.

PART SEVEN
CACTI

# Arizona Queen of the Night

Peniocereus greggii [PEEN-EE-OH-SER-EE-US GREG-EE-EYE]

The Arizona Queen of the Night belongs to the Cactaceae (cactus) family. This plant is also called the Night-blooming Cereus or Reina de la Noche. The plant was first documented by Josiah Gregg, a 19th-century explorer and naturalist, in the mid-1800s.

It's a fascinating plant that is native to the southwestern United States. It can be found in Arizona, New Mexico, Nevada, and Utah. This plant grows wild in rocky, dry areas and thrives in hot, arid climates.

Identification:

GROWTH/SIZE: can grow up to 2-3 feet tall.

ROOT/STEM: The stem is narrow and long, growing up to 6 inches in diameter, with a woody exterior and soft interior.

ARM: has long, spiny arms that can grow up to 4 inches long and are grayish-green.

SPINE: The spines of this plant are straight and grow up to 1 inch in length. They are white or grayish.

FLOWER: The flowers are large, white, and fragrant, growing up to 8 inches in diameter. It blooms for only one night yearly, typically in June or July.

FRUIT & HARVEST: The fruit starts as bright green, and as it ripens, it transforms into a rich, red hue and has surprisingly smooth skin. It's typically oval or elongated. It usually measures about 2 to 3 inches long and has a soft and fleshy interior. It is filled with small, black seeds mixed with juicy flesh. Handling the fruit gently is essential to avoid damaging its soft and succulent flesh. The window for harvesting this fruit is relatively short, as the ripe fruit can quickly become overripe in the desert summer's intense heat. Harvesting the fruit is considered unique, as this cactus does not bloom or fruit frequently.

Look-a-Like(s): Toxic: **Cholla Cactus** (*Cylindropuntia*) While not toxic in the same way as the others, Cholla cacti have extremely sharp spines that are painful and difficult to remove if they become embedded in the skin. *Differences:* They are usually more robust and have a 'jointed' appearance, with sections that look like they are strung together. The spines are much more prominent and numerous.

Non-Toxic: **White-fleshed Pitahaya or Dragon Fruit** (*Hylocereus undatus*) is sweet and crisp, with white flesh speckled with small black seeds. *Differences:* It's generally larger and has triangular-shaped stems with larger, more dramatic flowers. Its fruit is larger, with a spiky appearance, and it is usually bright pink or red on the outside. **Peruvian Apple Cactus** (*Cereus peruvianus*) The fruit is sweet and succulent, resembling a small apple or pear, with white flesh and small black seeds. *Differences:* It's a tall, columnar cactus that can reach impressive heights. The fruits are also more rounded, resembling a small apple or pear.

Cautions: There are no associated cautions with Arizona Queen of the Night.

Culinary Uses: If you can get your hands on one, you are in for a sweet treat. Here are a few things you can do with this fruit. *Fresh Fruit Snack:* Peel the skin off the ripe fruit and enjoy the soft, sweet flesh as a fresh and juicy snack. *Cactus Fruit Sorbet:* Blend the fruit's flesh with sugar and lemon juice, then freeze it to make a refreshing and light sorbet. *Cactus Fruit Smoothie:* Combine the fruit's flesh with yogurt, a banana, and a touch of honey in a blender. Blend until smooth for a nutritious and delicious breakfast or snack. *Cactus Fruit Jelly:* the fruit with sugar and pectin to create a sweet and vibrant jelly. Spread it on toast or use it as a topping for desserts. *Cactus Fruit Syrup:* Cook the fruit with sugar and water until it forms a syrup. This syrup can be drizzled over pancakes, waffles, or ice cream for a sweet and unique flavor. *Cactus Fruit Cocktails:* Use the fruit's juice as a cocktail base. Mix it with tequila or rum, a splash of lime juice, and a little sugar to create a delightful and exotic drink.

Medicinal Uses: Arizona Queen of the Night has been used for medicinal purposes by Native Americans for centuries. It has been used to treat various ailments like inflammation, arthritis, and digestive issues. Modern research has shown that the plant contains antioxidant and anti-inflammatory compounds.

Fun/Historical Fact: In Mexico, the Arizona Queen of the Night is known as Reina de la Noche, or Queen of the Night. Legend has it that the plant's beautiful flowers were a gift from the gods to a poor, indigenous girl who prayed for a way to impress her love interest. The girl could wear the flower to a dance, which was a hit, leading to her eventual marriage.

Dog Toxicity: Arizona Queen of the Night is not toxic to dogs.

rizona Rainbow

Echinocereus rigidissimus [EH-KY-NOH-SEER-EE-US RI-JID-ISS-I-MUS]

The Arizona Rainbow belongs to the Cactaceae (cactus) family. Interestingly, this cactus was discovered in 1827 by a German botanist, Franz von Paula Schrank.

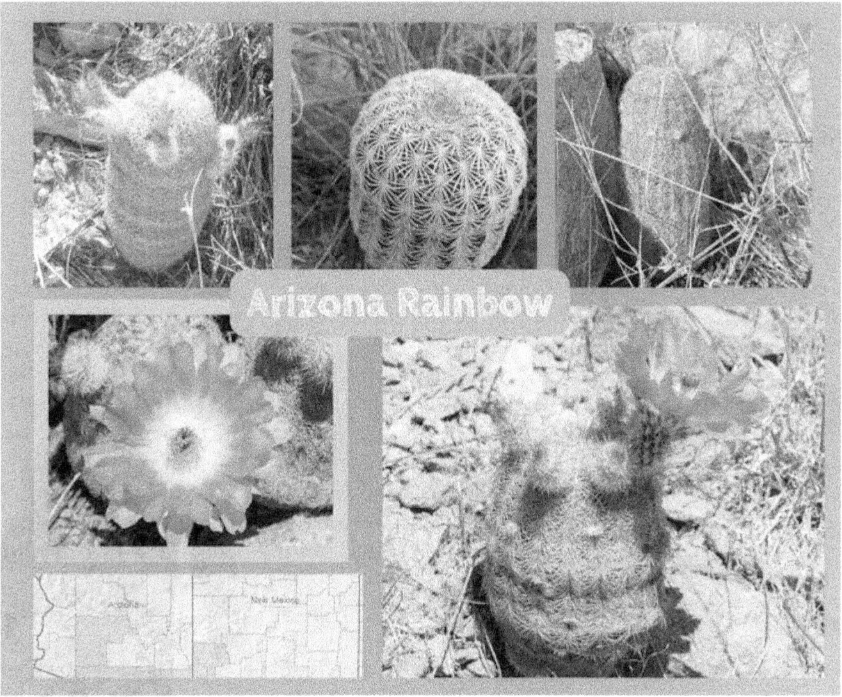

It's native to the southwestern United States, including Arizona, New Mexico, Nevada, and Utah, and can be found in the wild in dry, rocky, and sandy areas.

Identification:

GROWTH/SIZE: can grow up to 3 feet in height and 1 foot in width. ROOT/STEM: The plant has a thick, cylindrical stem and a shallow root system.

ARM: it does not have arms but instead has multiple stems that grow upwards in a columnar fashion.

SPIN: The cactus has short, stiff spines that grow in clusters on the stem. The spines can be white or yellow.

FLOWER: It produces beautiful, vividly-colored flowers about 2-3 inches in diameter. These flowers bloom in the late spring to early summer and can be pink, purple, yellow, or red.

FRUIT & HARVEST: After pollinating the flowers, they develop into deep red or purple fruits. Small, round, or slightly elongated, resembling a small berry or a mini oval-shaped ball. When it comes to harvesting, it is usually done in late spring to early summer when the fruits are ripe and full of seeds. People can pick them directly from the cactus by hand, but be careful of its sharp spines!

Look-a-Like(s): Toxic: it's challenging to find plants that look similar enough to be confusing and toxic.

Non-Toxic: **Fishhook Barrel Cactus** *(Ferocactus wislizeni)* The edible fruits resemble small, yellowish pineapples. They are sweet and can be eaten fresh or used in jams. *Differences*: It's larger and more barrel-shaped. Its spines are long and curved, resembling fishhooks. **Engelmann's Prickly Pear** *(Opuntia engelmannii)* The fruits, often called "tunas," are sweet and juicy. They can be eaten fresh, made into jelly, or used in drinks. The young pads of the cactus, called "nopalitos," are also edible and are a common ingredient in Mexican cuisine. *Differences*: This cactus has a distinct flat, paddle-like appearance. The flowers of Opuntia are also usually yellow, unlike the bright pink flowers of the Arizona Rainbow Cactus.

Cautions: There are no known cautions associated with the Arizona Rainbow plant.

Culinary Uses: Each of these culinary uses offers a unique and delicious way to enjoy this delightful desert treasure. Whether consumed fresh or transformed into a sweet treat, the fruit is versatile and adds a splash of the Southwest to various dishes! *Cactus Fruit Jelly:* The sweet, vibrant red fruit can be used to make a delicious jelly. Combine the fruit juice with sugar and pectin, then boil until it thickens. *Cactus Sorbet:* Puree the fruit, add sugar and water, and freeze it. *Dried Cactus Fruit:* The fruit can be dried for long-term storage. *Cactus Fruit Syrup:* To make syrup, cook the fruit with water and sugar until it reduces to a thick liquid. *Cactus Fruit Salad:* The fresh fruit can be chopped and mixed with other fruits, like oranges, apples, and berries, to create a vibrant and tasty fruit salad. It's a refreshing and healthy option for a side dish or dessert.

Medicinal Uses: No known medicinal uses.

Fun/Historical Fact: Did you know that the Arizona Rainbow cactus is also known as the Arizona hedgehog cactus? This is because its shape and spiny exterior resemble that of a hedgehog.

Dog Toxicity: The Arizona Rainbow plant is non-toxic to dogs and other pets. However, if ingested or stepped on, the spines can be sharp and cause physical injury.

B eavertail

Opuntia basilaris [OH-PUN-TEE-UH BAH-SUH-LAIR-IS]

The Beavertail belongs to the Cactaceae (cactus) family. It is also commonly known as the Beavertail prickly pear. Interestingly, the Beavertail was used as a food source by Native Americans for thousands of years.

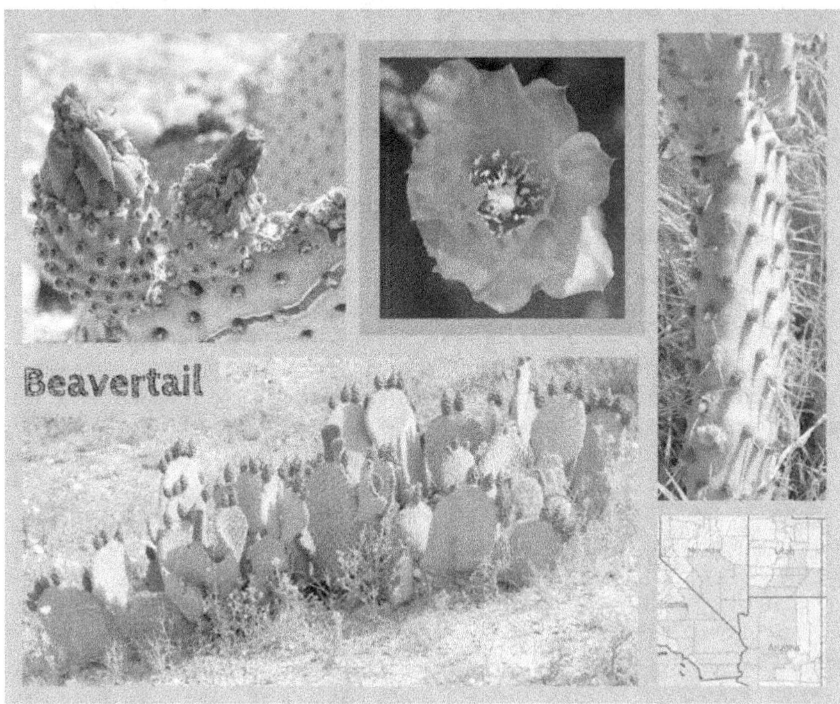

It's native to the southwestern United States. It grows wild in Arizona, New Mexico, Nevada, and Utah. It is often found in desert regions and rocky slopes.

Identification:

GROWTH/SIZE: typically grows up to 2 feet in height and can spread up to 6 feet wide.

ROOT/STEM: The stem is flat and paddle-shaped. It can grow up to 6 inches wide and 12 inches long.

ARM: The Beavertail does not have arms.

SPINE: The spines are small and grow up to 1 inch long. They are yellow or pink.

FLOWER: The flowers are pink to red and bloom in late winter or early spring. They can grow up to 2 inches in diameter.

FRUIT & HARVEST: As it matures, it produces a somewhat oval or pear-like fruit that is typically deep red or purplish. **It's** generally small to medium, about 1 to 2 inches long. Harvesting usually occurs in late spring to early summer when the fruit is ripe and has reached its deep red or purplish color. To harvest the fruit, it is best to use tongs or gloves, as the plant has tiny, hair-like spines called glochids that can easily embed themselves in the skin and are painful to remove.

Look-a-Like(s): Toxic: No known toxic look-a-likes.

Non-toxic: **Cow's Tongue Pricklypear** (*Opuntia engelmannii*) Sweet fruits can be eaten raw or made into jams and jellies. The young pads can be cooked and eaten as well. *Differences:* It has larger, more elongated pads that resemble the shape of a cow's tongue. The flowers of this species can range from yellow to red. **Pancake Prickly pear (Opuntia chlorotic***)* The fruits are edible and sweet. The pads are also edible when cooked. *Differences:* This cactus gets its name from its pads, which are round and flat like pancakes but usually thicker and more robust than those of Opuntia basilaris. Its flowers are typically yellow.

Cautions: The pads and fruits have small, sharp spines that need to be removed entirely, and it's a good idea to wear gloves while handling them.

Culinary Uses: A versatile cactus used in various culinary ways. Here are several ways you can use this cactus in your kitchen. *Nopales Salad:* The young, tender pads of Opuntia basilaris, called nopales, can be sliced into strips and cooked. They are mixed with tomatoes, onions, cilantro, and lime juice to create a refreshing and tangy salad. It's a popular dish in Mexican cuisine. *Pricklypear Jelly:* The red fruits of the cactus, known as prickly pears or tunas, can be used to make a sweet and vibrant jelly. The fruits are boiled, strained to remove the seeds, and then mixed with sugar and pectin to create a delicious jelly perfect on toast or as a glaze for meats. *Grilled Nopales:* The pads can be cleaned (removing all spines), marinated in olive oil and spices, and then grilled until they are tender and have nice char marks. They are a great meat substitute in fajitas or as a side dish. *Pricklypear Juice:* The red fruits can be juiced to create a sweet and tangy beverage. The skin is removed, and the inside fruit is blended and strained to remove seeds. It is then chilled and can be enjoyed as-is or used as a base for cocktails or other drinks.

Medicinal Uses: People have used different parts of this plant, including the pads and fruits, for various medicinal purposes. Here are a few potential medicinal uses. *Wound Healing & Skin Care:* The gel-like sap inside the pads has traditionally been used to soothe and help heal minor cuts, burns, and wounds and can be a soothing topical treatment. Applying the sap directly to the skin may create a protective barrier to help wounds heal more quickly. *Blood Sugar Regulation:* Some people consume the pads to help stabilize blood sugar levels. Research suggests that the fiber and pectin in the pads might help lower blood sugar by slowing the absorption of sugar in the stomach and intestines. *Lowering Cholesterol:* Studies have shown that the pads' fiber may help reduce levels of bad cholesterol (LDL) in the blood. *Digestive Health:* The pads are high in dietary fiber, which can promote healthy digestion.

Fun/Historical Fact: The prickly pear cactus family is a significant symbol in Mexican culture. It is featured prominently in the center of the Mexican national flag, where it is shown supporting an eagle holding a snake.

Dog Toxicity: The Beavertail is not toxic to dogs, but its spines can cause injury or irritation if ingested or lodged in the skin.

lack-Spined Prickly Pear

Opuntia violacea [OH-PUN-TEE-UH VY-OH-LAY-SEE-UH]

The Black-Spined Prickly Pear is a fascinating plant found in the southwestern region of the United States. This plant belongs to the Cactaceae (cactus) family and is commonly called the Violet Prickly Pear or Purple Cactus. The plant is native to Arizona, New Mexico, Nevada, and Utah.

The Black-Spined Prickly Pear is a native plant of the southwestern region of the United States. It grows wild in Arizona, New Mexico, Nevada, and Utah. This plant thrives in arid and semiarid areas and grows in rocky slopes, canyons, and deserts.

Identification:

GROWTH/SIZE: a medium-sized cactus that can grow up to 4 feet tall and spread to 6 feet wide.

ROOT/STEM: a thick and woody stem that can grow up to 12 inches in diameter.

ARMS: that can be up to 12 inches long.

SPINE: black and can be up to 2 inches long.

FLOWER: pink or purple and blooms in the late spring or early summer.

FRUIT & HARVEST: The cactus produces visually striking fruit with its deep magenta to violet hue, contrasting against the green pads. The fruit, referred to as "tuna," is elongated and measures approximately 1.5 to 2.5 inches long. This cactus fruit captivates with its vibrant color and provides a delightful, sweet, and juicy treat when fully ripe. To experience its optimal taste and texture, it is recommended to harvest the fruit during late summer to early fall, when it becomes slightly soft to the touch and its color intensifies.

Look-a-Like(s): A few look-a-like plants resemble the Black-Spined Prickly Pear. One toxic plant that looks similar is the Desert Rose. The Desert Rose has pink flowers, but its spines are shorter and lighter in color. Another similar toxic plant is the Jimsonweed, which has white or purple flowers and spiny leaves. On the other hand, a non-toxic plant that looks similar is the Cholla Cactus. The Cholla Cactus has longer spines and smaller flowers.

Cautions: The spines of the Black-Spined Prickly Pear can cause skin irritation if touched, so it is important to handle the plant with care.

Culinary Preparations: The Black-Spined Prickly Pear has been used as a food source by Native Americans for centuries. Here are some ways to prepare the plant as food: The fruit can be eaten raw or made into juice, jams, and jellies. The pads (nopales) can be cooked and eaten in salads, soups, and stews. The flowers can be eaten raw or cooked and used as a garnish.

Medicinal Uses: The Black-Spined Prickly Pear has been used for its medicinal properties for centuries. Traditional uses include treating wounds, reducing inflammation, and relieving digestive issues. Modern research has shown that the plant may have antioxidant and anti-inflammatory properties and help manage diabetes.

Fun/Historical Fact: The Black-Spined Prickly Pear has a long history of use by Native Americans. The plant was used for food, medicine, and textile dye.

Dog Toxicity: The Black-Spined Prickly Pear is not toxic to dogs, but the spines can cause injury if ingested or get stuck in their skin. Symptoms may include pain, swelling, and infection at the injury site. It is important to keep pets away from the plant to avoid injury.

Buckhorn Cholla

Cylindropuntiaacanthocarpa [SILL-IN-DRO-PUN-TEE-UHUH-KAN- THUH-KAR-PUH]

The Buckhorn Cholla is a unique plant found in the Southwest region of the United States. It belongs to the Cactaceae (cactus) family. Other common names include Buckhorn Cactus, Fishhook Cactus, and Horse Crippler.

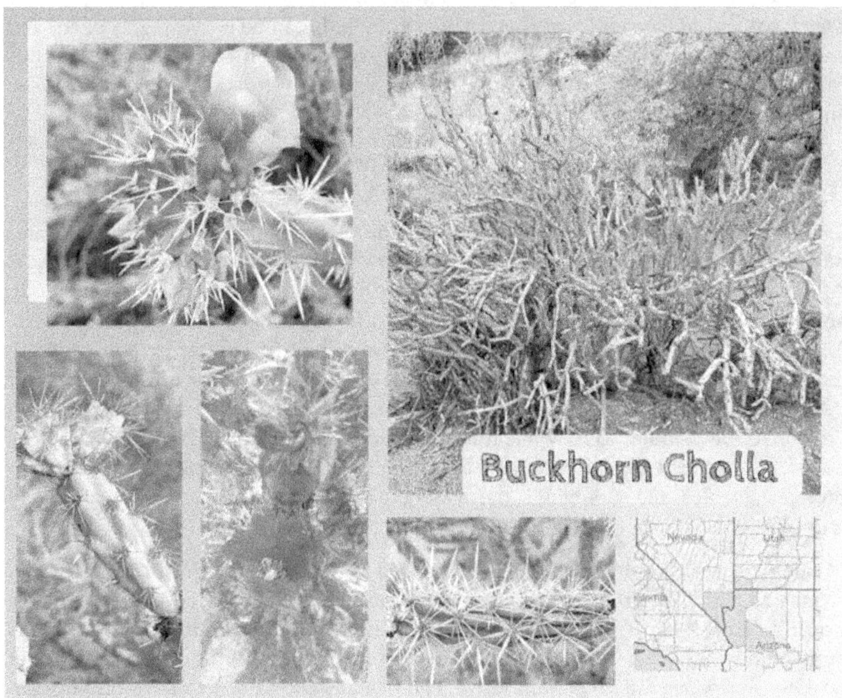

The Buckhorn Cholla is native to the Southwest region of the United States, specifically in Arizona, Nevada, New Mexico, and Utah. It grows in deserts, rocky areas, and other arid habitats.

Identification:

GROWTH/SIZE: grows up to 5 feet tall and 3 feet wide.

ROOT/STEM: has a single stem that branches into several arms.

ARM: The arms are cylindrical and range from 1-6 inches in diameter to 1-2 feet long. It's green to bluish-green and has small, gray-colored bumps.

SPINE: The spines are long and hooked, ranging from 1-4 inches long. The color of the spines is yellow to brown.

FLOWER: It produces bright pink to purple flowers about 1 inch long and blooms from April to June.

FRUIT & HARVEST: When mature, the fruit is typically a bright yellow or reddish color and has a somewhat cylindrical or elongated shape. It's generally about 1 to 2 inches long. This is relatively small compared to the size of the whole cactus, but the fruit is quite noticeable due to its bright color. The best time to harvest the fruit is typically in the late spring to early summer.

Look-a-Like(s): Toxic: No known toxic look-a-likes.

Non-toxic: **Chain-fruit Cholla** (*Cylindropuntia fulgida*) produces hanging chains of fruit that are green when young and darken to a purplish color as they mature. *Differences:* it's known for its fruit that remains on the plant and forms long chains. **Tree Cholla** (*Cylindropuntia imbricata*) The young buds can be harvested, cooked, and eaten. They are known to have a mild, green-bean-like flavor. The mature fruit of this cactus is dry and not commonly consumed. *Differences:* It grows taller, more tree-like, and has distinctive purple or magenta flowers.

Cautions: The Buckhorn Cholla can be dangerous if you get too close. The sharp spines can easily penetrate your skin, causing irritation and pain.

Culinary Uses: Historically, indigenous people of the southwestern United States have used it as a food. Here are a few unique uses for this cactus. *Pickled Cholla Buds:* After boiling and cleaning the young buds, they can be pickled in vinegar, water, salt, and spices. The pickled buds can be a tasty addition to salads or a unique side dish. *Cholla Jam:* The fruits can be boiled, mashed, and combined with sugar and pectin to create a sweet, fruity jam. *Dried Cholla Buds:* They can be dried for preservation after being boiled and cleaned. These dried buds can later be rehydrated and used in various recipes, similar to how one might use dried mushrooms. *Cholla Bud Soup:* The boiled and cleaned young buds can be a key ingredient in soups. Combined with broth, vegetables, and seasonings, they can help to create a hearty and nutritious soup with a unique flavor.

Medicinal Uses: People have traditionally used various parts of this plant, including stems and fruits, for different medicinal purposes. Here are a few potential medicinal uses. *Wound Healing:* The sap from the stems has been used traditionally to treat cuts and wounds. It is believed to help soothe and protect the wound, promoting quicker healing. *Anti-inflammatory & Pain Relief:* The plant is considered to have anti-inflammatory properties. It's traditionally been made into a poultice from the stems and applied to swollen or painful areas to help reduce inflammation. *Skin Care:* The sap from the stems has been used traditionally to soothe skin irritations, such as burns and insect bites, similar to how aloe vera is used. *Digestive Health:* Native American tribes have reportedly used the stems of this cactus to help with digestion. They would prepare it as tea or consume it in other ways to help soothe an upset stomach.

Fun/Historical Fact: "buckhorn" comes from the cactus's resemblance to deer or elk antlers. The plant has long, branching arms that look a bit like the horns of a buck, especially when viewed from a distance.

Dog Toxicity: The Buckhorn Cholla is not toxic to dogs. However, the spines can cause irritation and pain if stuck in a dog's skin. Symptoms may include swelling, redness, and itching.

Grizzly Bear Prickly Pear

Opuntia erinacea [OH-PUN-TEE-UH ER-UH-NAY-SEE-UH]

The Grizzly Bear Prickly Pear belongs to the cactus family Cactaceae. It's also commonly known as the Robust Prickly Pear, among other names. This plant is native to Mexico but has since spread to the United States, where it can be found in Arizona, New Mexico, Nevada, and Utah.

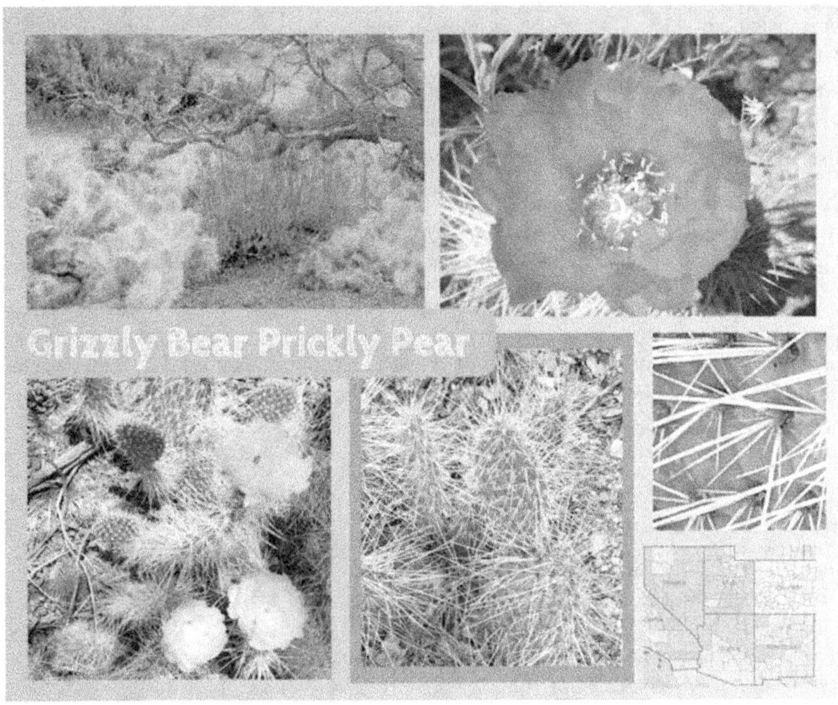

It's a native plant in the Southwest region of the United States. It can be found in Arizona, New Mexico, Nevada, and Utah, typically in dry, rocky terrain.

Identification:

GROWTH/SIZE: The Grizzly Bear Prickly Pear can grow up to 3-5 feet tall and 3-6 feet wide.

ROOT/STEM: The stems of this plant are thick and fleshy, with a greenish-brown color. They can grow up to 6 inches in diameter.

ARM: This plant has large, flattened pads that are typically bluish-green. They can grow up to 12 inches long and 6 inches wide.

SPINE: The Grizzly Bear Prickly Pear has sharp spines growing up to 3 inches long. The spines are typically a yellowish-brown color.

FLOWER: This plant produces beautiful yellow flowers growing up to 3 inches in diameter. The blooming season typically occurs in late spring to early summer.

FRUIT & HARVEST: The fruit typically displays a purple or deep red hue and has an egg or small oval shape, reaching 1 to 2 inches long. During late summer harvest, wearing thick gloves is recommended due to the plant's sharp spines.

Look-a-Like(s): Toxic plants: The Poison Hemlock and the Jimsonweed are toxic plants that may be mistaken for the Grizzly Bear Prickly Pear. Both plants have distinctive differences in their appearance and should not be consumed.

Non-toxic plants: The Cholla Cactus and the Saguaro Cactus are two non-toxic plants that may resemble the Grizzly Bear Prickly Pear. However, they have different appearances and are safe to consume.

Cautions: The spines on the Grizzly Bear Prickly Pear can cause skin irritation and discomfort, so handling this plant carefully is essential.

Culinary Preparations: The pads can be sliced and grilled or boiled, then used in salads, soups, or stews. The flowers can be used to make tea or syrup, which can be added to cocktails or used as a sweetener. The fruit can be peeled and eaten raw or used to make juice, jam, or jelly.

Medicinal Uses: It has been used in traditional medicine for centuries. It is said to have anti-inflammatory and antioxidant properties and has been used to treat various ailments such as diabetes, high cholesterol, and skin conditions. Modern research has also shown promising results for using the Grizzly Bear Prickly Pear in treating these conditions.

Fun/Historical Fact: The Grizzly Bear Prickly Pear is named after its large, furry spines resembling a grizzly bear's fur.

Dog Toxicity: The Grizzly Bear Prickly Pear is not toxic to dogs. However, the spines can cause discomfort and irritation if ingested, so keeping your pets away from this plant is essential. If your dog does come into contact with the Grizzly Bear Prickly Pear, remove any spines or needles that may be stuck in their skin and monitor them for any signs of discomfort or irritation.

Pancake Prickly Pear

Opuntia chlorotica [OH-PUN-TEE-UH KLOR-OH-TY-KUH]

The Pancake Prickly Pear belongs to the Cactaceae (cactus) family. It is also known as the Desert Prickly Pear or the Pancake Cactus. The plant is native to the southwestern region of the United States, including Arizona, New Mexico, Nevada, and Utah.

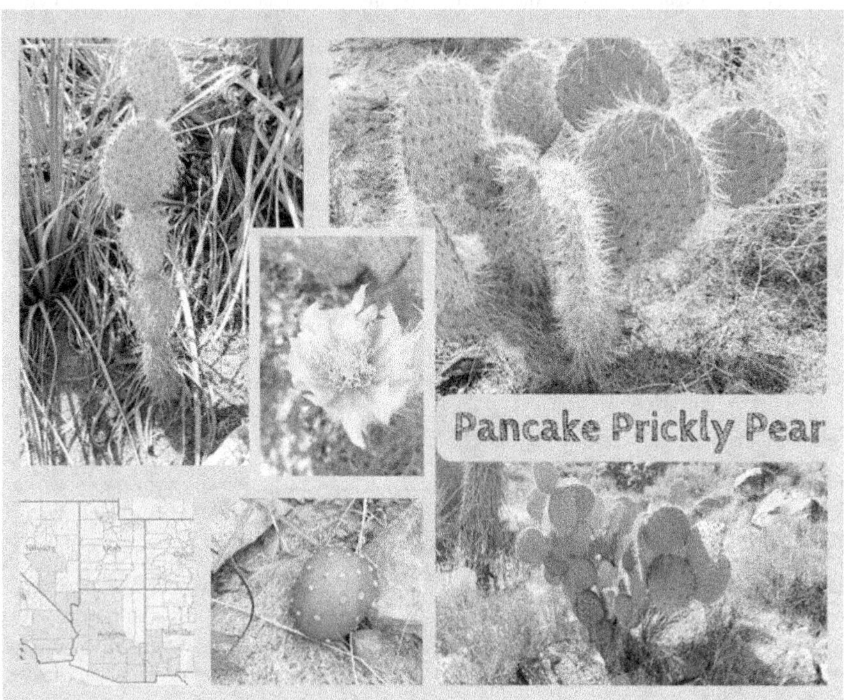

The Pancake Prickly Pear grows wild in various habitats in the southwest, including desert grasslands, rocky slopes, and canyon bottoms. It is a native plant to the region found in all four states mentioned above.

Identification:

GROWTH/SIZE: The Pancake Prickly Pear can grow up to 1-2 feet tall and 2-4 feet wide.

ROOT/STEM: The stem is flat and circular, with a 6-8 inches diameter. It has a green color and is covered in small spines.

ARM: This cactus does not have arms.

SPINE: The spines of the Pancake Prickly Pear are short, straight, and yellow. They can grow up to 1 inch long.

FLOWER: The flowers of this plant are a bright yellow or orange color and bloom in late spring and early summer. They are approximately 2 inches in diameter.

FRUIT & HARVEST: This oval-shaped fruit, typically 1 to 2 inches long, turns bright red or purple when ripe, usually in late summer or early fall. However, beware of the tiny, sharp spines called glochids on the fruit and plant.

Look-a-Like(s): Two toxic look-a-like plants to the Pancake Prickly Pear are the Cholla and the Saguaro. The Cholla has longer spines and a differently shaped stem, while the Saguaro is much larger and has a different flower shape. Two non-toxic look-a-like plants to the Pancake Prickly Pear are the Hedgehog Cactus and the Barrel Cactus. The Hedgehog Cactus has a smaller stem, while the Barrel Cactus has a more cylindrical shape.

Cautions: Pancake Prickly Pear can cause skin irritation if the spines come into contact with the skin. Care should be taken when handling the plant.

Culinary Preparations: The Pancake Prickly Pear is a popular food item in southwestern cuisine. Here are some ways it can be prepared:

- Sliced and grilled or roasted
- Used to make jelly or syrup
- Added to salads or salsa
- Used as a filling for tacos or burritos

Medicinal Uses: The Pancake Prickly Pear has been used for medicinal purposes for centuries. Traditional uses include treating wounds, burns, and inflammation. Modern research shows that the plant may treat diabetes, high cholesterol, and obesity.

Fun/Historical Fact: The Pancake Prickly Pear is called "pancake" because of its flat and circular shape. It is also known as the "cowboy's pancake" because it was a popular food item for cowboys on the range.

Dog Toxicity: The Pancake Prickly Pear is not toxic to dogs. However, the spines can cause discomfort and irritation if they come into contact with the dog's skin or mouth. Symptoms may include swelling, redness, and pain. If your dog comes into contact with the plant, removing any spines and seeking necessary veterinary care is important.

Scarlett Hedgehog

Echinocereus triglochidiatus [IH-KY-NOH-SEER-ee-us TRY-GLOH-KID-EE-AH-TUS]

The Scarlett Hedgehog belongs to the Cactaceae (cactus) family. Other common names for this plant include the Claret Cup cactus, kingcup cactus, the Mojave Mound cactus, and Crimson Hedgehog. Native Americans have known and used this cactus for centuries, highlighting its resilience and importance in the region's ecosystem.

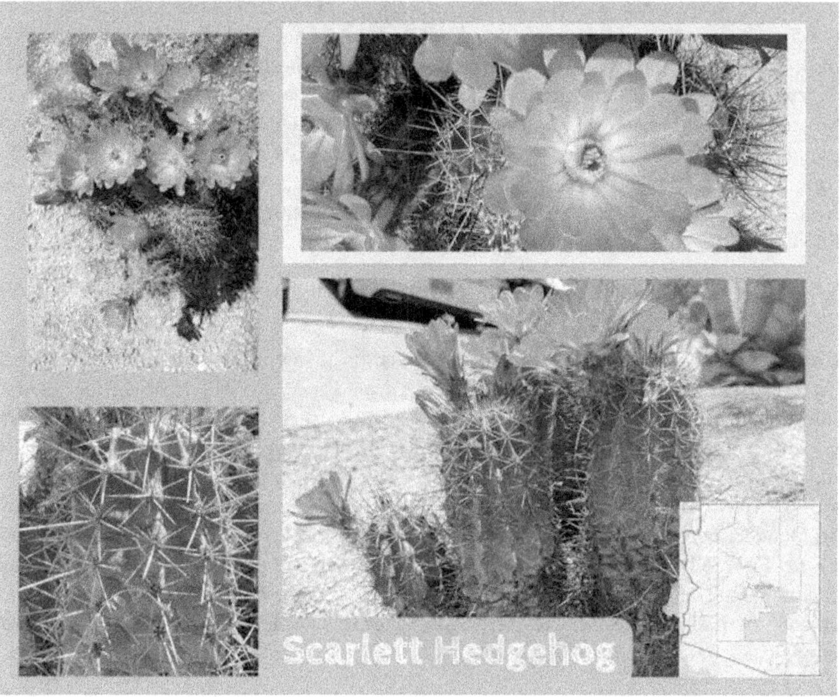

This plant calls the arid, sunny, and rocky environments of the Southwest its home. Keep your eyes peeled if you're in states like Arizona, New Mexico, Utah, Colorado, Nevada, or Texas! You might spot this cactus in deserts, on rocky slopes, or nestled among the shrubs and trees of a woodland.

Identification:

GROWTH/SIZE: grows up to 12 inches tall and 6 inches wide.

ROOT/STEM: This plant's root system is shallow, with a single columnar stem.

ARM: grows from the base of the stem and can reach up to 6 inches long. These arms are cylindrical and covered in tiny spines.

SPINE: The spines are short and come in various colors, including white, yellow, and red. They are typically less than an inch long.

FLOWER: produces bright red, bell-shaped flowers that bloom in the late spring and early summer. The flowers are about 2 inches in diameter.

FRUIT & HARVEST: When the fruit is ripe, it turns red. It's generally oval. It's like a small, plump barrel that sits atop the cactus's green, spiny stems. The fruit is relatively small, typically about 1 to 1.5 inches long. The best time to harvest the fruit is in late summer. Harvesting the fruit requires care to avoid the cactus's spines. It's gently twisted or snipped from the cactus using garden shears or scissors.

Look-a-Like(s): Toxic: No known toxic look-a-likes.

Non-Toxic: **California Barrel Cactus** (*Ferocactus cylindraceus*) produces yellow fruit that remains on the cactus long after the flowers are gone. This fruit is fleshy but not particularly tasty. Native people sometimes used the flesh of young plants as food. *Differences:* This cactus grows into a large, barrel-like shape with bright yellow or red flowers. It is significantly larger and more cylindrical than the Scarlett Hedgehog cactus. **Lace Cactus** (*Echinocereus reichenbachii*) produces small, dark red or purple fruits that are edible. They can be eaten fresh but are not as sweet as other cactus fruits. *Differences:* It's known for its smaller size and intricate, lace-like spines. The flowers are typically large and brightly colored, often in shades of pink or purple.

Cautions: Be careful when you're out and about and think you spot one. Its spines are needle-sharp and can easily poke you.

Culinary Uses: The fruit is edible and has been used in various culinary applications by indigenous peoples and modern cooks. *Cactus Fruit Jelly:* The fruit can be turned into a delicious jelly. The fruits are first boiled to extract their juice. Then, sugar and pectin are added to the juice to make a thick, sweet spread. *Cactus Syrup:* Similar to making jelly, the fruit's juice can be boiled down with sugar until it becomes a thick syrup. *Cactus Seed Smoothies:* Inside the fruit, there are numerous tiny seeds. These can be blended into smoothies and other fruits for added texture and nutrients. *Pickled Cactus Pads:* While this is more commonly done with the pads from the prickly pear cactus, young and tender pads can also be pickled. After cleaning and removing the spines, the pads are sliced and pickled in vinegar, salt, spices, and herbs, creating a tangy snack or side dish.

Medicinal Uses: Some Native American tribes have traditionally used parts of this plant for medicinal purposes. Here are some medicinal uses. *Pain Relief:* Traditionally, some Native American tribes have used the cactus as a pain reliever. A poultice is applied directly to painful areas, such as sore muscles or joints, to help reduce inflammation and ease pain. *Antiseptic Uses & Skin Treatments:* The pulp has been used as a natural antiseptic to treat minor skin ailments, including cuts, burns, and insect bites. The moist inside part of the cactus would be applied directly to the skin to promote healing, prevent infection, and reduce inflammation. *Respiratory Relief:* Some Native American tribes have used parts of the cactus to remedy respiratory problems, such as coughs and colds. They may prepare a tea or infusion using the cactus and consume it to help clear mucus and soothe sore throats.

Fun/Historical Fact: It's often considered a symbol of the American Southwest due to its widespread presence in that region. It is in Arizona, New Mexico, Utah, and Colorado.

Dog Toxicity: It isn't known to be toxic to dogs. However, the spines can be a problem. If your dog is a curious explorer like mine and loves to sniff (or taste!) everything, those sharp spines could hurt their nose, mouth, or paws.

Spiny Star

Escobaria vivipara [ES-KOH-BAIR-EE-UH VEE-VI-PAR-UH]

The Spiny Star belongs to the Cactaceae (cactus) family, specifically the Echinocactus genus. It is also known as the Horse Crippler, Mojave Mound Cactus, or the Golden Barrel Cactus.

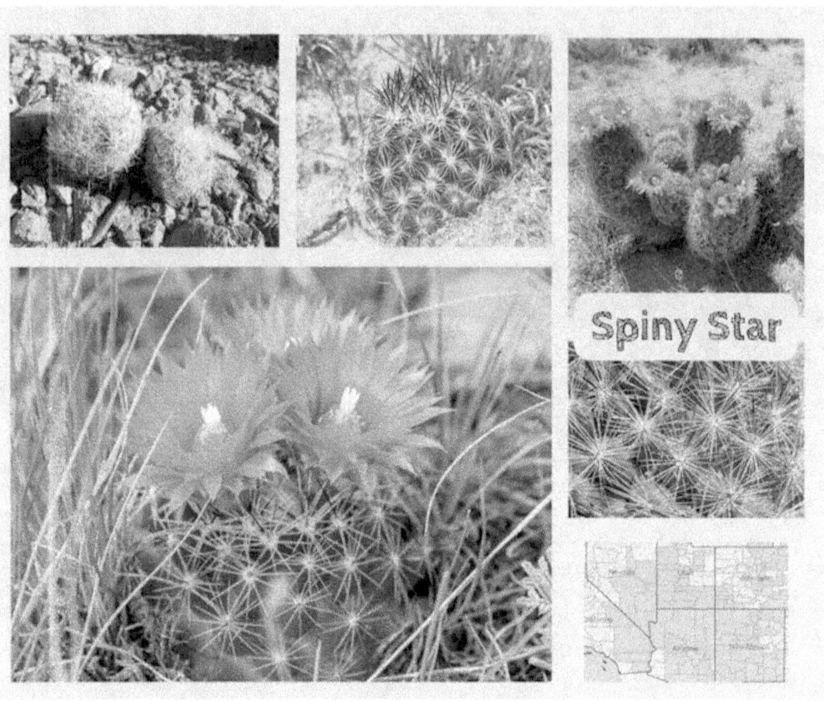

The Spiny Star is native to Mexico but can be found in Arizona, New Mexico, Nevada, and Utah. This cactus plant prefers hot and dry desert climates, and it can be found growing wild in rocky or sandy areas, as well as in gardens and parks.

Identification:

GROWTH/SIZE: The Spiny Star can grow up to three feet tall and two feet wide.
ROOT/STEM: The plant has a round stem with a shallow root system.

ARMS: The Spiny Star is round and flattened with no arms.

SPINE: The cactus has long, sharp spines that grow in clusters and are yellow or gold.

FLOWER: The Spiny Star produces yellow or red flowers that bloom in the summer and fall.

FRUIT & HARVEST: The small fruits are bright red and resemble miniature spheres with a size similar to that of a marble. These fruits ripen during the summer season, and collecting them when they are fully red is recommended, indicating their readiness for consumption.

Look-a-Like(s): Toxic plants: The Jimsonweed and Water Hemlock are toxic plants that can be mistaken for the Spiny Star. However, the Spiny Star has distinct spines, the Jimsonweed has large leaves and white or purple flowers, and the Water Hemlock has umbrella-shaped clusters of small white flowers.

Non-toxic plants: The Prickly Pear and Cholla cacti are non-toxic plants that resemble the Spiny Star, but they have distinct differences. The Prickly Pear has flat, paddle-shaped stems, while the Cholla has more arms that are more slender and have more pronounced spines.

Cautions: The spines of the Spiny Star are sharp and can cause injury if touched or stepped on. It is important to handle this cactus plant with care and keep it away from children and pets.

Culinary Preparations: The Spiny Star can be eaten in a variety of ways, including:

- Roasted and eaten as a vegetable
- Used as a taco filling
- Made into a salsa or relish
- Used in salads
- Dried and ground into a powder to be used as a spice
- Made into a juice or tea

Medicinal Uses: Native American tribes have traditionally used the Spiny Star to treat various ailments, including digestive and skin problems. Recent studies have shown that the plant may have anti-inflammatory and antioxidant properties.

Fun/Historical Fact: The Spiny Star has been used in many traditional Native American ceremonies, including the Hopi and Navajo tribes. The plant was also used as a water source and food for indigenous people in the Southwest.

Dog Toxicity: The Spiny Star is not toxic to dogs, but the sharp spines can cause injury to their paws if stepped on or ingested. Symptoms may include pain, swelling, and bleeding. Keeping this plant away from curious pets is important to avoid potential injuries.

S taghorn Cholla

Cylindropuntia versicolor [SIGH-LIN-DRO-PUN-tee-uh VUR-SI-KUH-LUR]

The Staghorn Cholla belongs to the Cactaceae (cactus) family. Other common names for this cactus include Club Cholla.

The Staghorn Cholla is native to the southwestern region of the United States, including Arizona, New Mexico, Nevada, and Utah. It grows in desert environments like the Sonoran and Mojave deserts.

Identification:

GROWTH/SIZE: The Staghorn Cholla can grow up to 13 feet in height and 4 inches in diameter.

ROOT/STEM: The plant has a woody stem covered in branches that grow cylindrical.

ARMS: The branches of the Staghorn Cholla are segmented and grow outwards, resembling the antlers of a stag.

SPINES: The plant is covered in spines ranging from light yellow to dark brown. The spines can grow up to 2 inches in length.

FLOWERS: The Staghorn Cholla blooms in the spring and summer, producing pink or purple flowers around 1 inch in diameter.

FRUIT & HARVEST: The fruit produced by this plant is genuinely stunning, boasting a vibrant red or reddish-purple color that contrasts beautifully with the green foliage. The fruits are cylindrical, resembling small barrels or elongated beads, and typically measure 1 to 1.5 inches in length. Harvesting these fruits in late spring to early summer is best when they have reached their full size and color for optimal flavor and ripeness.

Look-a-Like(s): Toxic plants: The Devil's Claw and the Jimson Weed are toxic plants that can be mistaken for the Staghorn Cholla. The difference is that the Devil's Claw has long, curvy spines, and the Jimson Weed has large, trumpet-shaped flowers.

Non-toxic plants: The Saguaro and the Barrel Cactus are non-toxic plants easily distinguished from the Staghorn Cholla by their shape and size.

Cautions: The spines of the Staghorn Cholla can cause irritation and injury if touched. Keeping a safe distance from this plant is important to avoid accidents.

Culinary Preparations: The fruit of the Staghorn Cholla is edible and has been used in traditional Native American cuisine. Here are some ways to prepare the fruit:

- Roasted over a fire
- Boiled and mashed into a paste
- Dried and ground into flour
- Used to make jelly or syrup
- Added to stews or soups

Medicinal Uses: The Staghorn Cholla has been used in traditional medicine to treat a variety of ailments, including:

- Wounds and injuries
- Digestive issues
- Respiratory problems
- Arthritis

More research is needed to understand the medicinal properties of this plant fully.

Fun/Historical Fact: The Staghorn Cholla has a unique defense mechanism where it breaks off segments of its branches and sticks them to animals that come into contact with it. This helps the plant to spread its seeds to new locations.

Dog Toxicity: The Staghorn Cholla is not toxic to dogs, but the spines can cause injury if touched. Symptoms can include pain, swelling, and infection. If your dog comes into contact with this plant, carefully remove any spines and monitor them for signs of discomfort.

Teddy Bear Cholla

Cylindropuntia bigelovii [SILL-IN-DROH-PUN-tee-uh by-geh-LOH-vee-eye]

The Teddy Bear Cholla is a Cactaceae (cactus) family member and is also commonly known as the jumping cholla. This plant is native to the Sonoran Desert in the southwestern United States and northwestern Mexico.

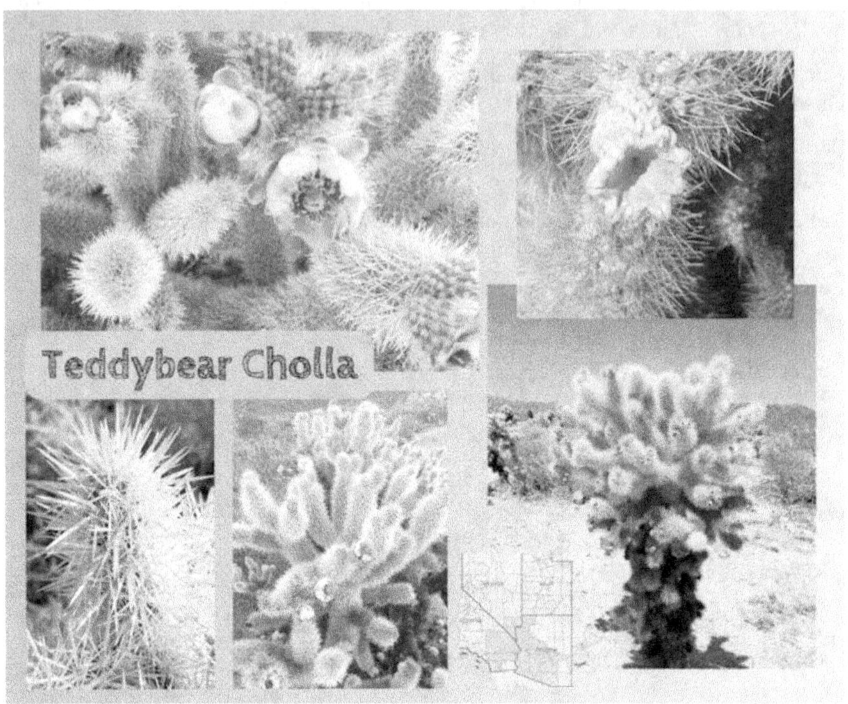

The Teddy Bear Cholla is native to Arizona, New Mexico, Nevada, and Utah. It can grow wild in these states' deserts, mountains, and valleys.

Identification:

GROWTH/SIZE: The Teddy Bear Cholla can grow up to 6 feet tall and 3 feet wide.

ROOT/STEM: The plant's stem is cylindrical and can be up to 6 inches in diameter.

ARMS: The plant has many arms, typically 4-6 inches long, and covered in fuzzy spines resembling teddy bear fur. The arms are a yellow-green color.

SPINES: The spines on the Teddy Bear Cholla are long and sharp and can range in color from yellow to red.

FLOWER: The plant produces beautiful pink to purple flowers in the late spring and early summer. The flowers can be up to 2 inches in diameter.

FRUIT & HARVEST: The fruit showcases a tubular shape and measures 1 to 1.5 inches long. Once mature, these fruits display a vibrant yellow-green color, creating a striking contrast against the cactus's spiky silhouette. Typically, the fruits emerge after the cactus's flowering season, from late spring to early summer. Waiting until late summer, when the fruit has fully matured, is advisable for optimal harvesting.

Look-a-Like(s): Two toxic plants that can be mistaken for the Teddy Bear Cholla are the Silver Cholla and the Jumping Cholla. The Silver Cholla has gray-green arms and spines that are silver in color. The Jumping Cholla has longer, more dangerous spines than the Teddy Bear Cholla.

Two non-toxic plants that resemble the Teddy Bear Cholla are the Buckhorn Cholla and the Staghorn Cholla. The Buckhorn Cholla has shorter spines and a more rounded shape, while the Staghorn Cholla has longer, thinner arms.

Cautions: The spines on the Teddy Bear Cholla can be very sharp and difficult to remove once they become embedded in skin or clothing. It is important to wear protective clothing and be cautious when near this plant.

Culinary Preparations: The fruit of the Teddy Bear Cholla can be harvested and used to make jelly or syrup. The plant can also be roasted, and the flesh can be eaten as a vegetable. Additionally, the seeds can be roasted and ground to make a nutritious flour.

Medicinal Uses: The Teddy Bear Cholla has been traditionally used by Native Americans to treat a variety of ailments, including wounds, infections, and digestive issues. Modern research has shown that the plant contains compounds with anti-inflammatory and antioxidant properties.

Fun/Historical Fact: The Teddy Bear Cholla got its name because the fuzzy spines on its arms resemble a teddy bear's fur.

Dog Toxicity: The Teddy Bear Cholla is not toxic to dogs, but the spines can cause physical harm if they become embedded in the dog's skin. Symptoms of exposure to the spines can include pain, swelling, and infection. It is important to keep dogs away from this plant and seek veterinary care if exposed.

Utah Prickly Pear

Opuntia polyacantha [OH-PUN-TEE-UH POL-EE-UH-KAN-THUH]

The Utah Prickly Pear belongs to the Cactaceae (cactus) family, and its other common names include Plains Prickly Pear, Missouri Prickly Pear, and Rocky Mountain Prickly Pear.

The plant's origins can be traced back to the Great Plains of North America, where Native Americans used it as a food source and for medicinal purposes. However, it is important to note that the fun fact about the plant is that it was introduced to the area by camels brought over by the U.S. Army in the mid-1800s.

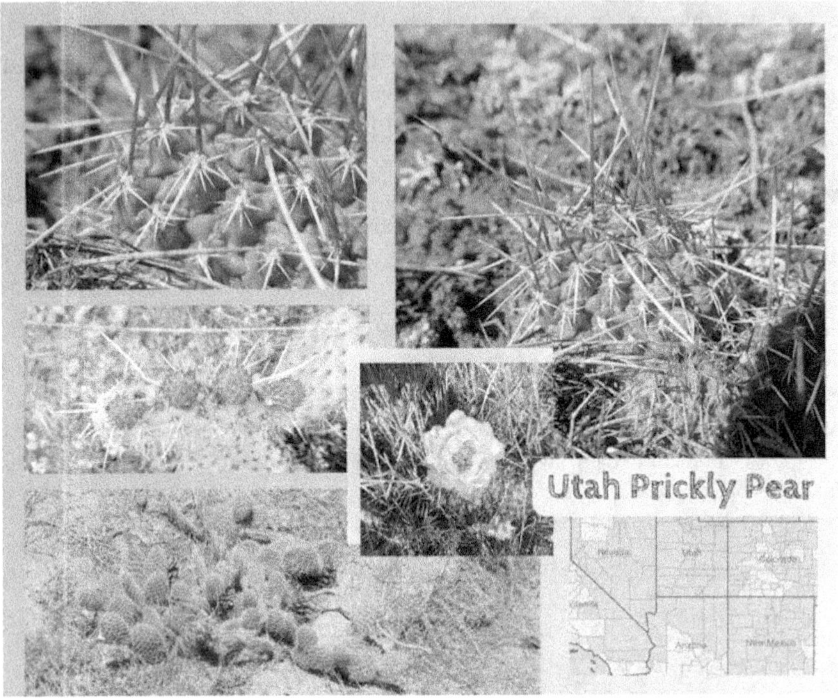

The Utah Prickly Pear is native to Arizona, New Mexico, Nevada, and Utah. It can be found in the wild in various habitats such as deserts, grasslands, and forests.

Identification:

GROWTH/SIZE: The Utah Prickly Pear can grow up to 2-6 feet in height and 2-4 feet in width.

ROOT/STEM: The stem of the plant is cylindrical and succulent. It can grow up to 10 inches in length and 3 inches in diameter. The roots are shallow and can spread up to 3 feet in diameter.

ARMS: The plant has no arms.

SPINES: The Utah Prickly Pear has spines that are 1-3 inches long, straight, and yellowish to reddish-brown.

FLOWER: The plant produces beautiful yellow flowers that are 2-3 inches in diameter and bloom from May to July.

FRUIT & HARVEST: These fruits, commonly known as "tunas," have an oval to cylindrical shape and can vary in color from green to reddish-purple when ripe. Their length usually ranges between 1 to 2 inches. The skin is covered in small spines called glochids, resembling hair, which require careful handling or removal before eating. The optimal period for harvesting these fruits is during late summer to early fall when they have fully ripened and developed a vibrant color. When picked at the perfect moment, they provide a delightful and distinctive sweetness that is truly rewarding.

Look-a-Like(s): Toxic plants that may resemble the Utah Prickly Pear include Jimsonweed and Nightshade. However, the Utah Prickly Pear can be easily distinguished by its spines and succulent stem. Non-toxic plants that may resemble it include the Christmas Cactus and the Easter Cactus, but they do not have spines.

Cautions: The spines of the Utah Prickly Pear can cause skin irritation, so it is essential to handle it with care.

Culinary Preparations: The Utah Prickly Pear is famous for many Southwestern dishes. It can be prepared in the following ways:

- The fruit can be eaten raw or cooked.
- The pads can be boiled or grilled and used in salads or as a side dish.
- The juice can be used to make jelly or syrup.

Medicinal Uses: The Utah Prickly Pear has been used for centuries to treat various health conditions such as diabetes, high cholesterol, and inflammation. Recent research has also shown that it may have anti-inflammatory and antioxidant properties.

Fun/Historical Fact: During World War II, the fibers of the Utah Prickly Pear were used to make rope for the war effort.

Dog Toxicity: The Utah Prickly Pear is not toxic to dogs. However, the spines can cause physical harm and irritation if ingested or come into contact with their skin. Symptoms may include vomiting, diarrhea, and skin irritation. If your dog has ingested any part of the plant, it is best to contact your veterinarian.

Walking-stick Cholla

Cylindropuntia spinosior [SILL-IN-DROH-PUN-TEE-UH SPI-NOH-ZEE-OR]

The Walking-stick Cholla is a member of the Cactaceae (cactus) family. It is commonly called the Cholla cactus, Chain-fruit Cholla, or Cholla. The Walking-stick Cholla is native to Mexico's Sonoran and Chihuahuan deserts and the southwestern United States.

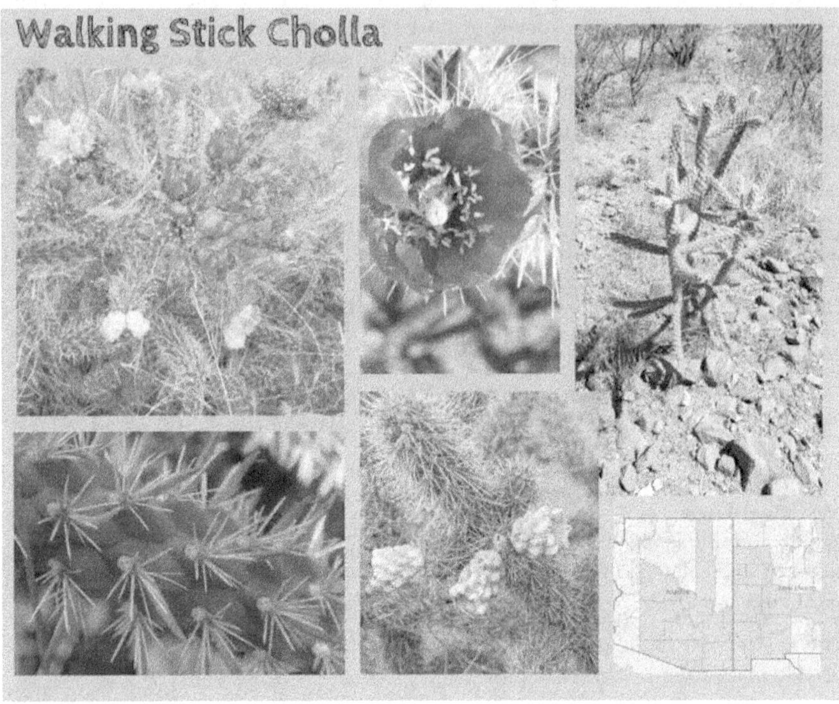

The Walking-stick Cholla is native to Arizona, New Mexico, Nevada, and Utah. It can also be found in other states, such as California and Texas. It typically grows in sandy, rocky, or gravelly soils in desert areas and can be found in elevations ranging from 1000 to 6000 feet.

Identification:

GROWTH/SIZE: Walking-stick Cholla can grow up to 10 feet tall and 5 feet wide.

ROOT/STEM: The plant has a woody base and cylindrical stems that are segmented, covered in spines, and grow up to 6 inches in diameter.

ARM: The Walking-stick Cholla has numerous arms that branch out from the main stem, each up to 2 feet long and covered in spines.

SPINE: The spines on the Walking-stick Cholla are long and slender, measuring up to 1 inch in length, and can be yellow, pink, or brown.

FLOWER: The Walking-stick Cholla produces small, vibrant, pink to magenta-colored flowers that bloom in the spring and summer. The flowers are approximately 1 inch in size.

FRUIT & HARVEST: This cactus fruit boasts a striking, deep magenta color that catches the eye. Its tubular shape can grow up to 1.5 inches long and is adorned with a few spines. The fruit's exterior has a slight texture, while its juicy and succulent flesh is a delight to taste. Wait until late summer to early fall for optimal harvesting when the fruit has matured and displays its most vibrant hue.

Look-a-Like(s): Two toxic plants that can be mistaken for the Walking-stick Cholla are the Jumping Cholla and the Teddy-bear Cholla. Both have spines and look similar to the Walking-stick Cholla, but the Jumping Cholla has barbed spines that detach easily, and the Teddybear cholla has shorter, thicker spines that resemble teddy bear fur. Two non-toxic plants that may be mistaken for the Walking-stick Cholla are the Joshua tree and the Saguaro cactus. The Joshua tree has spiky, green leaves and grows up to 40 feet tall, while the Saguaro cactus can grow up to 50 feet tall and has long, thick spines.

Cautions: The spines on the Walking-stick Cholla are sharp and can cause injury if not handled with care. They can easily attach to clothing, skin, or fur, making removal difficult and painful.

Culinary Preparations: The Walking-stick Cholla is edible, and its fruit is commonly used in traditional Mexican cuisine. Here are some ways to prepare the Walking-stick Cholla as food:

- Roasting the fruit over an open flame or in the oven
- Boiling the fruit to create a syrup or jelly
- Grinding the fruit into a powder to use as a spice or in baking
- Pickling the fruit in vinegar
- Using the fruit to make a refreshing drink

Medicinal Uses: The Walking-stick Cholla has a long history of use in traditional medicine. The fruit and stem have been used to treat various ailments, including inflammation, pain, and gastrointestinal issues. Modern research has shown that the Walking-stick Cholla may have anti-inflammatory, antioxidant, and antimicrobial properties.

Fun/Historical Fact: The Walking-stick Cholla gets its name from its long, slender arms that resemble walking sticks. Native Americans also used it as a source of food, medicine, and building materials.

Dog Toxicity: The Walking-stick Cholla is not considered toxic to dogs. However, the spines can cause significant injury and discomfort if embedded in the dog's skin or mouth. Symptoms of damage from the spines may include swelling, pain, bleeding, and infection. If a dog comes into contact with the Walking-stick Cholla, it's essential to remove any spines immediately and seek veterinary attention if necessary.

PART EIGHT
POISONOUS PLANTS

Angel Wings

Pleurocybella porrigens [Ploo-roh-si-BEL-uh PORE-rih-jenz]

Pleurocybella porrigens, known as the 'Angel's Wing' mushroom, is a unique and elegant fungus discovered mainly on decaying conifer logs in temperate forests. Its delicate, white appearance and wavy caps resembling wings have earned its celestial name. Although it was previously regarded as a desirable edible, recent concerns about its potential health risks have emerged. If you come across this ethereal beauty in its natural

habitat, it is advisable to appreciate its grace from a distance rather than considering it for culinary purposes.

Death Cap

Amanita phalloides [AH-MUH-NEE-tuh FUH-LOY-deez]

The Death Cap mushroom, or Amanita phalloides, is a highly toxic mushroom that belongs to the Amanitaceae family. It is also known as the Death Cap Amanita, the Death Cap fungus, or the Death Cap toadstool. The Death Cap mushroom is often mistaken for other edible mushrooms, which can be incredibly dangerous as it can cause severe illness or even death. Death Cap mushroom poisoning symptoms include nausea, vomiting, abdominal pain, and diarrhea, which can begin 6-12 hours after ingestion. As the toxin affects the liver, the symptoms can become more severe, leading to liver failure and death.

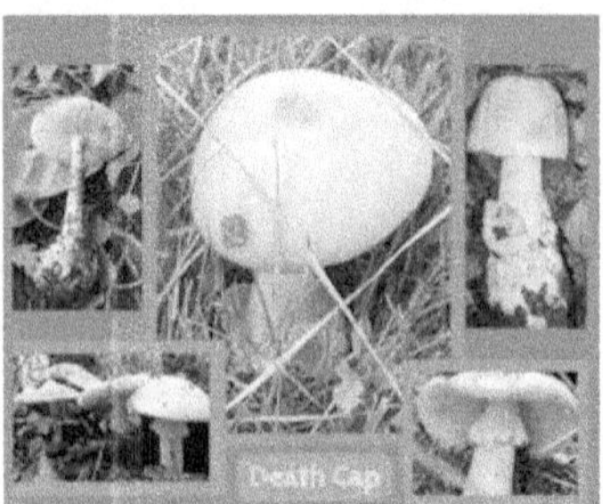

False Morel

Gyromitra esculenta [JEYE-ROH-MY-TRUH ES-KOO-LEN-TUH]

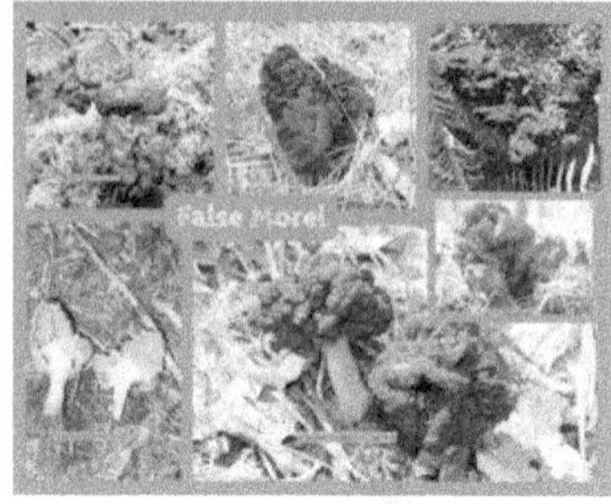

False Morels belong to the Helvellaceae family. These mushrooms have a distinctive wrinkled or brain-like cap and are often found growing in wood chips or near decaying wood. While they might look similar to other edible mushrooms, they are toxic and should not be consumed. They contain a toxic chemical called gyromitrin, which can cause symptoms like nausea, vomiting, diarrhea, and even liver damage if ingested. Symptoms may not appear for several hours after ingestion and can range from mild to severe.

Indian Tobacco

Lobelia inflata [LOH-BEE-LEE-UH IN-FLAY-TUH]

Indian Tobacco belongs to the Campanulaceae family. It is a native plant to North America and has been used for centuries by Native American tribes for its medicinal properties. Indian Tobacco is also known by other common names such as Asthma Weed, Pukeweed, and Vomitwort. The plant has a long history of traditional use for respiratory issues, such as asthma, bronchitis, and coughs. It's essential to use caution when using Indian Tobacco as a medicinal herb. Large doses can cause adverse side effects such as nausea, vomiting, and diarrhea. It's also important to note that Indian Tobacco can be toxic if ingested in large quantities.

Peyote Cactus

Lophophora williamsii [LOH-FOH-FOR-UH WIL-YAM-SEE-EYE]

The Peyote Cactus belongs to the Cactaceae family. It is native to the southwestern region of the United States and has been used for centuries by indigenous people for its psychoactive properties. The cactus has a distinctive button-like shape and is usually green or blue-green. It is important to note that the use of Peyote Cactus is highly regulated, and it is illegal to possess or use the plant without a permit from the government.

Additionally, it is essential to correctly identify the Peyote Cactus to avoid any toxic look-a-likes, as some cacti can be poisonous. Symptoms of consuming toxic cacti can include nausea, vomiting, and diarrhea.

Red Sage

Lantana camara [LAN-TAN-UH KUH-MAR-UH]

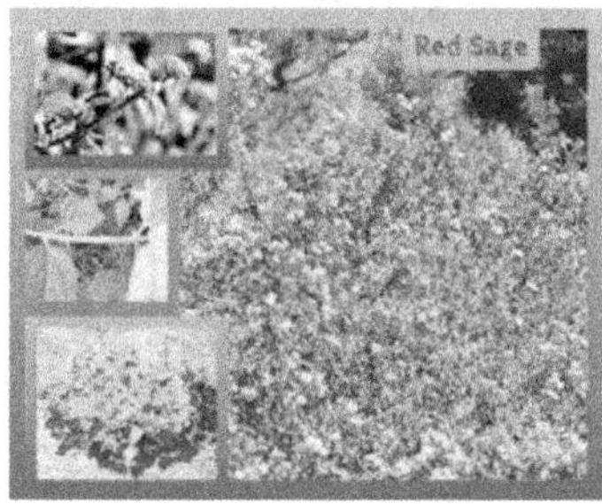

Red Sage belongs to the Verbenaceae family. It is also known as Lantana, Wild Sage, or Shrub Verbena. Red Sage is a beautiful plant that produces clusters of small, brightly colored flowers. However, it is essential to be cautious when handling Red Sage, as it can be toxic to humans and animals. There's a risk of vomiting, diarrhea, difficulty breathing, liver failure, and dermatitis from eating the flowers, fruits, and leaves.

Silverleaf Nightshade

Solanum elaeagnifolium [SO-LAY-NUM EL-EE-AGN-IH-FOH-LEE-UM]

The Silverleaf Nightshade is a small shrub that belongs to the Solanaceae family. It is a perennial plant native to the southwestern United States and northern Mexico. The plant gets its name from the silver-colored leaves that cover the plant. The Silverleaf Nightshade is toxic to both humans and animals, and all parts of the plant contain solanine, which can cause digestive issues and even death if ingested in large quantities. Symptoms of Silverleaf Nightshade poisoning can include nausea, vomiting, diarrhea, abdominal pain, and, in severe cases, hallucinations and coma.

Western Jack O'lantern

Omphalotus olivascens [OM-FA-LOH-TUS OH-LIV-AS-SENS]

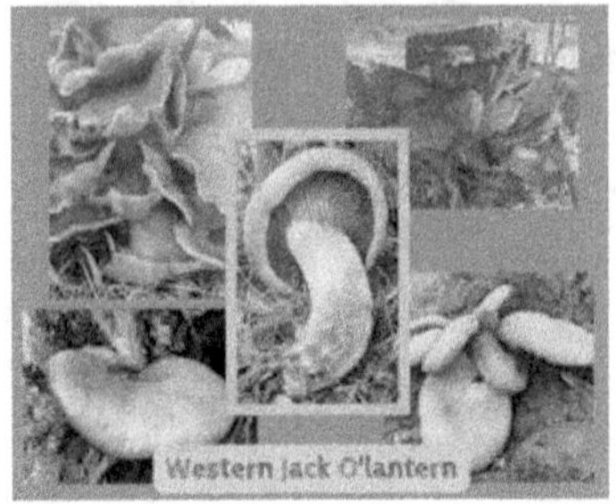

Western Jack O'Lantern belongs to the Omphalotaceae botanical family. Though it emits a captivating bioluminescent glow at night, this mushroom contains the toxin illudin, which, if consumed, can cause severe gastrointestinal distress, including nausea, vomiting, and cramping. While its luminescent properties might intrigue many, it's essential to approach this mushroom cautiously and avoid ingestion.

White Snakeroot

Ageratina altissima [AY-JER-UH-TEE-NUH AL-TIS-UH-MUH]

White Snakeroot is a plant that you may want to steer clear of. It's a member of the Asteraceae family and is commonly found in the eastern and central regions of the United States. White Snakeroot goes by many names, including Tall Boneset, Richweed, and White Sanicle. While White Snakeroot may look pretty with its clusters of small white flowers, it is toxic to humans and animals. It contains a toxin called tremetol, which can cause a range

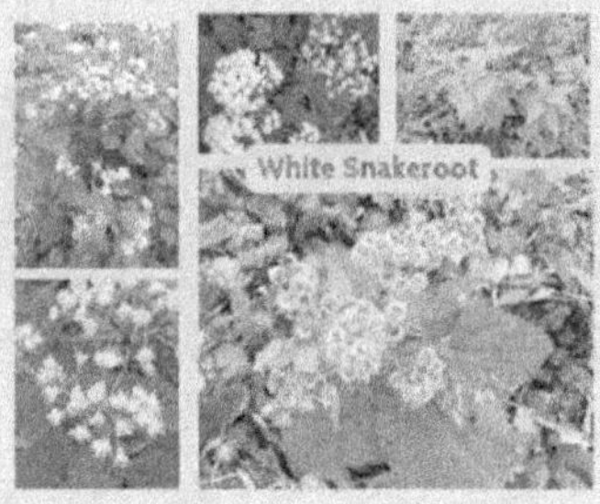

of symptoms such as vomiting, tremors, and even death in severe cases. The toxin is also present in the milk of animals who have eaten White Snakeroot, which can be dangerous for humans who consume that milk. Symptoms can range from mild to severe, depending on the amount ingested.

PART NINE
THE EDIBLE WILD
PREPPING AND STORING FOR OFF-SEASON USE

Nature has much to teach us. In today's fast-paced world, speed and convenience are paramount. But is this truly the case?

When it comes to foraging, connecting with nature is inherent. Therefore, adhering to these principles is important when handling the gifts it provides. Proper storage and preservation techniques can maximize the benefits of foraging. By taking care of your foraged food, you can savor it at your own pace. However, not all wild edibles are created equal, and certain preservation methods are better suited for specific types of food. To ensure the longevity of your foraged bounty, I'll provide a breakdown of preservation and storage methods.

Greens

After foraging in spring, you'll discover an abundance of delicious leafy greens. However, these greens can take up a significant amount of space. To make the most of your harvest, start by placing them in cool water when you return home. While this step isn't necessary for cleaning, it will refresh the greens. Ideally, you should consume most edible greens immediately, on the same day you harvest them. Delicate spring greens are perfect for salads, allowing you to appreciate the joy of foraging fully. However, if you come across hardier greens during your foraging adventure, they will last longer and are best enjoyed when cooked. Act quickly to maximize their flavor by making sauces and soups or adding them to stews. If you plan on cooking your greens a few days later or if they have a bitter taste, consider blanching them.

Blanching

Cooking large quantities of greens can be made easy with blanching. This method takes the edge off bitter greens and preserves their color and flavor, allowing them to last longer in the refrigerator and even be frozen for later use. To blanch, fill a large pot with salted water and bring it to a boil. Once boiling, cook the greens in batches until wilted, which should only take a few seconds. Immediately transfer them to a container of cold water to cool. If you want to freeze them, form them into balls after squeezing out excess water and store them in the freezer. Alternatively, for delicate greens or those you don't want to lose flavor, try freeze-wilting by placing them in a container in the freezer for 30 minutes and then letting them thaw.

Dehydration

Dehydration is an effective method for preserving foraged foods for an extended period. Depending on the type of greens, you can dehydrate them to create tea blends or utilize them as flavorful herbs. Keep in mind that wild herbs offer unique flavors that are not commonly found in grocery stores, making them perfect for enhancing your cooking.

You can employ several primary methods to dehydrate greens and herbs. The simplest approach is air drying, which works well for larger herbs like sage with thick stems. Bundle the herbs together and secure the stems at the bottom using a rubber band. Hang them upside down using butcher's twine or a hook in a well-ventilated, dry area.

Alternatively, you can lay the herbs flat on a wire rack that allows for proper air circulation. Within approximately a week, they should dry out completely.

If you want to expedite drying, place the herbs on a paper towel and microwave them for about 3 minutes. Be sure to monitor them closely to prevent burning, but they should dry out nicely. For those with a dehydrator, set it to 95°F and dry the herbs for 2-4 hours or until they crumble when touched. Once dried, store the leaves in a glass jar in a cupboard until you're ready to use them.

Berries

It is crucial to take certain measures to maintain the freshness of berries. Similar to greens, it is recommended to process the berry harvest immediately. This involves cleaning the berries to eliminate any factors that may accelerate spoilage. A simple method involves preparing a mixture of 3 cups of water and 2 tablespoons of white vinegar in a large bowl (adjust quantities for larger quantities of berries). After sorting through the berries and removing any debris or spoiled fruit, they should be placed in the bowl and soaked for up to 10 minutes, with occasional stirring. Subsequently, the berries should be drained in a colander and rinsed under cold running water. A salad spinner or dishtowel can be used to dry them, which should be stored in a container lined with paper towels. By following these steps, the berries can be kept fresh for an extended period of time in the refrigerator.

Freezing. Arrange the berries in a solitary layer on a baking sheet lined with a rim, and place them in the freezer for a few hours until they are completely frozen. After that, remove any excess air in freezer bags before returning them to the freezer. This technique guarantees that the berries will freeze individually, making them more convenient to use in future endeavors.

Canning. Put the cleaned berries in a cheesecloth, blanch them in boiling water for 30 seconds, and use the cheesecloth to remove them easily. Fill a canning jar with the fruit, process them in a boiling water bath for 15 minutes, and they will remain unopened for a year.

Dehydration. For optimal results, when working with bigger berries or fruit, it is recommended to slice them in half or into ¼-inch pieces. These should then be placed on dehydrator trays, and the temperature should be set to 135°F. Allow them to dry for a period of 10-14 hours until they are completely dry. Once cooled, transfer the dried berries to an airtight container for storage. To address any concerns regarding residual moisture, condition the berries by partially filling jars and shaking them daily for a week. In the event of condensation, dehydrate the berries for a few additional hours before storing them properly.

Roots

Root vegetables have a longer shelf life compared to greens or soft fruits. To ensure their longevity, it is important to store them correctly. An effective method for preserving large roots is to layer them in containers with damp sand, sawdust, or potting mix and then top them with the packing material. These containers should be placed in a cool and dark location, ensuring they do not freeze. This storage technique works best for large and flawless root vegetables. They can last for several weeks or even months in cooler weather conditions. Inspecting them regularly for any signs of rot or growth is advisable.

If the roots are damaged or imperfect, it is recommended to either utilize them promptly or dry them and reconstitute them later. Depending on the type of root, they can be dehydrated and transformed into powder for flavoring or incorporated into a tea blend.

If you intend to dry the roots, scrubbing them as soon as possible is crucial. If necessary, peel them before chopping or slicing them into equal pieces. The drying process can be done by air drying them on a wire rack, dehydrating them at 200°F for a few hours (with regular checks), or using a dehydrator at 140°F for 8-10 hours or until completely dry. The specific drying time may vary depending on the type of root. Once dried, they can be stored as they are or pulverized into powder form.

Nuts

Foraging and storing wild-harvested nuts can be a great way to enjoy them for months to come. While some nuts, like black walnuts, can be trickier to handle due to their staining juice, most can be easily stored by removing the husks and drying them in a well-circulated area. Freezing the nuts for 48 hours will kill off any bugs or eggs, and you can choose to store them in or out of the shell, depending on your preference. Shelled nuts can last for up to six months in the refrigerator and over a year in the freezer, making them a convenient and delicious snack to have on hand. If they become stale, roast them in the oven for 10 minutes to restore their flavor.

PART TEN
RECIPES

Buffaloberry Jam

Prep Time: 20 minutes. **Cook Time:** 30 minutes

Serving Size: About 2 cups

Ingredients:

- 4 cups fresh buffaloberries, cleaned and stemmed 2 1/2 cups granulated sugar
- 1/4 cup lemon juice, freshly squeezed
- 1 packet (about 1.75 oz) of fruit pectin (optional for a thicker consistency) 1/2 cup water

Instructions:

- After cleaning and stemming the buffaloberries, place them in a large bowl and mash them lightly to release their juices. This will aid in the cooking process and help to infuse the flavors.
- Combine the mashed buffaloberries, sugar, lemon juice, and water in a large, heavy-bottomed pot. Mix well to ensure the sugar is fully dissolved into the berry mixture.
- Bring the mixture to a boil over medium-high heat, stirring constantly to prevent sticking or burning. Once boiling, reduce the heat to medium-low and let the mixture simmer for about 20-25 minutes. The jam should thicken as it cooks.
- To test the jam's readiness, place a small amount on a cold spoon and let it cool for a moment. If it reaches your desired consistency, it's ready. If it's too runny, simmer for an additional 5 minutes and test again.
- Once the jam has reached the desired consistency, remove it from the heat and let it cool for about 10 minutes. Then, transfer it into clean, sterilized jars, leaving about 1/4 inch of space at the top. Seal the jars tightly and let them cool to room temperature. Once cooled, store in the refrigerator.

Note: If you want a thicker consistency for your jam, mix in the fruit pectin at this stage. Ensure it's thoroughly combined with the berry mixture.

Storage: The Buffaloberry Jam can be stored in the refrigerator for up to 3 weeks. For longer storage, consider processing the jars in a boiling water canner for 10 minutes and then storing them in a cool, dark place.

New Mexico Raspberry Delight

Prep Time: 15 minutes. **Cook Time:** 35 minutes.

Serving Size: 4 portions

Ingredients:

- 2 cups fresh New Mexico raspberries 1 cup granulated sugar
- 1 cup all-purpose flour
- 2 tsp baking powder 1/4 tsp salt
- 1 cup milk
- 1/2 cup unsalted butter, melted 1 tsp vanilla extract
- Optional: Whipped cream or vanilla ice cream for serving

Instructions:

1. Preheat your oven to 350°F (175°C). Lightly grease a 9-inch baking dish or pie pan.
2. In a medium-sized mixing bowl, whisk together flour, sugar (reserving 1/4 cup for the berries), baking powder, and salt.
3. Pour in the milk, melted butter, and vanilla extract. Mix until smooth. Transfer the batter to the prepared baking dish.
4. Evenly distribute the fresh New Mexico raspberries over the batter. They might sink, but that's okay. Sprinkle the reserved 1/4 cup of sugar over the raspberries.
5. Place the baking dish in the preheated oven and bake for 35-40 minutes or until the top is golden brown and a toothpick inserted into the center comes out mostly clean.
6. Let it cool for a few minutes. Serve warm, optionally topped with whipped cream or a scoop of vanilla ice cream to complement the tanginess of the raspberries.

Note: New Mexico raspberries are like any other raspberries, but the specific terroir of the region can enhance their flavor. If you cannot find New Mexico raspberries, regular raspberries will do, but the taste might slightly differ.

Enjoy your New Mexico Raspberry Delight, a dessert that pays homage to the rich flavors of the Southwest!

Stretchberry Delight

Prep Time: 20 minutes *Serving Size:* 4 servings

Ingredients:

- 2 cups fresh stretchberries (thoroughly washed and stems removed) 1 cup granulated sugar
- 1 tsp lemon zest
- 1 tbsp lemon juice 1/2 tsp vanilla extract 1 cup heavy cream
- 1/4 cup crushed graham crackers or biscuits (for garnish) Fresh mint leaves (for garnish)

Instructions:

1. Combine stretchberries, 3/4 cup of sugar, lemon zest, and lemon juice in a saucepan. Cook over medium heat, stirring occasionally, until the berries break down and the mixture thickens (about 10-15 minutes). Remove from heat and allow to cool. Stir in the vanilla extract.
2. Whisk the heavy cream with the remaining 1/4 cup sugar in a large mixing bowl until soft peaks form.
3. Layer the stretchberry compote and whipped cream in serving glasses or bowls. Begin with a spoonful of the compote at the base, followed by a dollop of whipped cream. Repeat layers until the glasses are filled.
4. Sprinkle the crushed graham crackers or biscuits over the top for a crunchy contrast. Finish with a fresh mint leaf.
5. Chill for at least an hour before serving, or enjoy immediately for a more relaxed dessert.

Bitterroot Herb Salad with Citrus Vinaigrette

Prep Time: 20 minutes

Serving Size: 4 servings

Ingredients:

- 1 cup fresh Bitterroot (Lewisia rediviva) leaves, cleaned and finely chopped 4 cups mixed salad greens (e.g., spinach, arugula, lettuce)
- 1/2 cup cherry tomatoes, halved 1/4 cup thinly sliced red onion 1/4 cup crumbled feta cheese 1/4 cup toasted pine nuts

For the Citrus Vinaigrette:

- Juice of 1 orange Juice of 1 lemon
- 2 tablespoons olive oil
- 1 tablespoon honey or agave nectar Salt and pepper to taste

Instructions:

1. Ensure the Bitterroot leaves are cleaned thoroughly. Remove any tough stems and finely chop the tender leaves.
2. Whisk together the orange and lemon juices, olive oil, and honey in a small bowl. Season with salt and pepper to taste. Adjust sweetness or tanginess based on your preference.
3. Combine the chopped Bitterroot, mixed salad greens, cherry tomatoes, and red onion slices in a large mixing bowl. Drizzle the citrus vinaigrette over the salad and toss gently to combine.
4. Divide the salad among four serving plates. Top each with an even amount of crumbled feta cheese and toasted pine nuts.
5. Serve immediately with crusty bread or as a refreshing side dish to your main course.

Note: While Bitterroot adds a unique flavor to dishes, always ensure you harvest and consume plants correctly identified and safely. Bitterroot is traditionally consumed for its starchy root, but we're using the leaves for a twist in this recipe. Adjust the quantity based on your taste preference.

Goldenrod Honey Tea

Prep Time: 10 minutes. **Brew Time:** 5 minutes

Serving Size: 2 cups

Ingredients:

- 2 tablespoons fresh Canadian Goldenrod leaves and flowers, finely chopped (Solidago canadensis)
- 2 cups boiling water
- 2 teaspoons honey (or to taste)
- Optional: a slice of lemon or a sprig of mint for added flavor

Instructions:

1. Ensure you've correctly identified Canadian Goldenrod before harvesting. Avoid areas that might have been treated with pesticides or other chemicals.
2. Wash the Goldenrod leaves and flowers thoroughly under cold water to remove any dust or small insects.
3. Place the chopped Canadian Goldenrod leaves and flowers in a teapot or heatproof container.
4. Pour the boiling water over the Goldenrod. Cover and steep for about 5 minutes.
5. While the tea is steeping, add honey to the serving cups and dissolve slightly with a small amount of hot water.
6. Strain the tea into the serving cups, ensuring no leaves or flowers make it into the final cup. Stir well to ensure the honey is fully dissolved.
7. Add a slice of lemon or a sprig of mint for added flavor, if desired.

Notes:

Goldenrod has a rich history in herbal medicine, known for its potential to support urinary tract health and as a remedy for seasonal allergies. Always consume in moderation and ensure you're not allergic before drinking in larger amounts.

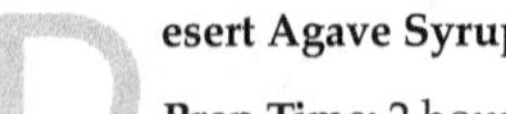

Desert Agave Syrup

Prep Time: 2 hours (including roasting and reducing time)

Serving Size: Approximately 1 cup

Ingredients:

- 1 large agave heart (from a mature plant; ensure that you have the necessary permissions and are harvesting sustainably)
- 2 quarts of water
- 1/4 teaspoon of sea salt (optional for enhanced flavor)

Instructions:

1. Using a sharp knife, trim away the sharp spines and outer leaves from the agave heart, revealing the inner piña (resembles a giant pineapple).

Roasting the Agave:

1. Preheat your oven to 325°F (165°C).
2. Cut the piña into eighths and place them on a baking tray.
3. Roast in the oven for 1 hour or until the pieces are soft and have a golden-brown hue. This process helps to convert the agave's natural inulin into fructose, adding to its sweetness.

Extracting the Sap:

1. Once roasted, allow the agave to cool slightly.
2. Using a spoon or knife, scrape off the soft, pulpy material from the inner part of each roasted section.
3. Place the pulp in a large pot and add the 2 quarts of water. Let it simmer on low heat for about 30 minutes.
4. Using a fine mesh strainer or cheesecloth, strain the liquid into a bowl, removing all solid residues.
5. Pour the strained liquid back into the pot. Bring to a boil, then reduce the heat, allowing it to simmer. Continue simmering until the liquid reduces by half and has a syrupy consistency. This might take around 20-30 minutes.
6. Remove from heat and stir in the sea salt, if using.
7. Once cooled, transfer your Desert Agave Syrup into a clean glass bottle or jar. Store in a cool, dry place. It should be kept for up to 6 months.

Desert Agave Glazed Salmon

Prep Time: 10 minutes. **Cooking Time:** 20 minutes. *Serving Size:* 4.

Ingredients:

- 4 salmon fillets (about 6 oz each) 1/4 cup Desert Agave syrup
- 2 tablespoons freshly squeezed lime juice 2 garlic cloves, minced
- 1 teaspoon ground cumin Salt and pepper to taste
- 1 tablespoon olive oil
- Fresh cilantro, chopped (for garnish) Lime wedges (for serving)

Instructions:

1. Mix the Desert Agave syrup, lime juice, minced garlic, cumin, salt, and pepper in a bowl. Place the salmon fillets in a shallow dish and pour the marinade over them. Ensure each fillet is well-coated. Allow them to marinate for at least 15 minutes.
2. While the salmon is marinating, heat the olive oil in a large skillet over medium-high heat.
3. Once the skillet is hot, place the salmon fillets skin side down. Cook for about 6-7 minutes or until the skin is crispy. Flip the fillets and cook for another 4-5 minutes, basting them occasionally with the remaining marinade.
4. Once the salmon is cooked through, transfer it to plates. Drizzle any remaining glaze from the skillet over the top. Garnish with fresh cilantro and serve with lime wedges on the side.

Chef's Note: Pair this Desert Agave Glazed Salmon with a side of roasted vegetables or a fresh Southwest-inspired salad for a complete meal. The sweet glaze contrasts beautifully with the hearty flavors of the salmon, offering a delightful culinary experience. Enjoy!

Tall Tumblemustard Greens & Garlic Sauté

Prep Time: 15 minutes **Cook Time:** 10 minutes *Serving Size:* 2

Ingredients:

- 2 cups of fresh Tall Tumblemustard greens, thoroughly washed and chopped
- 3 cloves of garlic, finely minced 2 tablespoons of olive oil
- 1/4 teaspoon of red chili flakes (optional for a little heat) Salt and pepper, to taste
- Juice of half a lemon
- Grated Parmesan cheese (optional)
- Toasted pine nuts or slivered almonds for garnish (optional)

Instructions:

1. After washing the Tall Tumblemustard greens, make sure to remove any tough stems. Chop the leaves roughly.
2. In a large skillet, heat the olive oil over medium heat. Add the minced garlic and red chili flakes (if using) and sauté for about a minute or until the garlic is fragrant but not browned.
3. Add the Tall Tumblemustard greens to the skillet. Sauté for about 5-7 minutes, stirring frequently. The greens will wilt and reduce in volume.
4. Season the sautéed greens with salt and pepper. Drizzle with fresh lemon juice and mix well.
5. Transfer the cooked greens to serving plates. Optionally, sprinkle with grated Parmesan cheese and garnish with toasted pine nuts or slivered almonds.

Serve immediately with a side of rustic bread or as a complement to grilled meats or fish.

Wild Bergamot Tea Infusion

Prep Time: 10 minutes. **Brewing Time:** 5-7 minutes

Serving Size: 2 cups

Ingredients:

- 2 tablespoons fresh wild bergamot flowers (or 1 tablespoon dried) 2 cups boiling water
- Optional: Honey or maple syrup to taste Optional: A slice of lemon

Instructions:

1. If you're using fresh bergamot flowers, gently rinse them to remove any dirt or bugs. If using dried, ensure they're free from any debris.
2. Bring the 2 cups of water to a rolling boil in a kettle or pot.
3. Place the wild bergamot flowers in a teapot or heat-resistant pitcher. Pour the boiling water over the flowers. Allow the mixture to steep for 5-7 minutes, depending on how strong you like your tea. The longer it steeps, the more pronounced the flavor will be.
4. Strain the tea into mugs, ensuring no flowers remain. If desired, add honey or maple syrup to sweeten and a slice of lemon for a citrusy touch.

Sip your wild bergamot tea slowly and savor the unique flavors of this wild herb.

A pache Plume Fruit Jam

Prep Time: 20 minutes. **Cook Time:** 30 minutes

Servings: About 2 cups

Ingredients:

- 3 cups of ripe Apache Plume fruits, cleaned and destemmed
- 1 cup granulated sugar
- 2 tbsp lemon juice 1/2 cup water
- A pinch of salt

Instructions:

1. Wash the Apache Plume fruits thoroughly under cold water to remove any debris. Remove the stems and any unwanted bits.
2. In a medium-sized saucepan, combine the Apache Plume fruits and water. Bring to a boil over medium heat, then reduce the heat and let it simmer for about 15 minutes or until the fruits become soft.
3. Using a potato masher or the back of a spoon, gently mash the fruits to release their juice and break them down further.
4. Add the granulated sugar, lemon juice, and a pinch of salt to the saucepan. Stir well to combine.
5. Let the mixture simmer for 10-15 minutes, stirring occasionally, until the jam thickens. You can test its consistency by placing a small amount on a cold plate; it's ready if it gels up after a few minutes.
6. Once done, remove it from heat and let it cool to room temperature. Transfer the jam into sterilized jars, seal tightly, and store in the refrigerator. Use within 2-3 weeks for the best flavor.

Serve on toasted bread, mix it into yogurt, or use as a topping for desserts. The unique flavor of Apache Plume will surely add a special touch to any dish.

Blue Palo Verde Bean Hummus

Prep Time: 30 minutes (excluding bean harvesting and drying)

Serving Size: 4-6 servings

Ingredients:

- 1 cup dried Blue Palo Verde beans (previously harvested, dried, and shelled)
- 2 cloves garlic, minced
- 1/4 cup tahini (sesame seed paste) 2 tbsp fresh lemon juice
- 2 tbsp olive oil, plus more for drizzling 1/2 tsp ground cumin
- Salt, to taste
- Freshly ground black pepper, to taste
- 1/4 cup fresh cilantro or parsley, chopped (for garnish) Paprika (for garnish)

Instructions:

1. Soak the dried Blue Palo Verde beans in water for 8 hours or overnight. After soaking, rinse them well and drain.
2. In a large pot, add the soaked beans and cover them with fresh water. Bring the water to a boil, then reduce the heat and simmer for 20-25 minutes or until the beans are tender. Drain and let them cool.
3. Combine the cooked beans, minced garlic, tahini, lemon juice, olive oil, ground cumin, salt, and pepper in a food processor. Blend until smooth. If the mixture is too thick, you can add a few tablespoons of water or olive oil for a creamier texture.
4. Taste and adjust seasonings as necessary.
5. Transfer the hummus to a serving bowl. Drizzle with a bit of olive oil, sprinkle with paprika, and garnish with chopped cilantro or parsley.

Serve with pita bread, vegetable sticks, or as a spread on sandwiches.

Note: While the Blue Palo Verde beans are naturally nutty and slightly sweet, it's essential to ensure they are cooked thoroughly to enhance their flavor and digestibility.

Enjoy your delightful and region-specific twist on a classic dish!

Screwbean Mesquite Honey Cookies

Prep Time: 25 minutes. **Cook Time:** 12 minutes *Serving Size:* Makes about 24 cookies

Ingredients:

- 1 cup Screwbean Mesquite flour 1 cup all-purpose flour
- 1/2 cup honey
- 1/2 cup unsalted butter, softened 1 large egg
- 1/2 tsp baking soda 1/4 tsp salt
- 1 tsp vanilla extract
- 1/2 cup chopped nuts (optional, like pecans or walnuts) 1/4 cup dried cranberries or raisins (optional)

Instructions:

1. Set your oven to 350°F (175°C). Line a baking sheet with parchment paper.
2. Combine Screwbean Mesquite flour, all-purpose flour, baking soda, and salt in a medium bowl. Whisk them together to ensure even distribution.
3. In a larger bowl, cream together the softened butter and honey until the mixture is smooth and light.
4. Beat in the egg and vanilla extract until the mixture is smooth.
5. Gradually blend the dry mixture into the wet mixture until just combined. If you're using nuts or dried fruits, fold them in now.
6. Drop the cookie dough by the spoonful onto the prepared baking sheet, ensuring there's enough space between each drop.
7. Place the baking sheet in the preheated oven and bake for about 10-12 minutes or until the edges are lightly golden. Remember, baking times might vary depending on your oven and the size of your cookies.
8. Once baked, remove the cookies from the oven and allow them to cool on the baking sheet for a few minutes before transferring them to a wire rack to cool completely.

These Screwbean Mesquite Honey Cookies are perfect for a light dessert or a midday snack. The mesquite's unique taste and honey's natural sweetness offer a delightful southwestern flavor twist to a traditional treat. Enjoy with a cup of tea or coffee!

Arizona Rainbow Cactus Salad

Prep Time: 30 minutes

Serving Size: 4 servings

Ingredients:

- 1 cup Arizona Rainbow Cactus pads (cleaned and diced) 1/2 cup cherry tomatoes (halved)
- 1/4 cup red onion (finely chopped) 1/2 cup cooked black beans
- 1/4 cup fresh cilantro (chopped)
- 1 lime (zested and juiced)
- 2 tablespoons extra-virgin olive oil Salt and pepper to taste
- 1 avocado (sliced)
- 1/4 cup crumbled queso fresco (or feta)

Instructions:

1. Carefully remove any remaining spines from the Arizona Rainbow Cactus pads using tongs and a sharp knife. Rinse thoroughly under cold water. Dice into small bite-sized pieces.
2. Bring a pot of salted water to a boil. Add the diced cactus and blanch for about 5-7 minutes or until tender. Drain and rinse under cold water to stop the cooking process.
3. Combine the blanched cactus, cherry tomatoes, red onion, black beans, and cilantro in a large mixing bowl.
4. Whisk together the lime zest, lime juice, olive oil, salt, and pepper in a small bowl. Pour the dressing over the salad mixture and toss gently to coat.
5. Divide the salad among serving plates. Top each serving with avocado slices and sprinkle with crumbled queso fresco.

Enjoy! Serve immediately, ideally with a refreshing iced tea or a crisp white wine.

Note: Always ensure the Arizona Rainbow Cactus you use is harvested sustainably and ethically. Remember to exercise caution when handling and prepping to avoid the spines.

Pickled Cholla Buds

Prep Time: 45 minutes (plus 1-2 days for pickling)

Serving Size: Makes about 2 pint jars.

Ingredients:

- 2 cups cholla buds, cleaned and spines removed 2 cups distilled white vinegar
- 1 cup water
- 2 tablespoons kosher salt 2 teaspoons sugar
- 4 garlic cloves, peeled 2 bay leaves
- 2 teaspoons black peppercorns 1 teaspoon coriander seeds
- 1/2 teaspoon red pepper flakes (optional for added heat)

Instructions:

1. Ensure that all spines and glochids (tiny spines) are removed from the cholla buds. Rinse them thoroughly under cold water.
2. In a large pot, bring water to a boil. Add cholla buds and blanch for about 3-4 minutes. Remove them with a slotted spoon and transfer them immediately to a bowl of ice water to halt the cooking process. Drain.
3. In a saucepan, combine distilled white vinegar, water, kosher salt, and sugar. Bring the mixture to a boil, ensuring the salt and sugar fully dissolve.
4. Divide the garlic cloves, bay leaves, black peppercorns, coriander seeds, and red pepper flakes (if using) between 2 sterilized pint jars. Pack the blanched cholla buds into the jars, leaving about a 1/2 inch of headspace at the top.
5. Carefully pour the hot brine over the cholla buds in the jars, ensuring they are fully submerged while maintaining the 1/2-inch headspace.
6. Wipe the rims of the jars with a clean cloth. Place the sterilized lids on the jars and screw on the rings until fingertip tight. Allow the jars to cool to room temperature. Once cooled, store them in the refrigerator.

Enjoying: Let the pickled cholla buds sit in the refrigerator for at least 1-2 days before consuming to allow the flavors to meld. Enjoy within a month for the best flavor and texture.

P ancake Prickly Pear Tacos

Prep Time: 30 minutes. **Cook Time:** 15 minutes

Servings: 4 servings (8 tacos)

Ingredients:

- 1 cup all-purpose flour
- 1 1/2 tsp baking powder 1/4 tsp salt
- 1 tbsp sugar
- 3/4 cup milk (or almond milk for a dairy-free version) 1 egg, beaten
- 1 tbsp butter or oil for frying
- 4 medium-sized prickly pears (tunas), peeled and diced 1/2 cup whipped cream or Greek yogurt
- 1 tbsp honey or maple syrup 1 tsp lime zest
- Fresh mint leaves for garnish

Instructions:

1. Whisk together the flour, baking powder, salt, and sugar in a large bowl.
2. Make a well in the center and pour in the milk and beaten egg. Mix until smooth. Let the batter rest for about 10 minutes.
3. Heat a non-stick skillet or griddle over medium heat. Add a little butter or oil.
4. Pour 1/4 cup of batter for each pancake. Cook until bubbles appear on the surface and the edges set, then flip and cook for 1-2 minutes. These pancakes should be slightly smaller, taco-sized.
5. Mix the diced prickly pear with honey or maple syrup and lime zest in a bowl.
6. Fold each pancake in half, resembling a taco shell.
7. Fill with a generous dollop of whipped cream or Greek yogurt.
8. Top with the prickly pear mixture.
9. Garnish with fresh mint leaves.

Serve immediately while the pancakes are warm. Enjoy the delightful fusion of soft pancakes and the exotic sweetness of prickly pear!

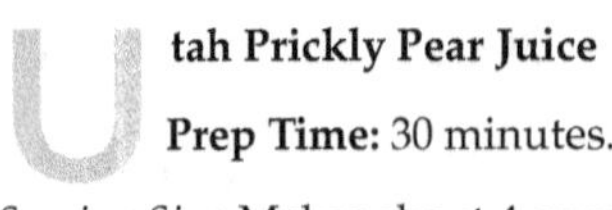 **tah Prickly Pear Juice**

Prep Time: 30 minutes.

Serving Size: Makes about 4 cups

Ingredients:

- 15-20 ripe prickly pears (look for a deep red or purple color)
- 4 cups cold water
- 2 tbsp fresh lime juice
- 2-3 tbsp honey or agave syrup (optional, adjust to taste) A pinch of salt

Instructions:

1. Begin by wearing gloves, as prickly pears have tiny, hair-like thorns. Lay down newspaper or plastic wrap on your work surface for easy cleanup.
2. Using a sharp knife, slice off both ends of the prickly pear. Make a shallow cut and peel back the skin from top to bottom. Discard the skin.
3. Place the peeled prickly pears in a blender and puree until smooth.
4. Pour the pureed prickly pear into a fine mesh strainer set over a large bowl. Use a spoon to press down and extract as much juice as possible. This step removes any seeds and remaining pulp.
5. Return the strained juice to the blender. Add cold water, fresh lime juice, honey or agave syrup (if using), and a pinch of salt. Blend until well combined.
6. Pour the Utah Prickly Pear Juice into glasses filled with ice. Garnish with a slice of lime if desired.
7. If you have leftover juice, store it in an airtight container in the refrigerator for up to 5 days. Shake or stir well before serving.

Tip: Adjust sweetness according to taste. Some prickly pears are naturally sweeter, so always taste before adding sweeteners.

Enjoy the refreshing taste of the Southwest right in your own home!

Banana Yucca Root Soup

Prep Time: 25 minutes. **Cook Time:** 35 minutes

Serving Size: 4

Ingredients:

- 2 medium-sized Banana Yucca roots, cleaned and diced 2 tablespoons olive oil
- 1 large onion, finely chopped 3 cloves garlic, minced
- 1 large carrot, diced 1 stalk celery, diced 1 bay leaf
- 5 cups vegetable broth Salt and pepper, to taste
- 1 tablespoon fresh lemon juice Fresh parsley or cilantro for garnish
- A dash of ground cumin (optional for added depth)

Instructions:

1. Begin by peeling the Banana Yucca roots, removing all the outer brown skin and fibrous parts. Dice the white inner flesh into bite-sized pieces.
2. Heat the olive oil over medium heat in a large pot or Dutch oven. Add the onions and sauté until they turn translucent, about 3-4 minutes.
3. Add the garlic, carrot, and celery to the pot, sautéing for another 5 minutes or until the vegetables start to soften.
4. Introduce the diced yucca root pieces to the pot. Stir occasionally and cook for 7-8 minutes until they take on a light golden hue.
5. Sprinkle in the ground cumin, ensuring the ingredients are well-mixed.
6. Pour in the vegetable broth and drop in the bay leaf. Increase the heat to bring the mixture to a boil. Once boiling, reduce the heat, cover, and let it simmer for 25-30 minutes or until the yucca root becomes tender.
7. After cooking, remove and discard the bay leaf. Using an immersion blender, carefully blend the soup until smooth. If you prefer a chunkier texture, blend only half of the soup and mix with the remaining half.
8. Season with salt, pepper, and lemon juice, adjusting according to your taste.

Serve hot, garnished with fresh parsley or cilantro.

Tip: Pair with crusty bread or a side salad for a complete meal. The mild taste of the yucca root provides a great canvas for adding other favored herbs or spices. Experiment and make the dish your own!

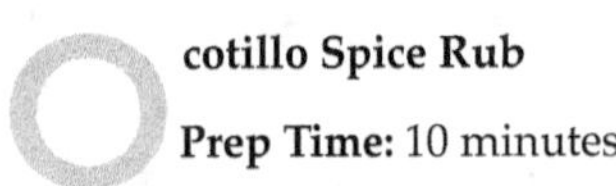 **cotillo Spice Rub**

Prep Time: 10 minutes

Serving Size: Enough rub for 3-4 lbs of meat or vegetables

Ingredients:

- 1 tbsp dried ocotillo flowers, finely ground
- 2 tbsp smoked paprika 1 tbsp garlic powder
- 1 tbsp onion powder 1 tsp ground cumin 1 tsp dried oregano
- 1 tsp ground coriander
- 1/2 tsp chili powder (adjust for desired heat) 1/2 tsp ground black pepper
- 1 tsp sea salt

Instructions:

1. Ensure the dried ocotillo flowers are free of any debris. Grind the flowers into a fine powder using a mortar and pestle or spice grinder.
2. Combine the finely ground ocotillo flowers in a medium-sized bowl with smoked paprika, garlic powder, onion powder, ground cumin, dried oregano, ground coriander, chili powder, black pepper, and sea salt. Mix thoroughly until all spices are well combined.
3. Store the Ocotillo Spice Rub in an airtight container, away from direct sunlight, for up to 6 months. This ensures the flavors remain potent and the rub stays fresh.
4. Generously sprinkle and press the rub onto your choice of meat or vegetables, ensuring an even coat. Allow the ingredients to marinate for at least 30 minutes to several hours before grilling, roasting, or pan-searing.

Note: Ocotillo flowers bring a subtle floral and earthy note, which beautifully complements the bold flavors of the other spices. Adjust the amount of chili powder based on your heat preference. Enjoy the distinct essence of the Southwest with each bite!

Wax Currant Salsa

Prep Time: 15 minutes *Serving Size:* 4-6 servings

Ingredients:

- 1 cup wax currants, rinsed and halved
- 2 medium tomatoes, diced
- 1 small red onion, finely chopped
- 1 jalapeño pepper, seeds removed and finely chopped (adjust based on heat preference)
- 2 tablespoons fresh cilantro, chopped 1 lime, juiced
- 1 teaspoon honey or agave nectar (optional for added sweetness) Salt and pepper, to taste

Instructions:

1. After rinsing the wax currants, cut them into halves. Dice the tomatoes and chop the red onion, jalapeño pepper, and cilantro.
2. In a mixing bowl, combine the wax currants, tomatoes, red onion, jalapeño, and cilantro.
3. Pour in the lime juice and mix well. If you prefer a sweeter salsa, add honey or agave nectar. Season with salt and pepper to taste.
4. For best flavor, let the salsa sit in the refrigerator for at least 30 minutes before serving. This allows the flavors to meld together.

Enjoy your Wax Currant Salsa with tortilla chips atop grilled chicken or as a refreshing side to any dish!

Note: Wax currants have a naturally tangy flavor, which pairs beautifully with the savory and spicy ingredients of this salsa. Adjust the heat and sweetness levels according to your preference.

Arrowleaf Balsamroot Cough and Cold Syrup

Prep Time: 20 minutes. **Cook Time:** 1 hour

Serving Size: Makes about 1 cup (8 oz) of syrup. Use 1-2 teaspoons as needed.

Ingredients:

- 2 cups of fresh Arrowleaf Balsamroot flowers and leaves, finely chopped 2 cups of filtered water
- 1 cup of raw honey
- 1/4 cup of lemon juice (for added Vitamin C and flavor)
- 1/2 tsp of ground ginger (optional, for added warmth and to soothe the throat)

Instructions:

1. Begin by washing the Arrowleaf Balsamroot flowers and leaves thoroughly. Pat them dry and finely chop them to release their natural juices.
2. Combine the chopped Arrowleaf Balsamroot in a saucepan with filtered water. Bring the mixture to a boil, then reduce heat to a simmer. Let it simmer until the volume is reduced by half (about 1 hour).
3. Once the mixture has reduced, remove from heat. Using a fine mesh strainer or cheesecloth, strain the liquid into a clean bowl, pressing down to get all the liquid out. Discard the plant material.
4. While the liquid is still warm (but not boiling), stir in the raw honey and lemon juice. If using, add the ground ginger. Mix until everything is thoroughly combined.
5. Pour the syrup into a sterilized glass bottle or jar with a tight-fitting lid. Allow it to cool to room temperature before sealing it.

Usage: Take 1-2 teaspoons of syrup for coughs and cold symptoms as needed. The syrup can be stored in the refrigerator for up to 6 weeks.

Note: Before using Arrowleaf Balsamroot or any other wild plant for medicinal purposes, it's essential to positively identify the plant and ensure you're not allergic to it. Consult with a healthcare professional or local herbalist before consuming. Pregnant or nursing women and people on medications should be particularly cautious.

P urplenerve Spring Parsley Herb Butter

Prep Time: 10 minutes

Serving Size: Makes about 1 cup

Ingredients:

- 1 cup unsalted butter, softened to room temperature
- 2 tablespoons fresh Purplenerve Spring Parsley leaves, finely chopped
- 1 small garlic clove, minced (optional for an added kick)
- Zest of 1 lemon
- 1/2 teaspoon sea salt (or to taste)
- A pinch of freshly ground black pepper

Instructions:

1. Ensure the butter is soft but not melted. Wash the Purplenerve Spring Parsley leaves thoroughly and pat them dry with a paper towel. Finely chop the leaves.
2. In a mixing bowl, combine the softened butter, chopped Purplenerve Spring Parsley, garlic (if using), lemon zest, salt, and black pepper. Use a fork or a hand mixer on low speed to blend all the ingredients until they're well incorporated.
3. Transfer the herb butter mixture onto a piece of parchment paper or plastic wrap. Shape it into a log, then roll it up in the paper or wrap, twisting the ends to seal. Place in the refrigerator for at least 2 hours to solidify and let the flavors meld.
4. Once chilled and set, slice the Purplenerve Spring Parsley herb butter into rounds and serve on warm bread, roasted vegetables, grilled meats, or any dish that would benefit from a flavorful buttery touch.

Storage: Store any leftover herb butter in the refrigerator for up to a week, or in the freezer for up to a month.

AFTERWORD

As we conclude our exploration of the "Wild Edible Plants of the Southwest," it is crucial to pause and appreciate this region's vast assortment of flora. This expansive and rugged terrain, often characterized by deserts, canyons, and plateaus, hides a treasure trove of nourishing plants that have sustained indigenous communities for countless generations. From the succulent pads of the prickly pear cactus to the nutritious beans of the mesquite tree, the Southwest presents an abundance of flavors, textures, and nutritional advantages.

While this book has provided us with comprehensive insights into identifying, gathering, and preparing these wild edibles, it is of utmost importance to approach foraging with reverence and caution. By preserving these natural habitats and practicing sustainable foraging methods, we can ensure that future generations will enjoy the bounties of the Southwest.

The knowledge within these pages serves as a guide to unlocking the culinary secrets of the Southwest and as a reminder of the profound connection we share with the land. May every expedition into the wilderness bring us closer to comprehending the intricate relationships between humans, plants, and the environment. Let us celebrate the discovery, respect, and enjoyment of the wild edibles of the Southwest!

PART ELEVEN
APPENDIX

UNIVERSAL EDIBILITY TEST

If you are in an unfamiliar area or a survival situation, you may be unable to identify edible plants. In this case, you'd want to use the universal edibility test. As the name suggests, this test will help determine whether a plant is edible. It should only be used as a last resort, as you should ideally never be in a situation where you can't find an identifiable plant or mushroom. Always check the edibility of your harvest, even if you're sure it's safe to eat. This is important when foraging and Identifying an edible plant you've never tried before.

Everyone will come across this scenario at some point. Even if you're confident that you've identified an edible plant, only try a small amount first. Even something safe to eat can make you feel unwell if you have digestive issues. Sometimes a food you haven't tried before doesn't agree with you, and you don't want to discover this after having a large portion. It's also possible to have an undiagnosed food allergy. Suppose you eat a lot of plant food on an empty stomach. In that case, you can quickly end up with cramps, nausea, diarrhea, or other gastrointestinal issues. An upset stomach is a quick way to ruin an otherwise enjoyable foraging trip.

Step 1: Fast for eight hours. You likely haven't eaten for at least eight hours in a survival situation like this. Still, it's essential to start on an empty stomach so that you know whether or not the plant you are testing is what has made you unwell. You can and should drink plenty of clean water, if possible.

Step 2: Check for common poisonous traits. Most toxic plants have distinguishing characteristics that are unlikely to be found on edible plants. These include shiny, waxy leaves, spines, fine hairs, milky sap, umbrella-shaped flowers, and green or white berries. If it looks like dill or parsley, avoid it, and steer clear of anything that smells like almonds. Not every plant with these characteristics is toxic, edible dandelions have milky sap, for example, but it's an excellent rule of thumb. Rule out anything with those traits.

Step 3: Once you find a plant without any of those traits, ensure you can find plenty of specimens. Remember, the edibility test takes time, so there's not much point in going through the whole process if you can't find any more plants of that type. When you find a likely plant, break it down into sections: flower, leaf, stem, etc. Not every plant part is edible, even if one part is. For example, potato tubers are edible, but the plant's stem is toxic. You will need to test every aspect of the plant individually.

Step 4: Now, it's time to start testing. Select a plant part and rub it on your skin. Most people rub it on their inner forearm, the inside of their elbow, or their outer lip. Wait for fifteen minutes. Continue with the test if you don't experience tingling, burning, or other adverse reactions. If any of the above persist, you will want to choose a different plant part.

Step 5: If all is well from the step above, do a taste test with the same plant part. Put it in your mouth and don't chew or swallow; leave it for five minutes. Spit it out and wash your mouth if you have any adverse reactions. Do the same if you taste bitterness, soapy flavors, or experience numbness. If nothing happens, continue with the test.

Step 6: Do a more extensive taste test. Now put the plant part in your mouth and chew for five minutes. Wait for any of the adverse effects mentioned above and spit out excess saliva (don't swallow anything yet). If everything seems okay after five minutes, swallow the plant part. Now the waiting begins. You need to fast for another eight hours before the next step.

Step 7: If you haven't experienced any digestive issues, you can prepare and eat one tablespoon of the plant part. If possible, it's usually safer to cook the plant part. If there are no poisoning symptoms after another eight hours of waiting, you can be sure this plant part is edible as you prepared. It would be best if you still didn't gorge yourself, but at least you have a relatively dependable food source. You'll reduce the chance of accidental poisoning by sticking with small amounts and waiting eight hours between tasting and eating. Suppose you have significant gastrointestinal symptoms in a survival situation, like vomiting or diarrhea. In that case, you may not be able to seek medical attention.

Glossary

Plant Families

Actinidiaceae [AK-TIN-UH-DIE-UH-SEE-EE] - This flowering plant family has three genera and about 355 species. It consists of shrubs, small trees, and lianas. It is primarily tropical and is particularly common in Southeast Asia.

Anacardiaceae [AN-UH-KAR-DEE-AY-SEE-EE] - The cashew or sumac family of flowering plants includes 83 genera and 860 species. Several species bear drupes and sometimes produce *urushiol*, which can cause skin irritation.

Apiaceae [AY-PEE-AY-SEE-EE] - These primarily aromatic flowering plants are known as the celery, carrot, and parsley family, or umbellifers. They are named after the genus Apium.

Araliaceae [UH-RAH-LEE-AY-SEE-EE] - This family includes approximately 43 genera and about 1500 flowering plants; most are woody, and some are herbaceous.

Asparagaceae [UH-SPAR-UH-GAY-SEE-EE] - the asparagus family of flowering plants based on the edible garden asparagus, *Asparagus officinalis*.

Aspleniaceae [AS-PLEE-NEE-AY-SEE-EE] - The spleenwort family **is** a family of ferns

Asteraceae [AS-TER-AY-SEE-EE] - The Compositae family was first described in the year 1740. They are called daisies, sunflowers, asters, composites, or sunflowers. With more than 32,000 species and 1,900 genera, it is the world's largest flowering plant group, rivaled only by the Orchidaceae family.

Berberidaceae [BER-BUH-RID-UH-SEE-EE] - Generally known as the Barberry family, this group of flowering plants contains 18 genera.

Brassicaceae [BRAS-IH-KAY-SEE-EE] - These medium-sized flowering plants are economically important. They are commonly known as the mustards, crucifers, or cabbage family.

Caryophyllaceae [KAR-EE-OH-FUH-LAY-SEE-EE] - The carnation family is a family of flowering plants with about 2,625 known species.

Elaeagnaceae [EE-LEE-AG-NAY-SEE-EE] - The Oleaster family comprises small trees and shrubs.

Ericaceae [EH-RI-KAY-SEE-EE] - The heath or heather family consists of flowering plants that flourish in acidic and infertile environments. Cranberries, blueberries, huckleberries, rhododendrons (including azaleas), and a wide range of heaths and heathers are examples of well-known members.

Euphorbiaceae [YOO-FOR-BEE-AY-SEE-EE] - Among flowering plants, the spurge family is one of the largest. They are also commonly known as euphorbias in English, their genus name. Most spurges are herbs, such as Euphorbia paralias, but some are shrubs or trees, particularly in the tropics.

Lamiaceae [LAY-MEE-AY-SEE-EE] The mint or deadnettle family is aromatic in all parts. They include widely used culinary herbs like basil, mint, rosemary, sage, savory, marjoram, oregano, hyssop, thyme, lavender, and perilla. Catnip, salvia, bee balm, wild dagga, and oriental motherwort are medicinal herbs.

Malvaceae [MAL-VAY-SEE-EE] - The Mallow family of flowering plants is estimated to contain 244 genera and 4225 known species. Among its well-known members are okra, cotton, cacao, and durian.

Menispermaceae [MEN-EE-SPER-MAY-SEE-EE]- The moonseed family comprises 440 species, most of which are found in low-lying tropical regions, with some species also found in temperate and arid regions.

Morchellaceae [MOR-KEL-EE-AY-SEE-EE]- This family includes the well-known morel mushrooms, which are highly prized for their culinary value. Members of the Morchellaceae family are characterized by their distinctive fruiting bodies, which typically have a sponge-like, honeycomb appearance. These fungi are found in a variety of habitats, often in forests, and are known to form symbiotic relationships with trees, helping in nutrient exchange. They are ascomycetes, meaning they produce spores in specialized cells called asci.

Oxalidaceae [OKS-UH-LUH-DAY-SEE-EE] - The wood sorrel family comprises five genera of herbaceous plants, shrubs, and small trees, with about 570 species in the Oxalis genus.

Plantaginaceae [PLAN-TUH-JIH-NAY-SEE-EE] - The Plantain family and order Lamiales include common flower species such as snapdragon and foxglove.

Polygonaceae [PUH-LIG-UH-NAY-SEE-EE] - The knotweed or smartweed-buckwheat family is an informal name for a family of flowering plants. There are about 1200 species within about 48 genera. Members of this family are found worldwide, but they are most abundant in the North Temperate Zone.

Portulacaceae [POR-CHUH-LUH-KAY-SEE-EE]- The purslane family is a family of flowering plants with 115 species in one genus, Portulaca.

Ranunculaceae [RUH-NUN-KYOO-LAY-SEE-EE]- the buttercup or crowfoot family is a family of over 2,000 known flowering plants in 43 genera distributed worldwide.

Rosaceae [ROH-ZAY-SEE-EE] - The rose family includes 4,828 species of flowering plants.

Viburnaceae [VY-BUR-NAY-SEE-EE] - was previously known as the Adoxaceae family and is commonly known as the Moschatel family. About 150–200 species belong to this family of flowering plants.

Plant Types

Annual [AN-YOO-UHL] - Plants without a permanent woody stem. They are usually flowering garden plants or potherbs.

Deciduous [DIH-SIJ-OO-UHS] - After the growing season, the plant sheds leaves and turns dormant.

Dioecious [DAHY-EE-SHUHS] - having the male and female organs in separate and distinct individuals, having different sexes.

Herbaceous [HUR-BEY-SHUHS] - low-growing plants with soft green stems. Their above-ground growth is often seasonal.

Monoecious [MUH-NEE-SHUHS] - having the stamens and the pistils in separate flowers on the same plant.

Perennial [PUH-REN-EE-UHL] - It usually lasts for more than two years. These plants don't have a lot of woody growth.

Plant Parts

Achene [UH-KEEN] - a small, dry, one-seeded fruit that does not open to release the seed.

Anther [AN-THER] - the pollen-bearing part of a stamen.

Filament [FIL-UH-MUHNT] - the stalklike portion of a stamen, supporting the anther.

Ligulate [LIG-YUH-LIT] - strap-shaped, such as the ray florets of daisy family plants.

Peltate [PEL-TEYT] - fixed to the stalk by the center or by some point distinctly within the margin.

Petiole [PET-EE-OHL] - the slender stalk by which a leaf is attached to the stem; leafstalk.

Pistil [PIS-TL] - the ovule-bearing or seed-bearing female organ of a flower, consisting when complete of the ovary, style, and stigma.

Pith - The soft central cylinder of tissue in the plant's stem.

Sepal [SEE-PUHL] - The outer parts of the flower (often green and leaf-like) that enclose a developing bud.

Sessile [SES-IL] - attached directly by its base without a stalk or peduncle.

Stamen [STEY-MUHN] - the pollen-bearing organ of a flower, consisting of the filament and the anther.

Staminodia [STAM-UH-NOH-DEE-UH] - A stamen that is sterile or abortive.

Whorled - The arrangement of like parts around a point on an axis, such as leaves or flowers;

Leaf Types

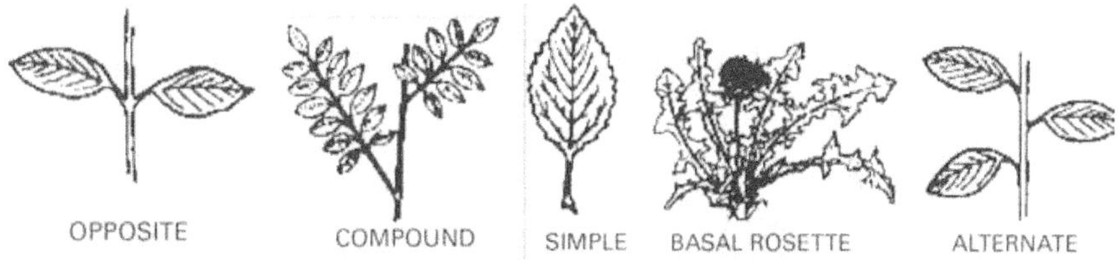

Alternate - The leaves are single at each node and spiral upwards along the stem.

Basal leaf - a leaf that grows lowest on the stem of a plant or flower.

Compound - composed of two or more leaflets that are attached to a single leaf stalk or petiole.

Opposite - When two leaves are attached at the same node, one on either side of the stem.

Palmate [PAL-MEYT] - Having four or more lobes or leaflets.

Palmately compound - A petiole's tip is attached to a leaflet.

Pinnate [PIN-EYT] - Each side of a stalk is divided into leaflets

Rosette [ROH-ZET] - a circular arrangement of leaves or structures resembling leaves.

Simple - Leaves with a single, undivided lamina

Tripinnately compound - Leaf made up of three pinnate parts.

Leaf Shapes

Cordate [KAWR-DEYT] - heart-shaped.

Elliptical [IH-LIP-TI-KUHL] - Planar, shaped like a flattened circle, symmetrical about the long and short axes, tapering equally to the tip and the base; oval.

Lanceolate [AN-SEE-UH-LEYT] - shaped like the head of a lance, having a rounded base and a tapering apex.

Long-pointed - Lying close and flat and pointing toward the plant's apex or structure.

Oblanceolate [OB-LAN-SEE-*UH*-LIT] - having a rounded apex and a tapering base.

Oblong [OB-LAWNG]- Having a length a few times greater than the width, with sides almost parallel and ends rounded.

Ovate [OH-VEYT] - egg-shaped, having such a shape with a broader end at the base.

Triangular - Planar with three sides.

Wedge - narrowly triangular, wider at the apex, and tapering toward the base.

Flower Types

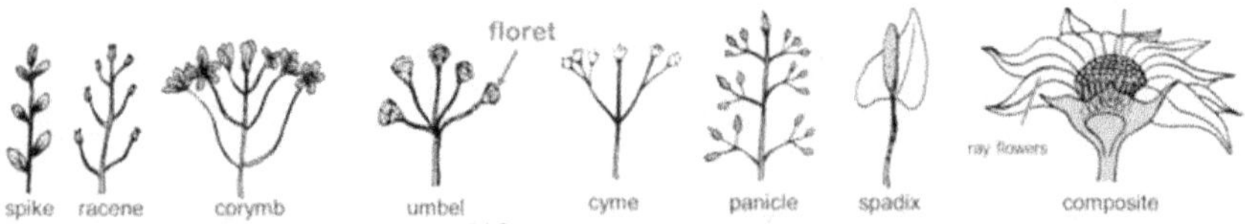

Corymb [KAWR-IMB] - a form of inflorescence in which the flowers form a flat-topped or convex cluster, the outermost flowers being the first to open.

Composite - is characterized by alternate, opposite, or *whorled* leaves and a whorl of bracts surrounding its flower heads. These flower heads typically extend from a disk containing tiny petal-less flowers and from the disk's rim to a ray of petals.

Cyme [SAHYM] - an inflorescence in which the primary axis bears a single central or terminal flower that blooms first.

Inflorescence [IN-FLAW-RES-UHNS] - the complete flower head of a plant, including stems, stalks, bracts, and flowers.

Panicle [PAN-I-KUHL] - any loose, diversely branching flower cluster.

Raceme [REY-SEEM] - a flower cluster with separate flowers attached by short equal stalks at equal distances along a central stem. The flowers at the base of the main stem develop first.

Spike - a type of racemose inflorescence.

Spadix [SPEY-DIKS] - an inflorescence consisting of a spike with a fleshy or thickened axis, usually enclosed in a spathe.

Umbel or Subumbel [UHM-BUHL] - consisting of several short flower stalks that spread from a common point, like umbrella ribs.

Seaweed

Blade - refers to the flattened and elongated portion of the seaweed that is similar to a leaf. The blade is the main photosynthetic organ of seaweed and is responsible for capturing light energy for photosynthesis.

Float - refers to a gas-filled bladder or sac that helps the seaweed stay afloat and near the water's surface, where it can receive maximum sunlight for photosynthesis.

Stipe - the stem-like structure that supports the leafy fronds. It is the main axis of the seaweed body and is analogous to the stem of a land plant.

Holdfast - a structure that anchors the seaweed to a solid surface, such as a rock or the ocean floor. Holdfasts are a critical part of the seaweed's anatomy as they provide stability and allow the seaweed to withstand the strong currents and waves of the ocean.

Fruit/Berry

Aggregate fruit [AG-RI-GIT FROOT] - composed of a cluster of carpels belonging to the same flower as the raspberry.

Dehiscent [DIH-HIS-UHNT] - opens to release seeds or pollen

Drupe [DROOP] - a fleshy fruit with thin skin and a central stone containing the seed, e.g., a plum, cherry, almond, or olive.

Globoid [GLOH-BOID] - approximately globular. Globe-shaped; spherical.

Infructescence [IN-FRUC-TES-CENCE] - an aggregate fruit.

Syconium [SAHY-KOH-NEE-UHM] - a fleshy hollow receptacle that develops into a multifruit.

Bark

Acaulescent [AK-AW-LES-UHNT] - stemless

Lenticel [LEN-TUH-SEL] - One of the many holes in a woody plant's stem that allows air to exchange between the inside and outside.

Myrmecochory [MUR-MUH-KOH-REE]- the dispersal of fruits and seeds by ants.

Elaiosome [IH-LAY-UH-SOHM] - an oil-rich body on seeds or fruits that attract ants and act as dispersal agents.

Medical Terms

Amygdalin [UH-MIG-DUH-LIN] - White, bitter-tasting glycosidic powder usually obtained from the leaves and seeds of plants of the genus Prunus and related genera: used mainly as an expectorant in medicine.

Anthocyanins [AN-THUH-SAHY-UH-NIN] - These flavonoids are known for their pigmentation properties, responsible for fruits, vegetables, flowers, and cereals' red, purple, and blue colors.

Astringent [UH-STRIN-JUHNT] - Contracting the body's tissues or canals reduces mucus or blood discharges.

Berberine [BUR-BUH-REEN] - Known as an antipyretic, antibacterial, and stomachic, this crystalline, water-soluble alkaloid is derived from barberry or goldenseal.

Carotenoid [KUH-ROT-N-OID] - Red or yellow pigments, similar to carotene, found in animal fat and some plants.

Cyanogenic glycosides - chemical compounds contained in foods that release hydrogen cyanide when chewed or digested.

Demulcent [DIH-MUHL-SUHNT] - a substance that relieves irritation of the mucous membranes in the mouth by forming a protective film.

Depurative [DEP-YUH-REY-TIV] - herbs considered to have purifying and detoxifying effects.

Flavonoids [FLEY-VUH-NOID] - An antioxidant, antiviral, anticancer, anti-inflammatory, and anti-allergenic group of water-soluble polyphenols found in plants.

Hydrocyanic acid - scientific word for cyanide.

Lutein [LOO-TEEN] - is known to have anti-inflammatory and immune-boosting properties and is important for maintaining healthy eyes and skin.

Lycopene [LAHY-KUH-PEEN] - Red crystalline substance found in some fruits, including tomatoes and paprika.

Odontalgic [OH-DON-TAL-JUH] - toothache.

Prunasin [PROO-NUH-SIN] - A cyanogenic glucoside related to amygdalin found in Prunus species.

Urolithiasis [YOOR-OH-LI-**THAHY**-UH-SIS] - A disease where stones form in the urinary tract.

Urushiol [OO-**ROO**-SHEE-AWL] - The active irritant principle in several plant species in the Rhus genus.

Zeaxanthin [ZEE-UH-ZAN-THIN] - is found in the macula of the eye, where it plays a role in protecting the eye from oxidative damage and age-related macular degeneration.

General definitions

Anthropogenic [AN-THR*UH*-P*UH*-JEN-IK] - caused by humans.

Decoction - concentrated herbal extracts that are made by boiling the plant material in water.

Glaucous [**GLAW**-K*UHS*] - covered with a whitish bloom, as a plum.

Siliceous [S*UH*-**LISH**-*UHS*] - growing in soil rich in silica.

Calcareous [KAL-**KAIR**-EE-*UHS*] - occurring on chalk or limestone.

Monoecious [M*UH*-**NEE**-SH*UHS*] - The stamens and pistils are in separate flowers on the same plant.

Mucilaginous [MYOO-S*UH*-**LAJ**-*UH*-N*UHS*] - having a viscous or gelatinous consistency.

ABOUT THE AUTHOR

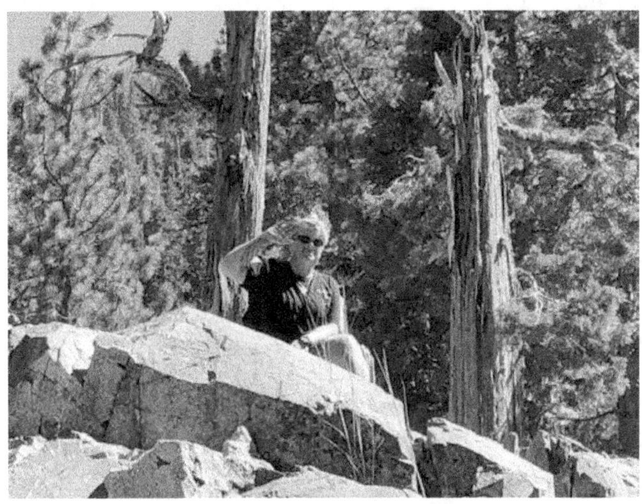

Shannon Warner is a long-time forager and survivalist with a deep love for the outdoors. She has spent countless hours exploring the wilderness, learning about the plants and animals that inhabit it, and honing her skills in sustainable harvesting and ethical foraging. She has embarked on many adventures with her two loyal dogs by her side, from hiking and camping to hunting and fishing.

One of her core beliefs is in sustainable harvesting and ethical foraging. She firmly believes that it is possible to enjoy the bounty of nature without causing harm to the environment or depleting its resources. In her books, she provides practical tips and advice on how to forage in a way that is both sustainable and respectful of the natural world.

Whether you are an experienced forager or a beginner looking to learn more about the plants that grow in your backyard, Shannon's book is an invaluable resource that will inspire and inform you. With her expert guidance, you, too, can discover the many benefits of wild edible plants and unlock the secrets of the natural world.

PLANT INDEX

BIBLIOGRAPHY

Photo Attributions

Vauquelinia californica subsp. _californica_observed in the United States of America by Daniel McNair (licensed under http://creativecommons.org/licenses/by/4.0/)

Vauquelinia californica subsp. _californica_ observed in the United States of America by Matthew Zappa (licensed under http://creativecommons.org/licenses/by/4.0/)

Vauquelinia californica subsp. _californica_ observed in the United States of America by Rachel Stringham (licensed under http://creativecommons.org/licenses/by/4.0/)

Vauquelinia californica subsp. californica observed in the United States of America by Matt Berger (licensed under http://creativecommons.org/licenses/by/4.0/)

Vauquelinia californica subsp. _sonorensis_ W.J.Hess & Henrickson observed in the United States of America by Isaac Krone (licensed under http://creativecommons.org/licenses/by/4.0/)

Shepherdia argentea (Pursh) Nutt. observed in the United States of America by Chloe and Trevor Van Loon (licensed under http://creativecommons.org/licenses/by/4.0/)

Shepherdia argentea (Pursh) Nutt. observed in the United States of America by Chloe and Trevor Van Loon (licensed under http://creativecommons.org/licenses/by/4.0/)

Shepherdia argentea (Pursh) Nutt. observed in the United States of America by Craig Whippo (licensed under http://creativecommons.org/licenses/by/4.0/)

Symphoricarpos orbiculatus Moench observed in the United States of America by Annika Lindqvist (licensed under http://creativecommons.org/licenses/by/4.0/)

Prunus andersonii Gray observed in the United States of America by Jim Morefield (licensed under http://creativecommons.org/licenses/by/4.0/)

Prunus andersonii Gray observed in the United States of America by Justin Paulin (licensed under http://creativecommons.org/licenses/by/4.0/)

Prunus andersonii Gray observed in the United States of America by Janel Johnson (licensed under http://creativecommons.org/licenses/by/4.0/)

Vaccinium membranaceum Douglas ex Hook. observed in the United States of America by John A Haskins (licensed under http://creativecommons.org/licenses/by/4.0/)

Vaccinium membranaceum Douglas ex Hook. observed in the United States of America by Nolan Exe (licensed under http://creativecommons.org/licenses/by/4.0/)

Vaccinium membranaceum Douglas ex Hook. observed in the United States of America by John Brew (licensed under http://creativecommons.org/licenses/by/4.0/)

Rubus neomexicanus A.Gray observed in the United States of America by CK Kelly (licensed under http://creativecommons.org/licenses/by/4.0/)

Rubus neomexicanus A.Gray observed in the United States of America by psweet (licensed under http://creativecommons.org/licenses/by/4.0/)

Prunus persica (L.) Stokes observed in the United States of America by Sydney Dragon (licensed under http://creativecommons.org/licenses/by/4.0/)

Prunus persica (L.) Stokes observed in the United States of America by Asher P Higgins (licensed under http://creativecommons.org/licenses/by/4.0/)

Prunus persica (L.) Stokes observed in the United States of America by Cody Stricker (licensed under http://creativecommons.org/licenses/by/4.0/)

Leccinum aurantiacum (Bull.) Gray observed in the United States of America by Richard Jacob (licensed under http://creativecommons.org/licenses/by/4.0/)

Leccinum aurantiacum (Bull.) Gray observed in the United States of America by Sigrid Jakob (licensed under http://creativecommons.org/licenses/by/4.0/)

Lophophora williamsii observed in the United States of America by Michelle (licensed under http://creativecommons.org/licenses/by/4.0/)

Lophophora williamsii observed in the United States of America by Michelle (licensed under http://creativecommons.org/licenses/by/4.0/)

Lophophora williamsii observed in the United States of America by Alan Rockefeller (licensed under https://creativecommons.org/licenses/by-sa/4.0/

Lophophora williamsii observed in the United States of America by Alan Rockefeller (licensed under https://creativecommons.org/licenses/by-sa/4.0/

Lophophora williamsii observed in the United States of America by Francisco Martínez González (licensed under https://creativecommons.org/licenses/by-sa/4.0/

Pleurocybella porrigens (Pers.) Singerobserved in the United States of America by Cricket Raspet (licensed under http://creativecommons.org/licenses/by/4.0/)

References

Amanita phalloides – Mushrooms Up! Edible and Poisonous Species of Coastal BC and the Pacific Northwest. (n.d.). https://explore.beatymuseum.ubc.ca/mushroomsup/A_phalloides.html

Annual Reports | CAM at the NCI | OCCAM. (n.d.). https://cam.cancer.gov/cam_at_nci/annual_report/2010/red_sage.htm

Aon, O. (2022, December 5). Oyster Mushrooms, Pleurotus species. *Forage Colorado.* https://www.foragecolorado.com/post/oyster-mushrooms-pleurotus-species

Apache Plume (Fallugia paradoxa) - Petrified Forest National Park (U.S. National Park Service). (n.d.). https://www.nps.gov/pefo/learn/nature/apache-plume.htm

Armillaria solidipes – Mushrooms Up! Edible and Poisonous Species of Coastal BC and the Pacific Northwest. (n.d.). https://explore.beatymuseum.ubc.ca/mushroomsup/A_solidipes.html

Arrowleaf Balsamroot. (n.d.). https://www.fs.usda.gov/wildflowers/plant-of-the-week/balsamorhiza_sagittata.shtml

Banana yucca. (n.d.). https://www.fs.usda.gov/wildflowers/plant-of-the-week/yucca_baccata.shtml Bergo, A. (2023, March 25). *Black Trumpet mushrooms.* Forager | Chef. https://foragerchef.com/the-horn-of-death-black-trumpet-mushrooms/

Bitterroot. (n.d.). https://www.fs.usda.gov/wildflowers/plant-of-the-week/lewisia_rediviva.shtml

Bitterroot - Lewis & Clark National Historic Trail (U.S. National Park Service). (n.d.). https://www.nps.gov/lecl/learn/nature/bitterroot.htm

bladderpod | UC Davis Arboretum and Public Garden. (n.d.). https://arboretum.ucdavis.edu/plant/bladderpod

Blog, G. (2023, July 24). *Queen of the Night in Bloom.* Desert Botanical Garden. https://dbg.org/queen-of-the-night-in-bloom/

Boise National Forest - Nature & Science. (n.d.). https://www.fs.usda.gov/detail/boise/learning/nature-science/?cid=fsed_009700

Bouteloua gracilis Blue Grama PFAF Plant Database. (n.d.). https://pfaf.org/User/Plant.aspx?LatinName=Bouteloua+gracilis

Broadwater County Blog - Broadwater County Extension | Montana State University. (n.d.). https://www.montana.edu/extension/broadwater/blog-article.html?id=22097

Bromus tectorum. (n.d.). https://www.fs.usda.gov/database/feis/plants/graminoid/brotec/all.html

Chilopsis linearis Desert Willow PFAF Plant Database. (n.d.). https://pfaf.org/User/Plant.aspx?LatinName=Chilopsis+linearis

Cholla.(n.d.).https://www.saguaro-juniper.com/i_and_i/cacti/opuntias/cylindropuntia/cylindropuntia.html

Cinnabar chanterelle (Cantharellus cinnabarinus) - mushrooms of Eastern Texas. (n.d.). https://www.texasmushrooms.org/en/cantharellus_cinnabarinus.htm

Cirsium ochrocentrum Yellow Spined Thistle PFAF Plant Database. (n.d.). https://pfaf.org/user/Plant.aspx?LatinName=Cirsium+ochrocentrum

Colorado Hardy Plants. (2023, July 2). *PURSHIA TRIDENTATA (Antelope Bitterbrush) - ColoradoHardyPlants.com.* ColoradoHardyPlants.com. https://www.coloradohardyplants.com/product/purshia-tridentata-antelope-bitterbrush/

Colorado Plant Database, Colorado State University Extension, Jefferson County. (n.d.). https://colorado plants.jeffco.us/plant/details/834

Control Cholla Cactus | New Mexico State University - BE BOLD. Shape the future. (n.d.). https://pubs.nmsu.edu/_b/B804/

Desert peach. (n.d.). Tmparksfoundation. https://www.tmparksfoundation.org/plants-fungi/desert-peach

DesertUSA.com. (n.d.). *Tumbleweed, - Russian Thistle - DesertUSA.* https://www.desertusa.com/flowers/tumbleweed.html

details. (n.d.). http://www.tsusinvasives.org/home/database/salsola-tragus

Dickinson, A. (2023a, August 16). *The complete guide to lobster mushrooms.* Shroomer. https://www.shroomer.com/lobster-mushrooms/

Dickinson, A. (2023b, September 27). *The complete guide to Elm Oyster mushrooms.* Shroomer. https://www.shroomer.com/elm-oyster-mushroom/

Eldridge, A. (2022, December 19). *Death cap | Description, Mushroom, Poisoning, Symptoms, & Facts.* Encyclopedia Britannica. https://www.britannica.com/science/death-cap

Find Trees & Learn | University of Arizona Campus Arboretum. (n.d.-a). https://apps.cals.arizona.edu/arboretum/taxon.aspx?id=1188

Find Trees & Learn | University of Arizona Campus Arboretum. (n.d.-b). https://apps.cals.arizona.edu/arboretum/taxon.aspx?id=281

Find Trees & Learn | University of Arizona Campus Arboretum. (n.d.-c). https://apps.cals.arizona.edu/arboretum/taxon.aspx?id=66

Find Trees & Learn | University of Arizona Campus Arboretum. (n.d.-d). https://apps.cals.arizona.edu/arboretum/taxon.aspx?id=770

Find Trees & Learn | University of Arizona Campus Arboretum. (n.d.-e). https://apps.cals.arizona.edu/ arboretum/taxon.aspx?id=72

Find Trees & Learn | University of Arizona Campus Arboretum. (n.d.-f). https://apps.cals.arizona.edu/ arboretum/taxon.aspx?id=233

Forager Chef. (n.d.). *Chicken of the Woods Archives.* Forager | Chef. https://foragerchef.com/category/ wild-mushroom-recipes-2/chicken-of-the-woods/

Forestiera pubescens | Landscape Plants | Oregon State University. (n.d.). https://landscapeplants.oregon state.edu/plants/forestiera-pubescens

Fouquieria splendens Ocotillo. Coach whip PFAF Plant Database. (n.d.). https://pfaf.org/user/Plant.aspx? LatinName=Fouquieria+splendens

Grizzly Bear Cactus (Opuntia polyacantha var. erinacea) — Cactus World. (n.d.). Cactus World. https:// www.cactusworld.com/shop/p/grizzly-bear-cactus-opuntia-polyacantha-var-erinacea

Gyromitra esculenta – Mushrooms Up! Edible and Poisonous Species of Coastal BC and the Pacific Northwest. (n.d.). https://explore.beatymuseum.ubc.ca/mushroomsup/G_esculenta.html

Harris, J. C. (2018, April 24). *Wonders in the Woodchip! The Black Morel.* The Mushroom Diary - UK Wild Mushroom Hunting Blog. https://www.mushroomdiary.co.uk/2012/04/black-morel-mushroom- morchella-elata/

Honey mushroom | fungus. (n.d.). Encyclopedia Britannica. https://www.britannica.com/science/honey-mushroom

Horehound — Northern Arizona Invasive plants. (n.d.). Northern Arizona Invasive Plants. https://nazinva siveplants.org/horehound

Hydnum repandum. (2019, July 3). Midwest American Mycological Information. https://midwestmycol ogy.org/hydnum-repandum/

Jack-O-Lantern - Bay Area Mycological Society. (n.d.). Text and Images Copyright Bay Area Mycological Society and the Authors Except Where Noted. All Rights Reserved. https://bayareamushrooms.org/ mushroommonth/jackolantern.html

Jenny. (2022, August 23). *Elm Oyster mushroom: identification, foraging, and lookalikes - Mushroom apprecia- tion.* Mushroom Appreciation. https://www.mushroom-appreciation.com/elm-oyster- mushroom.html

Jenny. (2023, September 25). *Angel Wings: Identification and Controversy - Mushroom appreciation.* Mushroom-Appreciation.https://www.mushroom-appreciation.com/angel-wings- identification.html

Johnson, J. (2020, June 24). *What to know about peyote.* https://www.medicalnewstoday.com/articles/ peyote

Juglans major. (n.d.). https://www.fs.usda.gov/database/feis/plants/tree/jugmaj/all.html

Juniperus monosperma (Cherrystone Juniper, New Mexico Juniper, One-seed Juniper, Oneseed Juniper, Sabina, Single-seeded Juniper, West Texas Juniper) | North Carolina Extension Gardener Plant Toolbox. (n.d.). https:// plants.ces.ncsu.edu/plants/juniperus-monosperma/

Juniperus monosperma One-Seed Juniper PFAF Plant Database. (n.d.). https://pfaf.org/user/Plant.aspx? LatinName=Juniperus+monosperma

Kansas Wildflowers and Grasses - Yellow-spine thistle. (n.d.). https://kswildflower.org/flower_details.php? flowerID=700

Kinsey, T. B. (2011, May 27). *Cymopterus multinervatus - Purplenerve Springparsley, Arizona Springparsley, Wild Parsnip - Southeastern Arizona Wildflowers and Plants.* https://www.fireflyforest.com/flowers/ 2742/cy-mopterus-multinervatus-purplenerve-springparsley/

Kris. (2023, April 23). *Buffaloberry - Discover Lewis & Clark.* Discover Lewis & Clark. https://lewis-clark.org/sciences/plants/buffaloberry/

Lady Bird Johnson Wildflower Center - The University of Texas at Austin. (n.d.-a). https://wildflower.org/ plants/result.php?id_plant=vaca5

Lady Bird Johnson Wildflower Center - The University of Texas at Austin. (n.d.-b). https://www.wildflower. org/plants/result.php?id_plant=FAPA

Lady Bird Johnson Wildflower Center - The University of Texas at Austin. (n.d.-c). https://www.wildflower. org/plants/result.php?id_plant=vaca5

Lady Bird Johnson Wildflower Center - The University of Texas at Austin. (n.d.-d). https://www.wildflower. org/plants/result.php?id_plant=basa3

Lady Bird Johnson Wildflower Center - The University of Texas at Austin. (n.d.-e). https://www.wildflower. org/plants/result.php?id_plant=yuba

Lady Bird Johnson Wildflower Center - The University of Texas at Austin. (n.d.-f). https://www.wildflower. org/plants/result.php?id_plant=opba2

Lady Bird Johnson Wildflower Center - The University of Texas at Austin. (n.d.-g). https://www.wildflower. org/plants/result.php?id_plant=OPMAM2

Lady Bird Johnson Wildflower Center - The University of Texas at Austin. (n.d.-h). https://www.wildflower. org/plants/result.php?id_plant=pafl6

Lady Bird Johnson Wildflower Center - The University of Texas at Austin. (n.d.-i). https://www.wildflower. org/plants/result.php?id_plant=boda2

Lady Bird Johnson Wildflower Center - The University of Texas at Austin. (n.d.-j). https://www.wildflower. org/plants/result.php?id_plant=soca6

Lady Bird Johnson Wildflower Center - The University of Texas at Austin. (n.d.-k). https://www.wildflower.org/plants/result.php?id_plant=syor

Lady Bird Johnson Wildflower Center - The University of Texas at Austin. (n.d.-l). https://www.wildflower.org/plants/result.php?id_plant=agde

Lady Bird Johnson Wildflower Center - The University of Texas at Austin. (n.d.-m). https://www.wildflower.org/plants/result.php?id_plant=PRFA

Lady Bird Johnson Wildflower Center - The University of Texas at Austin. (n.d.-n). https://www.wildflower.org/plants/result.php?id_plant=PUGL2

Lady Bird Johnson Wildflower Center - The University of Texas at Austin. (n.d.-o). https://www.wildflower.org/plants/result.php?id_plant=pran2

Lady Bird Johnson Wildflower Center - The University of Texas at Austin. (n.d.-p). https://www.wildflower.org/plants/result.php?id_plant=chli2

Lady Bird Johnson Wildflower Center - The University of Texas at Austin. (n.d.-q). https://www.wildflower.org/plants/result.php?id_plant=OPPOE

Lady Bird Johnson Wildflower Center - The University of Texas at Austin. (n.d.-r). https://www.wildflower.org/plants/result.php?id_plant=LOIN

Lady Bird Johnson Wildflower Center - The University of Texas at Austin. (n.d.-s). https://www.wildflower.org/plants/result.php?id_plant=RUNE

Lady Bird Johnson Wildflower Center - The University of Texas at Austin. (n.d.-t). https://www.wildflower.org/plants/result.php?id_plant=jumo

Lady Bird Johnson Wildflower Center - The University of Texas at Austin. (n.d.-u). https://www.wildflower.org/plants/result.php?id_plant=CYMU2

Lady Bird Johnson Wildflower Center - The University of Texas at Austin. (n.d.-v). https://www.wildflower.org/plants/result.php?id_plant=SPCR

Lady Bird Johnson Wildflower Center - The University of Texas at Austin. (n.d.-w). https://www.wildflower.org/plants/result.php?id_plant=ECCOP

Lady Bird Johnson Wildflower Center - The University of Texas at Austin. (n.d.-x). https://www.wildflower.org/plants/result.php?id_plant=prpu

Lady Bird Johnson Wildflower Center - The University of Texas at Austin. (n.d.-y). https://www.wildflower.org/plants/result.php?id_plant=soel

Lady Bird Johnson Wildflower Center - The University of Texas at Austin. (n.d.-z). https://www.wildflower.org/plants/result.php?id_plant=esvi2

Lady Bird Johnson Wildflower Center - The University of Texas at Austin. (n.d.-aa). https://www.wildflower.org/plants/result.php?id_plant=fopu2

Lady Bird Johnson Wildflower Center - The University of Texas at Austin. (n.d.-ab). https://www.wildflower.org/plants/result.php?id_plant=pied

Lady Bird Johnson Wildflower Center - The University of Texas at Austin. (n.d.-ac). https://www.wildflower.org/plants/result.php?id_plant=CYSP8

Lady Bird Johnson Wildflower Center - The University of Texas at Austin. (n.d.-ad). https://www.wildflower.org/plants/result.php?id_plant=RICE

Lady Bird Johnson Wildflower Center - The University of Texas at Austin. (n.d.-ae). https://www.wildflower.org/plants/result.php?id_plant=agal5

Lady Bird Johnson Wildflower Center - The University of Texas at Austin. (n.d.-af). https://www.wildflower.org/plants/result.php?id_plant=mofi

Lai, P., Naidu, M., Sabaratnam, V., Wong, K., David, R. P., Kuppusamy, U. R., Abdullah, N., & Malek, S. N. A. (2013). Neurotrophic Properties of the Lion's Mane Medicinal Mushroom, Hericium erinaceus (Higher Basidiomycetes) from Malaysia. *International Journal of Medicinal Mushrooms, 15*(6), 539–554. https://doi.org/10.1615/intjmedmushr.v15.i6.30

Lara Hartley for DesertUSA.com. (n.d.). *Desert Peach, Prunus andersonii - DesertUSA.* https://www.desertusa.com/flowers/Desert-Peach.html

Leccinum aurantiacum: The Ultimate Mushroom Guide. (n.d.). 1102 Mushroom Identifications: The Ultimate Mushroom Library. https://ultimate-mushroom.com/edible/46-leccinum-aurantiacum.html

Lewisia rediviva Bitter-Root PFAF Plant Database. (n.d.). https://pfaf.org/user/Plant.aspx?LatinName=Lewisia+rediviva

Lobelia inflata (Indian Tobacco): Minnesota Wildflowers. (n.d.). https://www.minnesotawildflowers.info/flower/indian-tobacco

Lobelia inflata Indian Tobacco PFAF Plant Database. (n.d.). https://pfaf.org/user/Plant.aspx?LatinName=Lobelia+inflata

Lobster mushroom. (n.d.). Missouri Department of Conservation. https://mdc.mo.gov/discover-nature/field-guide/lobster-mushroom

Lobster Mushroom (hypomyces lactiflourum) - Mushroom-Collecting.com. (n.d.). http://mushroom-collecting.com/mushroomlobster.html

Marrubium vulgare (Horehound, White Horehound) | North Carolina Extension Gardener Plant Toolbox. (n.d.). https://plants.ces.ncsu.edu/plants/marrubium-vulgare/

McCrae, A. (2022, April 2). *How to find Morel mushrooms in the city: A breakdown on Landscape Morels!* Mushroom Marauder. https://mushroommarauder.com/blogs/morel-mushroom-hunting/how-to-find-landscape-morels

Monarda fistulosa - Plant Finder. (n.d.). https://www.missouribotanicalgarden.org/PlantFinder/PlantFinderDetails.aspx?kempercode=g560

Monarda fistulosa (Bee Balm, Eastern Bergamot, Wild Bergamot) | *North Carolina Extension Gardener Plant Toolbox.* (n.d.). https://plants.ces.ncsu.edu/plants/monarda-fistulosa/

Mushroom. (2023a, January 30). *Oyster mushroom: identification, foraging, and cooking - Mushroom appreciation.* Mushroom Appreciation. https://www.mushroom-appreciation.com/oyster-mushroom.html

Mushroom. (2023b, January 30). *Oyster mushroom: identification, foraging, and cooking - Mushroom appreciation.* Mushroom Appreciation. https://www.mushroom-appreciation.com/oyster-mushroom.html

Mushroom. (2023c, April 17). *False Morel Mushrooms - Everything you need to know - Mushroom appreciation.* Mushroom Appreciation. https://www.mushroom-appreciation.com/false-morel.html

Mushroom. (2023d, May 5). *Chasing the Chicken of the Woods (Facts, identification, and Recipes) - Mushroom appreciation.* Mushroom Appreciation. https://www.mushroom-appreciation.com/chicken-of-the-woods.html

Mushroom. (2023e, July 13). *The Jack O'Lantern Mushroom - Mushroom appreciation.* Mushroom Appreciation. https://www.mushroom-appreciation.com/omphalotus-olearius.html

Mushroom. (2023f, July 18). *Black Trumpet Mushrooms: Identification and Foraging Guide - Mushroom appreciation.* Mushroom Appreciation. https://www.mushroom-appreciation.com/black-trumpet.html

MushroomExpert.Com. (n.d.). *Cantharellus cinnabarinus (MushroomExpert.Com).* https://www.mushroomexpert.com/cantharellus_cinnabarinus.html

Mycognostic. (2017, September 11). *Elm Oyster (Hypsizygus/Pleurotus ulmarius) mix-up between growers & foragers.* MycoGnosis. https://mycognosis.com/elm-oyster-hypsizygus-ulmarius-mix-up/

Natural Heritage Program and Montana Fish, Wildlife & Parks. (2023a, October 31). *MTNHP.* https://fieldguide.mt.gov/speciesDetail.aspx?elcode=PMPOA151H0

Natural Heritage Program and Montana Fish, Wildlife & Parks. (2023b, October 31). *MTNHP.* https://fieldguide.mt.gov/speciesDetail.aspx?elcode=PDCAC0X0G0

Natural Heritage Program and Montana Fish, Wildlife & Parks. (2023c, October 31). *MTNHP.* https://fieldguide.mt.gov/speciesDetail.aspx?elcode=PDBRA2C010

Natural Heritage Program and Montana Fish, Wildlife & Parks. (2023d, October 31). *MTNHP.* https://fieldguide.mt.gov/speciesDetail.aspx?elcode=PDGRO02080

Night Blooming Cereus cactus - Queen of the Night - DesertUSA. (n.d.). https://www.desertusa.com/cactus/night-blooming-cereus.html

Nocturnal scene fact sheet. (n.d.). https://www.desertmuseum.org/kids/oz/long-fact-sheets/Buckhorn%20cholla.php

Ocotillo - Fouquieria splendens - DesertUSA. (n.d.). https://www.desertusa.com/flora/ocotillo.html *Ocotillo fact sheet.* (n.d.). https://www.desertmuseum.org/kids/oz/long-fact-sheets/Ocotillo.php *Opuntia eastern prickly pear, Prickly pear cactus PFAF Plant Database.* (n.d.). https://pfaf.org/user/Plant.aspx?LatinName=Opuntia

Oyster mushroom. (n.d.). Missouri Department of Conservation. https://mdc.mo.gov/discover-nature/field-guide/oyster-mushroom

Oyster Mushroom Identification: Pictures, Habitat, Season & Spore Print | *Pleurotus ostreatus.* (n.d.). https://www.ediblewildfood.com/oyster-mushroom.aspx

Oyster mushrooms | *Mushroom varieties 101.* (2023, March 16). Mushroom Council. https://www.mushroom-council.com/mushroom-101/varieties/oyster/

Pancake Prickly Pear | *Desert Mountain, AZ.* (n.d.). https://www.desertmthoa.com/336/Pancake-Prickly-Pear

Pinus Edulis | *Capitol Reef Field Station* | *Utah Valley University.* (n.d.). https://www.uvu.edu/crfs/native-plants/pinus-edulis.html

Pinus edulis (Colorado Pinyon, Colorado Pinyon Pine, Nut Pine, Pino Dulce, Pinyon Pine, Two-leaf Pinyon, Two-needle Pine) | *North Carolina Extension Gardener Plant Toolbox.* (n.d.). https://plants.ces.ncsu.edu/plants/pinus-edulis/

Plants of Texas Rangelands » Silverleaf nightshade. (n.d.). https://rangeplants.tamu.edu/plant/silverleaf-nightshade/

Pleurocybella toxin - North American Mycological Association. (n.d.). https://namyco.org/pleurocybella_toxin.php

Prosopis glandulosa Honeypod mesquite. Glandular mesquite PFAF Plant Database. (n.d.). https://pfaf.org/user/Plant.aspx?LatinName=Prosopis+glandulosa

Prunus andersonii Desert Peach PFAF Plant Database. (n.d.). https://pfaf.org/User/Plant.aspx?LatinName=Prunus+andersonii

Prunus fasciculata Desert Almond PFAF Plant Database. (n.d.). https://pfaf.org/user/Plant.aspx?LatinName=Prunus+fasciculata

Quaking Aspen | *National Wildlife Federation.* (n.d.). National Wildlife Federation. https://www.

nwf.org/Educational-Resources/Wildlife-Guide/Plants-and-Fungi/Quaking-Aspen

Quaking Aspen - Populus tremuloides - PNW Plants. (n.d.). Copyright (C) 2006 Filaret Ilas. All Rights Reserved. http://www.pnwplants.wsu.edu/PlantDisplay.aspx?PlantID=340

Red–capped scraber stalk (Leccinum aurantiacum) : Photos, Diagrams & Topos : SummitPost. (n.d.). SummitPost.org. https://www.summitpost.org/red-capped-scraber-stalk-leccinum-aurantiacum/362642

Ringless honey mushroom. (n.d.). Missouri Department of Conservation. https://mdc.mo.gov/discover-nature/field-guide/ringless-honey-mushroom

Rockland-Miller, A. (2020a, September 4). *Leccinums: Insipid or Inspiring? — The Mushroom Forager*. The Mushroom Forager. https://www.themushroomforager.com/blog/2020/9/4/leccinums-insipid-or-inspiring

Rockland-Miller, A. (2020b, October 2). *Lion's Mane: A Foolproof Fungus — The Mushroom Forager*. The MushroomForager.https://www.themushroomforager.com/blog/2010/9/29/ tncikqd1y4b0a6hgdzx0ypn-hcq018o

Rockland-Miller, A. (2021a, March 3). *Cinnabar-red Chanterelle: As Good as Gold — The Mushroom Forager*. The Mushroom Forager. https://www.themushroomforager.com/blog/2013/8/13/cinnabar-red-chanterelle-as-good-as-gold

Rockland-Miller, A. (2021b, March 3). *Tastes like Chicken — The Mushroom Forager*. The Mushroom Forager. https://www.themushroomforager.com/blog/2012/6/19/tastes-like-chicken

Rockland-Miller, A. (2021c, October 28). *Hedgehog Mushroom: The Safer Chanterelle — The Mushroom Forager*. The Mushroom Forager. https://www.themushroomforager.com/blog/2012/9/2/hedge hog-mush-room-the-safer-chanterelle

Russian thistle — Northern Arizona Invasive Plants. (n.d.). Northern Arizona Invasive Plants. https://nazin vasiveplants.org/russian-thistle

Salvia greggii "Radio Red" - Plant Finder. (n.d.). https://www.missouribotanicalgarden.org/PlantFinder/PlantFinderDetails.aspx?taxonid=443866&isprofile=0&

Selemin, J. (2023, July 20). *The complete guide to the hedgehog mushroom*. Shroomer. https://www.shroomer.com/hedgehog-mushroom/

Shepherdia argentea Buffalo Berry, Silver Buffaloberry, PFAF Plant Database. (n.d.). https://pfaf.org/user/Plant.aspx?LatinName=Shepherdia+argentea

Sisymbrium altissimum (Tall Tumble Mustard): Minnesota Wildflowers. (n.d.). https://www.minnesotawild flowers.info/flower/tall-tumble-mustard

Solidago canadensis (Canada Goldenrod, Canadian Goldenrod, Common Goldenrod, Goldenrod, Meadow Goldenrod,, Tall Goldenrod) | North Carolina Extension Gardener Plant Toolbox. (n.d.). https://plants.ces. ncsu.e-du/plants/solidago-canadensis/

Solidago canadensis Canadian Goldenrod, Shorthair goldenrod, Harger's goldenrod, Rough Canada goldenrod, Common Goldenro PFAF Plant Database. (n.d.). https://pfaf.org/User/Plant.aspx? LatinName=Solidago+canadensis

Species Detail Woody, Cacti, Succulent. (n.d.). https://cals.arizona.edu/yavapaiplants/SpeciesDetail.php?genus=Forestiera&species=pubescens

Sporobolus cryptandrus (Sand Dropseed): Minnesota Wildflowers. (n.d.). https://www.minnesotawildflow ers.info/grass-sedge-rush/sand-dropseed

Sporobolus cryptandrus Sand Dropseed PFAF Plant Database. (n.d.). https://pfaf.org/User/Plant.aspx? LatinName=Sporobolus+cryptandrus

Stevens, M. W. &. F. (n.d.). *California Fungi: Omphalotus olivascens*. https://www.mykoweb.com/CAF/species/Omphalotus_olivascens.html

Sturla, E. (n.d.-a). *Cirsium ochrocentrum, Yellowspine Thistle, Southwest Desert Flora*. https://southwestde sertflora.com/WebsiteFolders/All_Species/Asteraceae/Cirsium%20ochrocentrum,%20Yel-lowspine%20Thistle.html

Sturla, E. (n.d.-b). *Cylindropuntia acanthocarpa, Buckhorn Cholla, Southwest Desert Flora*. https://southwest desertflora.com/WebsiteFolders/All_Species/Cactaceae/Cylindropuntia%20acanthocarpa,%20Buck-horn%20Cholla.html

Sturla, E. (n.d.-c). *Cylindropuntia bigelovii, Teddy Bear Cholla, Southwest Desert Flora*. https://southwestde sertflora.com/WebsiteFolders/All_Species/Cactaceae/Cylindropuntia%20bigelovii,%20Ted-dy%20Bear%20Cholla.html

Sturla, E. (n.d.-d). *Echinocereus coccineus, Scarlet Hedgehog Cactus, Southwest Desert Flora*. https://south west-desertflora.com/WebsiteFolders/All_Species/Cactaceae/Echinocereus%20coccineus,%20Scar-let%20Hedgehog%20Cactus.html

Sturla,E.(n.d.-e).*Genusspecies,commonname,SouthwestDesertFlora*.https:// southwestdesertflora.-com/WebsiteFolders/All_Species/Fabaceae/Prosopis% 20pubes-cens,%20Screw%20Bean%20Mesquite.html

Sturla, E. (n.d.-f). *Juglans major, Arizona Walnut, Southwest Desert Flora*. https://southwestdesertflora. com/WebsiteFolders/All_Species/Juglandaceae/Juglans%20major,%20Arizona%20Walnut.html

Sturla, E. (n.d.-g). *Juniperus monosperma, Oneseed Juniper, Southwest Desert Flora*. https://southwestdesert

flora.com/WebsiteFolders/All_Species/Cupressaceae/Juniperus% 20monosperma,%20Oneseed%20Juniper.html

Sturla, E. (n.d.-h). *Rubus neomexicanus, New Mexico Raspberry, Southwest Desert Flora.* https://southwest desertflora.com/WebsiteFolders/All_Species/Rosaceae/Rubus%20neomexicanus,%20New%20Mexico%20Raspberry.html

Sturla, E. (n.d.-i). *Solanum elaeagnifolium, Silverleaf Nightshade, Southwest Desert Flora.* https://southwest desertflora.com/WebsiteFolders/All_Species/Solanaceae/Solanum%20elaeagnifolium,%20Silverleaf%20Nightshade.html

Sturla, E. (n.d.-j). *Thelesperma megapotamicum, Hopi Tea Greenthread, Southwest Desert Flora.* https://south westdesertflora.com/WebsiteFolders/All_Species/Asteraceae/Thelesperma% 20megapotamicum,%20Hopi%20Tea%20Greenthread.html

Symphoricarpos orbiculatus (Buckbrush, Coralberry, Indian Currant, Snowberry, Waxberry) | North Carolina Extension Gardener Plant Toolbox. (n.d.). https://plants.ces.ncsu.edu/plants/symphoricarpos-orbiculatus/

Symphoricarpos orbiculatus Coralberry PFAF Plant Database. (n.d.). https://pfaf.org/user/Plant.aspx?LatinName=Symphoricarpos+orbiculatus

The American Southwest. (n.d.-a). *Agave deserti, desert agave.* https://www.americansouthwest.net/plants/agavoideae/agave-deserti.html

The American Southwest. (n.d.-b). *Cacti of Utah.* https://www.americansouthwest.net/plants/cacti/utah.html

The American Southwest. (n.d.-c). *Cylindropuntia acanthocarpa, buckhorn cholla.* https://www.american southwest.net/plants/cacti/cylindropuntia-acanthocarpa.html

The American Southwest. (n.d.-d). *Cylindropuntia bigelovii, teddy bear cholla.* https://www.americansouth west.net/plants/cacti/cylindropuntia-bigelovii.html

The American Southwest. (n.d.-e). *Cylindropuntia spinosior, cane cholla.* https://www.americansouthwest.net/plants/cacti/cylindropuntia-spinosior.html

The American Southwest. (n.d.-f). *Cylindropuntia versicolor, staghorn cholla.* https://www.americansouth west.net/plants/cacti/cylindropuntia-versicolor.html

The American Southwest. (n.d.-g). *Escobaria vivipara, common beehive cactus.* https://www.americansouth west.net/plants/cacti/escobaria-vivipara.html

The American Southwest. (n.d.-h). *Opuntia chlorotica, pancake prickly pear.* https://www.americansouth west.net/plants/cacti/opuntia-chlorotica.html

The American Southwest. (n.d.-i). *Opuntia erinacea, Mojave prickly pear.* https://www.americansouthwest.net/plants/cacti/opuntia-erinacea.html

The Editors of Encyclopaedia Britannica. (1998a, July 20). *Horehound | Plant, Herb, Uses, & Facts.* Encyclopedia Britannica. https://www.britannica.com/plant/horehound

The Editors of Encyclopaedia Britannica. (1998b, July 20). *Indian tobacco | Herbal Medicine, Medicinal Uses, Nicotine-Free.* Encyclopedia Britannica. https://www.britannica.com/plant/Indian-tobacco

The Editors of Encyclopaedia Britannica. (1998c, July 20). *Quack grass | Invasive Weed, Perennial Grass, Creeping Rhizomes.* Encyclopedia Britannica. https://www.britannica.com/plant/quack-grass

The Editors of Encyclopaedia Britannica. (1999a, May 4). *Buffalo berry | Description, Plant, Berry, Uses, & Facts.* Encyclopedia Britannica. https://www.britannica.com/plant/buffalo-berry

The Editors of Encyclopaedia Britannica. (1999b, May 4). *Ocotillo | Description, distribution, & Facts.* Encyclopedia Britannica. https://www.britannica.com/plant/ocotillo

The Editors of Encyclopaedia Britannica. (1999c, May 27). *Bitterroot | Native, edible, medicinal.* Encyclopedia Britannica. https://www.britannica.com/plant/bitterroot

The Editors of Encyclopaedia Britannica. (2023a, September 29). *Prickly pear | Description, Uses, & Species.* Encyclopedia Britannica. https://www.britannica.com/plant/prickly-pear

The Editors of Encyclopaedia Britannica. (2023b, September 29). *Prickly pear | Description, Uses, & Species.* Encyclopedia Britannica. https://www.britannica.com/plant/prickly-pear

The Editors of Encyclopaedia Britannica. (2023c, October 11). *Peyote | Description, Distribution, & Uses.* Encyclopedia Britannica. https://www.britannica.com/plant/Lophophora-williamsii

The Great Morel. (2023, March 16). *False Morels - The Great Morel.* https://www.thegreatmorel.com/false-morels/

Thelesperma megapotamicum Navajo Tea PFAF Plant Database. (n.d.). https://pfaf.org/USER/Plant.aspx?LatinName=Thelesperma+megapotamicum

Theodore Payne Foundation. (n.d.). *Peritoma arborea - Bladderpod (Plant).* https://store.theodorepayne.org/products/theodore-payne-foundation-peritoma-isomeris-arbore

Trust, W. (n.d.). *Deathcap (Amanita phalloides) - Woodland Trust.* Woodland Trust. https://www.wood landtrust.org.uk/trees-woods-and-wildlife/fungi-and-lichens/deathcap/

Tumble mustard — Northern Arizona Invasive Plants. (n.d.). Northern Arizona Invasive Plants. https://nazin-vasiveplants.org/tumble-mustard

Tuttle, C. (2023, May 9). Opuntia macrocentra "Black-spined Pricklypear" | Succulents and

Sunshine. *Succulents and Sunshine*. https://www.succulentsandsunshine.com/types-of-succulents/opuntia-macrocentra-black-spined-pricklypear/

USDA Plants Database. (n.d.). https://plants.usda.gov/DocumentLibrary/factsheet/pdf/fs_fopu2

Valley Bladderpod, Peritoma arborea var. globosa. (n.d.). https://calscape.org/Peritoma-arborea-var.- globosa-()

Viess, D. (n.d.). *California Morels - Bay Area Mycological Society*. Text and Images Copyright Bay Area Mycological Society and the Authors Except Where Noted. All Rights Reserved. https://bayarea mush-rooms.org/mushroommonth/index.html

Wang, L., Ma, R., Liu, C., Liu, H., Zhu, R., Guo, S., Tang, M., Yu, L., Niu, J., Fu, M., S, G., & Zhang, D.

(2017). Salvia miltiorrhiza: A Potential Red Light to the Development of Cardiovascular Diseases. *Current Pharmaceutical Design, 23*(7), 1077–1097. https://doi.org/10.2174/1381612822666161010105242 *White snakeroot*. (n.d.). Missouri Department of Conservation. https://mdc.mo.gov/discover-nature/field-guide/white-snakeroot

White Snakeroot (Ageratina altissima). (n.d.). https://www.illinoiswildflowers.info/woodland/plants/ wh_s-nakeroot.htm

Wildflowers of Joshua Tree Country. (2023, March 1). *Prunus fasciculata – "Desert Almond" - Wildflowers of Joshua Tree Country*. Wildflowers of Joshua Tree Country - a Field Guide Featuring Animal Associations, Native American Ethnobotany & Translations of Scientific Names. https://wildflower sofjoshua-treecountry.com/plant-entry/desert-almond-prunus-fasciculata/

WoS. (2023, August 9). *Echinocereus rigidissimus (Arizona Rainbow Cactus)*. World of Succulents. https://worldofsucculents.com/echinocereus-rigidissimus-arizona-rainbow-cactus/

Young, T. K. a. G. (2016, June 28). *Ancient native plant relationships*. Wild About Utah. https://wildaboutu tah.org/ancient-native-plant-relationships/

Yucca baccata Spanish Bayonet, Banana yucca, Blue Yucca, Spanish Yucca PFAF Plant Database. (n.d.). https://pfaf.org/user/plant.aspx?LatinName=Yucca+baccata